THE PARANORMAL SOURCEBOOK

THE PARANORMAL SOURCEBOOK

A Complete Guide to All Things Otherworldly

Charles E. Sellier

Joe Meier

ROXBURY PARK

LOWELL HOUSE

LOS ANGELES

NTC/Contemporary Publishing Group

Published by Lowell House
A division of NTC/Contemporary Publishing Group, Inc.
4255 West Touhy Avenue,
Lincolnwood (Chicago), Illinois 60646-1975 U.S.A.

Lowell House books can be purchased at special discounts when ordered
in bulk for premiums and special sales. Contact Department CS
at the following address:

4255 West Touhy Avenue
Lincolnwood, IL 60646-1975
1-800-323-4900

Library of Congress Cataloging-in-Publication Data
Sellier, Charles E.
        The paranormal sourcebook: a complete guide to all things
otherworldly/Charles E. Sellier with Joe Meier.
        p.   cm
        "A Roxbury Park Book"
        Includes bibliographical references and index.
        ISBN 1-56565-961-9
        1. Parapsychology. I. Meier, Joe. II. Title
    BF1031.S44   1999   99-15023
    133—dc21   CIP

Roxbury Park is a division of NTC/Contemporary Publishing Group, Inc.

Managing Director and Publisher: Jack Artenstein
Editor in Chief, Roxbury Park Books: Michael Artenstein
Director of Publishing Services: Rena Copperman
Editorial Assistant: Nicole Monastirsky
Interior Design: Robert S. Tinnon
Typesetting: Ken Trickey

Printed and bound in the United States of America

10 9 8 7 6 5 4 3 2 1

This book is gratefully dedicated to "Gayle," who so graciously and

generously gave of her life experiences and her vast library,

and to Pete Liakakis, of Savannah, Georgia,

without whose lifelong inspiration this

book might never have been written.

Contents

PREFACE
XI

SECTION ONE
PSYCHIC SCIENCE
1

Chapter One
THE PSYCHIC IN SOCIETY
5

Chapter Two
THE QUEEN OF SCIENCES
19

Chapter Three
IN THE PALM OF YOUR HAND
31

SECTION TWO
PSYCHIC PATTERNS
47

Chapter Four
PHYSICIAN, POET, PROPHET
51

Chapter Five
THE SLEEPING PROPHET
63

Chapter Six
CRYSTAL CLEAR
77

SECTION THREE
THE PSYCHIC HEALERS
93

Chapter Seven
THE HEALING MIND
99

Chapter Eight
MEDICAL MYSTERIES
109

SECTION FOUR
A PSYCHIC POTPOURRI
121

Chapter Nine
THE PSYCHIC DETECTIVES
127

Chapter Ten
GOVERNMENT PSYCHICS
135

Chapter Eleven
TRUTH *IS* STRANGER THAN FICTION
157

Chapter Twelve
GHOSTS, APPARITIONS, AND THE AFTERLIFE
173

SECTION FIVE

PROPHECIES AND PREDICTIONS
189

Chapter Thirteen
PROPHETS, PSYCHICS, AND SEERS
191

Chapter Fourteen
THE TELESCOPE OF TIME
205

Chapter Fifteen
THE FATE OF NATIONS
221

Chapter Sixteen
THE END TIME
239

FURTHER READING
255

ORGANIZATIONS AND WEB SITES
261

NOTES
275

INDEX
281

Preface

Par·a·nor·mal (ˌpar-ə-ˈnȯr-məl) *adj.*
    of or pertaining to events or perceptions
    occurring without scientific explanation, as
    clairvoyance or extrasensory perception.

When this definition appeared in the *Random House College Dictionary,* it pretty well covered everything that anybody knew or cared to know about the paranormal. Today it is quite a different matter, for the gap between the paranormal and normal is rapidly closing. Events that would have caused snorts of derision or (at the very least) polite laughter just a few years ago are viewed today not only as commonplace but as worthy of serious consideration. It is not uncommon to hear someone talking about "the sense of things" or giving a fairly comprehensive analysis of someone's "vibes." This is now the sort of thing heard in both private and professional conversation.

When carefully analyzed, the definition of what constitutes the paranormal, almost anything for which there is not an immediate and clear explanation is included. And yet, events and perceptions that defy *scientific* conclusions are all around us.

Perhaps it is too heavy a burden to place upon our scientists. After all, in many respects, today's science was yesterday's paranormal perception. Within the past half century, while science scoffed at the idea of an "aura" surrounding the human body, a Russian photographer was busy devising a method of photographing it.

While mainstream scientists have universally rejected the notion that the brain has the power to move objects, bend metals, and otherwise control things and circumstances, certain industrialists and even governments have gone about the business of using those same brain "waves" to control tons of high-tech metal flying through the air at supersonic speeds.

Explaining the paranormal may simply be beyond the scope of the scientific community. But the fact that science cannot explain certain events and that most scientists do not accept the evidence of even firsthand paranormal experiences has not diminished the reported number and scope of these events. If anything, the number of reported experiences is growing as more and more people ignore the once dreaded public ridicule that invariably accompanies such reports.

Still, most of us remain skeptical and tend to regard as simply coincidence the small events that nearly everyone experiences at one time or another. An old friend you haven't seen in years is abruptly and inexplicably very much on your mind. Suddenly the phone rings and your friend's voice is in your ears.

"Oh, what a coincidence," you say, laughing. "I was just thinking about you."

But was it a coincidence that a famous psychic predicted, a decade before it happened, that a Democrat would be seated as president in 1960 and would die while in office?

Could it be that the same processes and/or abilities that brought that vision to Jeane Dixon actually reside in all of us?

Some societies rely entirely on the prophecies, or predictions, of their priests, shamans, or soothsayers. By whatever name they go by, these people have a remarkable record of successful performance that has engendered enormous confidence in what they have to say. Prophets of the Old Testament were perhaps the most severely tested. If their prophecies didn't come to pass, they were stoned to death.

It is also true that a good case can be made for the contributions made by practitioners of the "occult sciences." The alchemists of the Middle Ages, while unsuccessful in their attempts to change base metals into gold, were almost certainly the forerunners of modern chemistry. Astrologers needed to map the heavens in order to perform their magic, and in so doing, they mapped out the science of astronomy. History is filled with men and women who pitted themselves against traditional thought and were destroyed in the process, only to be vindicated, long after their death, by the same science that ridiculed them.

Then, of course, there is the concept of the "unbound" mind—the area of paranormal activity that at once raises the greatest criticism and the most admiration and wonder. Is there such a thing as "telepathy"? Can thought be transmitted outside the accepted senses? Is "clairvoyance" a reality? Can a person know that some event, large or small, will in fact happen? Precognition and retrocognition are opposite sides of the same coin—a knowledge of future and past events.

This activity, while part of the "paranormal," is more specifically defined as "psychic phenomena." The *Random House College Dictionary* tells us that the term *psychic* refers to events that are:

- of or pertaining to the human soul or mind
- outside of natural or scientific knowledge; spiritual
- of or pertaining to some apparently nonphysical source or agency
- sensitive to influences or forces of a nonphysical or supernatural nature

When we call a person a psychic, we are saying that the person "is sensitive to psychic influences or forces." These definitions are principally concerned with the ability of the mind to overcome or in some cases control physical forces. But the ancient Greek language, from which the term is taken, seemed to indicate that it was more of an activity of the soul.

This area of psychic awareness leads us to the concept of *teleportation*, the ability to move an object (including your body) from one place to another by purely psychic means; *levitation, materialization, out-of-body-projection, astral flight,* and *long-distance viewing* are all examples. All of these phenomena come about through the power of the mind. We will also look closely at a number of psychic objects, such as the several *crystal skulls* that have been found at various locations around the world.

Then, of course, there is the matter of ghosts and poltergeists (the latter known for their boisterous and mischievous activities), some of whom have achieved great notoriety. Many of them seem to be locked into their own specific haunts, but as Lloyd Auerbach, a famed paranormal psychologist, said recently in a convocation at Weber State University in Ogden, Utah, "They always show up where people are." Ghosts, it seems, seldom appear in cemeteries. When asked if he feared ghosts Auerbach replied, "Not in the least. People carry guns and knives, ghosts don't."

The fact that people do carry guns and knives and other instruments of destruction brings us to yet another area of paranormal investigation: the *psychic detectives.* As a writer, producer, and director of films for thirty years, I have had the opportunity to meet a number of truly remarkable people. During the course of one of my projects, I actually filmed perhaps the most famous psychic detective of all time—Peter Hurkos. The Los Angeles Police Department had, for some time, very quietly been using psychic detectives to help them solve particularly difficult cases—cases in which there were no leads of any kind. The LAPD had hired Mr. Hurkos and graciously allowed us to be present and film one of his sessions for our movie. The results were startling, and we'll share them with you in Chapter Nine. Today, even small, rural police departments do not hesitate to include a psychic investigator in a case that is otherwise unsolvable. What is perhaps even more amazing is that they seem to have little trouble finding psychics willing to take on even the most difficult case.

You will meet a number of remarkable people in the following pages. Some of them, like Joan of Arc and Edgar Cayce, may be familiar to you. Others, like Mother Shipton, the Brahan seer, and Malachi O'Morgain, will likely be new acquaintances, but we think you'll find them fascinating. And there are some, like Drs. Caroline Myss and Richard Johnson, who offer a thoroughly modern view of the ancient concepts. All of these individuals have something important to add to your understanding of the paranormal. We think you'll find them interesting and entertaining and an ongoing source of inspiration.

It is perhaps our twenty-first-century conceit that makes us believe that we have the answers to all the important questions. Before you have finished this book, you may decide that we're not even sure of the questions.

PSYCHIC SCIENCE

Man is most ignorant of those things
Which are most manifest.
ZOLAR

No one is quite so certain of the truth of things as he whose ideas have never been challenged. So long as a person can move within a circle of agreeable friends, it is folly to challenge the "group think" that determines the order of life.

Yet there is almost always someone who does.

The setting is a small town in the West, known for spectacular tourist attractions in the nearby canyons and gorges of the Colorado River. A group of broadcasters has gathered for their annual convention, and one of the vendors has opened a hospitality suite, much to the chagrin of the local bar owners. On this particular evening, a large crowd has gathered in the suite for the usual conversation and cocktails before dinner. But something is different. The crowd, usually two and three deep at the bar, is instead gathered around a young woman, the wife of one of the attendees. She is seated on a couch, "reading" jewelry. The group is largely silent, listening intently to what the woman tells each person who, in their turn, presents an item of jewelry to the woman. She takes the item in her hand, holds it for a few moments, then hands it back with some enlightening comment that, without exception, is confirmed by the owner of the jewelry.

The head of one of the national news bureaus sits on the couch and hands the young woman a ring. She takes it and closes her hand around it, but almost instantly she drops it and begins to rub her hand vigorously against her hip, as if the ring were hot. Looking up at the man, puzzled, she tries again with the same result. Without further ado, she returns the ring and informs the owner that he is in constant pain.

"Yes," he whispers, almost embarrassed by the revelation, "I hurt my back seventeen years ago. The doctors have been unable to fix it. I just live with the pain."

From among the men and women who surround him and have known and worked with him for years, there is an audible gasp. None of them has had the slightest idea of his condition.

Another man steps up, a station owner who still spends a good deal of time "on the air." He offers a watch with a silver band embedded with turquoise nuggets. It is, he says, the piece of jewelry he has owned the longest. This time the woman takes the watch in both hands in order to encompass as much of the watch and band as possible. The room falls silent as she holds the watch much longer than usual. At last she returns it to the owner, saying, "I don't get anything from this." Later, in private, she asks the man if his wife knows of his lover *and the son* she has borne him.

"I think," he says, ignoring the question, "I need another drink."

The history of the paranormal reads like a history of humankind. From 20,000-year-old cave paintings of ancient shamans dressed up in animal skins to the horoscope printed in the daily newspaper, it is clear that people have always sought to know the future. Despite the power of kings and priests and the threat of divine retribution, people have continued to seek out those who have the "gift." Whether it's the ability to read jewelry, the stars, the cards, the palm of the hand, or the liver or entrails of sheep, there has always been a ready market for those who can demonstrate they have such power. Paradoxically, it seems that the paranormal is actually quite normal.

By the way, if you think this sounds like ancient superstition and unworthy of a world where scientific proof has become the rule, then you should know that today in New York City (and probably New Orleans, San Francisco, and just about every other major city), you can buy a wax effigy, complete with its own supply of pins suitable for making your enemies miserable. You can also buy wax candles set in small dishes to be filled with cold water so that the shape of the drippings can be easily "read." And who has not seen the barrage of ads for "phone psychics." Thousands, perhaps millions, of very modern citizens are finding, often to their surprise, that these psychics do indeed have satisfying answers to their questions, and those answers alone are frequently enough to provide a sense of comfort and well-being. Interestingly, it is not the psychics themselves who tout their abilities; for the most part it is the client, the person calling in, who is the most vocal supporter of these services.

There is, of course, a worldwide debate over whether any of the so-called psychic sciences have any validity. It is not, as you might suspect, a new argument. Dante, in the fourteenth century, reserved a special place for fortune-tellers in his version of hell. Their heads were all twisted backward as an eternal punishment because they dared to assume the power of God by trying to see into the future.

It is not our intent here to play advocate for one position or another. In fact, the line between normal and paranormal is becoming increasingly blurred—in good point due to the interest of science. But as you will see, science has a lot of ground to cover.

CHAPTER ONE

THE PSYCHIC IN SOCIETY

IN 1994, A SMALL FLORIDA TOWN WAS SHOCKED by the disappearance of one of its longtime citizens. An older man living with his girlfriend and with family nearby, he seemed an unlikely candidate for foul play, but nevertheless he was gone. Early one morning, this man (we'll call him Charlie) told his girlfriend that he was going out and that he would see her later. He climbed into the cab of his old pickup truck and drove away. He was never seen or heard from again.

The police and fire departments were called in almost immediately, and according to Charlie's brother, they worked diligently over the next sixteen months to try to find some trace or uncover some clue as to what might have happened to him. Their combined efforts were completely unsuccessful. Finally, in desperation, the detective assigned to the case called a professional psychic detective, a woman who made a living working with various law enforcement agencies as well as with private individuals.

The woman told the detective that it would be a month before she could fit his case into her busy schedule, and in the meantime she asked the officer to gather up any of Charlie's personal possessions that might still be available. That was the easy part. Charlie had left everything behind except his pickup truck. When the psychic detective finally arrived on the scene, the officer provided her with Charlie's wallet and all his credit and identity cards, a pair of shoes, and even some of his medications.

The woman used a technique known as *psychometry* to help her discover what had happened to Charlie. This is a process that presupposes that all personal items will attract and maintain some portion of the owner's energy field. By handling these items, the psychic picks up images created by that person's energy. The woman, in the presence of the police officer, began to work with Charlie's personal things, and the sessions were recorded to provide the officer with an ongoing reference. It is fair to say that even though the police had called her in, there was a healthy degree of skepticism on the part of most city officials; but since nearly a year and a half had gone by without a single clue as to Charlie's whereabouts, the feeling was one of "What can it hurt?"

The psychic detective began to give the officer in charge a series of clues. She was certain that wherever Charlie was, he was still in his truck; she had a strong feeling, she said, of metal. She also thought that the truck, with Charlie in it, had gone over a cliff or high ledge of some kind, since she had the sensation of falling through the air. She told the officer to look for red bricks, railroad tracks, and an old bridge or something that looked like a bridge. She also drew a quadrant on a map and said confidently that Charlie would be found somewhere in that quadrant. As a final clue, she told the officer to be sensitive to the numbers 1, 2, 4, and 5.

Armed with a tape recording and little else, the police detective began a meticulous search of the quadrant outlined on the map. The area was dotted with deep, water-filled quarries and lime pits, open fields, and thick woods. For nearly two months, the detective tramped across the terrain on foot, fighting his way through the brush, bugs, and snakes. Discouraged and just about ready to chalk the whole thing up to experience, he walked up to the edge of one of the old quarries and found himself standing on a bed of broken red bricks. So far this was the only one of the psychic's clues he had seen. He began a serious search of the surrounding area and quickly discovered an old truck scale that in its abandoned state looked very much like a bridge. A little further on he discovered what was left of an old railroad track, now nearly covered by grass and brush. The detective walked to the edge of the quarry. It was at least 50 to 75 feet straight down to the water, certainly enough to give the impression of falling through the air. Encouraged, he called in some local divers, but the water was so murky and choked with weeds, they could find nothing.

At this point, all the clues seemed to come together. This particular quarry was just off route 45, and it was exactly 2.1 miles from Charlie's driveway to the edge of the water. The detective, without telling them he was working with psychic clues, called in the navy. They arrived on the scene with sensitive, deepwater metal detectors and after two days of searching found a large metal mass about 25 feet under the surface. The following day, Charlie's old truck was pulled up from the murky waters of the quarry with Charlie's body still inside, just as the psychic predicted.

A professor from a nearby university was called in to evaluate what appeared to be the psychic's astonishing feat. Was he impressed? Not at all. According to the professor, "after the fact events always favor the psychic." After all, he reminded them, the psychic had nearly a month to prepare. In his view, it would have been an easy matter to deduce that Charlie had driven off into one of the many quarries in the surrounding area. Choosing one with red bricks, the old scale, and railroad tracks was just a lucky guess. In the professor's opinion, going to see a psychic or astrologer was fine (and probably even fun) so long as one kept firmly in mind that there was no scientific basis for any of it.

Some observers thought that the professor's theory of a "lucky guess" was more fantastic than the psychic's clues, especially in view of the fact that the police and fire departments had nearly a year and a half to make the same lucky guess and had failed to do so. In any event, Charlie was found in a place and condition outlined in astonishing detail by someone who calls herself a psychic detective. Neither the fire chief nor the police officer on the case were willing to accept the idea of "psychic powers," but both had to admit that, at least in this instance, there could be little doubt that the clues given them by the psychic were directly responsible for finding Charlie.

We are reminded of the story of the old farmer whose son persuaded him to call the agricultural scientists at the university to help him improve the yield from his farm. The experts arrived, tested the soil, water, and fertilizer the farmer used, and in precise detail pointed out to him that corn simply wouldn't grow on that land.

"Well, thank you," the farmer replied. "I can see you are well intentioned, well educated and I respect your opinion." He then hoisted his bag of seed corn onto his shoulder and started for the field.

"Wait! Where are you going?" the scientists asked.

The farmer turned back patiently. "It's springtime, I have to plant."

"But I thought you said you respected our opinions."

"Oh I do," the farmer replied, "but sometimes the corn grows anyway."

It is entirely possible to respect the work of the rational scientist, who works very hard to discover the how and why of things, and still keep in mind that the scientific community has been known to make mistakes. Louis Pasteur, for example, the great nineteenth-century chemist, discovered the microscopic organisms we now call bacteria and tried to explain to his fellow scientists that it was these tiny villains that caused much of the sickness in the world. You might think that his discovery would be hailed as a great achievement. Instead, the man who is probably the world's first bacteriologist and the inventor of pasteurization, the process that kills harmful bacteria, was hounded and ridiculed by his colleagues to his dying day. Then there's the case of Galileo, whose intense observations of the moon and nearby planets led him to invent the first telescope. With it he was able to confirm the Copernican theory that the earth and other planets move around the sun, instead of the other way around. He made his findings known, expecting, no doubt, the accolades that accompany such a great discovery. Instead, he was forced to recant the evidence of even direct observation upon threat of being disfellowshipped by the scientific community and excommunicated from the church. Those, of course, are just two of history's more glaring examples.

The great strength of science is that it restricts itself to what is observable—to those things that can be weighed, measured, and analyzed. But that is also the great weakness of science. The fact is, scientific assurances notwithstanding, history is replete with examples that "sometimes the corn grows anyway."

Like most of the people we interviewed for this book, we came to an understanding of the paranormal by the skeptical route. At one time we believed that these things simply did not happen—or if they did, there had to be a logical, "scientific" explanation. That attitude in and of itself is probably very healthy, but there is a world of surprises awaiting the person who approaches the paranormal with an open mind.

My own reason for getting involved with the paranormal was twofold. I had developed a growing interest in the subject through personal contact with a number of people both in and out of the movie industry whose personal experiences seemed incredible. Two highly successful movies, which I produced, *UFO, Fact or Fiction* and *Bigfoot, the Mysterious Monster,* served to heighten that interest.

The second reason was more practical. In 1977, I accepted a contract to produce a show entitled "The Amazing World of Psychic Phenomena." I was looking forward to the project because it was an opportunity to work with David Wolper, the world-famous producer of *Roots.* My previous work had undoubtedly brought me to the attention of this production group, but my personal leanings were still to the side of the skeptics. Little did I know that this show would change my life forever.

Until I read the script for "The Amazing World of Psychic Phenomena," I was unacquainted with most of the people whose names might have some "marquee" value in this area. I was living in Park City, Utah, at the time; David Wolper, of course, was living in Los Angeles and was in close contact with many of the psychics who would appear on the show. My own research was focused primarily on getting acquainted with what these people did and, insofar as it was possible to determine, how they did it.

One morning, during preproduction, I received a phone call from a young man by the name of Uri Geller. It was a name I recognized from my research, but at the time his fame was still well into the future, so I was surprised that someone so obscure thought he had a contribution to make to the picture. As it turned out, Wolper had told him about the show, and he wanted an opportunity to meet with me and any members of my staff I would care to bring along. He was, he said, on his way from Los Angeles to England, but he could arrange his flight plans to accommodate a brief stopover at the Salt Lake City airport.

I agreed to the meeting and arranged to be at the airport when Geller's flight came in. I took two of my staff with me—Jerry Fleck, a longtime assistant who is now an assistant director on the *Star Trek* television series at Paramount, and a young man by the name of Tom Chapman, one of our staff writers and a close personal friend. The meeting took place as scheduled, in the second-floor restaurant of the Salt Lake City airport, overlooking the runways.

Uri Geller turned out to be a very likable young man, good-looking, intelligent, and very perceptive. It didn't take him long to discover that I was still skeptical regarding things of a psychic nature. My attitude at the time was fairly typical: "If you can't put it in my hand, it probably doesn't exist." That seemed to suit Geller just fine. If all it took was a demonstration, he was glad to oblige. He leaned back and with just a trace of a smile asked if anyone had a key. Jerry reached in his pocket and came out with a leather, zippered key case full of keys and started to hand it to Uri.

"No," Geller said, "don't give it to me, you hold it."

Jerry kept possession of the case, unzipped it, and held it open. "Okay?" he said.

"Fold out the longest key in there," Geller instructed, "then zip it back up and hold it tightly."

Jerry selected the key, zipped up the case around it, and, as he had been instructed, held onto the case very tightly.

"Now," Uri said, "put it in front of Mr. Sellier."

The leather case was now being firmly held in Jerry's hand, the key that was selected protruding from between his thumb and forefinger. He was holding it in front of Tom and myself, just a few inches from our eyes. We can see it very clearly and in every detail. Uri now took his index finger and positioned it about 2 inches *above* the key. In fact, at no time did he touch the key during the entire demonstration. Instead, he began moving his finger back and forth, stroking the air in a petting motion just above the key.

"You've got to be kidding," I thought, and glanced up to see if Mr. Geller weren't actually putting us on just a bit. His dark eyes were focused intently on the task at hand. He was not smiling now, and I got the distinct impression that two airplanes could have collided on the runway just outside the window and he wouldn't have noticed. I looked back down at the key. It was a stout, brass key, similar to those used in Yale locks. It was, in fact, the key to Jerry's post office box. I was still staring intently at the key, trying to imagine what in the world this young man was up to when suddenly it began to curl, to bend upward. I looked up at Jerry, still holding the key firmly between thumb and forefinger. His eyes began to widen, as I'm sure did mine. Tom bent in closer, as if he couldn't quite believe what he was seeing.

Uri dropped his hands, leaned back, and with a big smile asked, "Well, what do you think?"

I took the key from Jerry and examined it closely. I'm not sure I could have bent it in a vice, yet it had just curled up like a Christmas ribbon right before our eyes, *with no one touching it.* Trickery was out of the question. Geller could not have known what key Jerry would pull out of the case, and in any event, all of us were within inches of both the key and the case, when the key began to curl. There were no diversions, no substitutions possible. The three of us had witnessed, firsthand and very close-up, the amazing power of the mind.

Later, Uri Geller and I struck a deal to include him in the show, and over the years we have become good friends. Unfortunately for the film, the decision was made to use existing university footage that documented his amazing skills. I have always regretted not taking the time to shoot new footage. It would have been fun, for example, to re-create the scene at the airport.

Speaking of fun, there is an interesting sidelight to this story. The United States Post Office takes a very dim view of people who lose or otherwise destroy or disable the keys they are issued. Getting a replacement is a very big deal. The postmaster was neither convinced nor amused when Jerry applied for a new one and tried to explain what had happened. The bad news is that he had to pay for a replacement; the good news is that he still has that key, and yes, it is still bent. Not too surprisingly, perhaps, he has no better luck today explaining to his friends how it got bent than he did to the postmaster.

I was subjected to a major attitude adjustment that day, and while it was just the beginning, the first step down a long road of paranormal investigation, it had the lasting effect of opening up my mind to new and previously unthinkable possibilities. "The Amazing World of Psychic Phenomena" was no longer just a project. It was the world in which I lived, in which we all live. I had just witnessed an amazing demonstration of what is called *psychokinesis,* and like the detective's experience with psychometry, it was impossible to deny.

The skeptic, of course, will smile and say, "I live in a world that is material; it is made up of matter and energy, nothing more and certainly nothing less." We are familiar with that attitude, and it demands respect. But we must also respect the history that contests the point. There is no place for something like clairvoyance or extrasensory perception (ESP) in the materialistic concept, yet clairvoyance and ESP in various forms exist and have existed for thousands of years.

To the average person interested in finding out just exactly what the paranormal is about, all of this is probably very confusing. But that shouldn't come as any great surprise. It is easy to be confused by a society that accepts psychic readings over the telephone, buys books on every metaphysical subject imaginable, and yet joins in a chorus of ridicule when the press pokes fun at a president because his wife consults an astrologer. Yet, just about every metaphysical or paranormal practice and device known to exist is openly supported by some highly placed person or group. Official government and religious institutions are, if not more broad-minded, certainly more tolerant of those who exercise their gifts both in public and private.

It is confusing when a famous psychic is widely accepted because of her prediction concerning the assassination of an important government figure, but when the same psychic forecasts a similar fate for the man's younger brother, not even his mother will accept the warning phone call. On the other hand, one of the most often used pickup lines of the eighties was, "What's your sign?"—referring, of course, to the signs of the zodiac.

To the serious investigator of the paranormal, these seemingly conflicting attitudes are difficult to reconcile. Why is it, for example, that there appears to be such widespread acceptance of the notion of psychic gifts, and yet the official institutions of government and higher learning tend to scoff at these ideas while devoting enormous resources trying to discover if they are in fact valid? Could it be that we are simply dealing with the natural skepticism of a scientific community that accepts nothing until it can be proven by empirical standards? Or is it that they have already made up their mind and are simply trying to bolster their position?

We thought it might be worthwhile, in view of the growing popularity of almost all the psychic sciences, to try to reconcile these apparently irreconcilable views. To that end, we will examine the "mechanics," if you will, of the more popular psychic sciences: Is it just a matter of someone becoming skilled at reading the position of the stars, the lines in the hand, the turn of the cards? Or is there something more to it than that? We will also be looking at different *kinds* of psychics: those who accept the gift with a certain degree of passion and devote their lives to it; those who have perhaps only one psychic experience in their entire lives; and those who have the gift thrust upon them in spite of all they do to avoid it.

If we accept the notion that virtually all psychic phenomena has as its ultimate goal an ability to catch a glimpse of the future, we have a benchmark by which to measure the success or failure of a particular psychic skill. It is undeniable that at least some of these gifted people have changed lives, redirected the fate of nations, even changed the course of the entire world. That being the case, it probably makes sense to try and determine where the psychic gifts come from. Is it a learned skill? Are we all capable of "knowing" what will happen in our lives? Or did Daniel in the Old Testament have it right? Remember, the king was surrounded by magicians, soothsayers, and astrologers, but none of them could tell him his dream. Daniel admitted that it was beyond his skill also, but there was a God in heaven, he told the king, who could reveal all things. You might be surprised to discover just how many of the most famous psychics, both ancient and modern, profoundly believed, like Daniel, that their gift came directly from God.

Science and the government, of course, are less interested in where the information comes from than in how accurate it is. We will look at some of the efforts that have been made to determine the validity and accuracy of psychic science. It may interest you to know, for example, that long after Hitler's astrologers became nothing more than a historical footnote, both sides in the Cold War were spending millions of dollars seeking out, verifying, and employing a number of psychics of varying skills.

But looking into the future, whether 5 minutes or 500 years, is only one of the many areas of psychic phenomena this book will explore. We will also examine what many practitioners call "the queen of sciences"—*astrology*, a discipline based on hundreds, perhaps thousands of years of the procession of stars across the heavens. Mathematically precise in its origins, astrology boldly claims that it can not only tell you who you are and what you will likely become, but with imperious arrogance tell you why.

Astrology has been practiced for thousands of years. Ancient Babylonian kings, rulers of everything they surveyed, co-opted an entire culture to this purpose. The Chaldeans were brought to the court specifically to divine the nature of things by reading the stars. Nor was any subject too small to merit their attention, from great battles to simple dreams that sometimes turned out to be nightmares. Is it possible there is something to it?

There is another very interesting and perhaps more practical avenue of psychic discovery that many people are finding works to their advantage. (I say "works" advisedly, since there is a large and influential body of thought that is unalterably opposed to anything other than their own conventions.) This is in the area of psychic health practices. It seems nothing more than a flight of fanciful imagination (see *Indiana Jones and the Temple of Doom*) that a man from the Philippine Islands can actually reach into the human body, without instruments or anesthesia, and repair diseased or injured parts. Yet, hundreds of this psychic surgeon's patients swear by his skills. Trained medical doctors have closely observed him at work, with film crews recording the entire "operation." The patient emerges seemingly cured and none the worse for wear. Yet, so far, rational explanations have eluded all observers.

Nothing raises the ire of the scientific community quite like claims of "psychic healing." But today, as perhaps at no other time in history, people are seeking alternatives to the scientifically approved methods of healing. More and more people, weary of needles and knives and pills, seek the cure for their ills among practitioners of such healing arts as kinesiology, hypnotherapy, energy manipulation, even psychic surgery, and the oldest method of all, faith healing. After all, didn't Christ tell his apostles that they could perform all the miracles he performed, even the raising of the dead, if they would only have faith?

There is a rather large body of thought that suggests that everyone comes into this world with a high degree of "psychic awareness." Gradually, we are taught to neglect these faculties, and eventually, like an old friend who is always ignored, they simply go away. There are ways, however, to "test" your own psychic skills, and from time to time throughout this book, we will invite you to participate in these tests. There is, for example, a simple way to discover your own ability to sense bodily ills. The following steps will give you an idea of how sensitive you are to the body's ability to communicate from the subconscious to the conscious mind through the muscular system:

1. Have a friend stand facing you, with one arm relaxed at his side and the other held out, horizontal to the floor. (It doesn't matter which arm is used.)

2. Place one of your hands on the shoulder of the arm that is hanging relaxed at your friend's side. Place your other hand, with just two or three fingers extended, on the extended arm just above the wrist.

3. Tell your friend that you are going to try to push his arm down and that he should resist with all his strength.

4. Ask your friend a question that can be answered with a simple yes or no. (Example: Is your name _____?) Tell your friend to answer out loud.

5. Upon hearing the answer, press down firmly on the extended arm.

6. Examine the result. If your friend answers truthfully, he will resist the downward pressure easily. If his answer is false, the arm will fall away easily no matter how hard he resists.

7. To confirm the finding, repeat the process, asking the same question but with the opposite answer.

Do not make a joke out of the process. Concentrate and avoid even smiling during the test. Then switch places and have your friend do the same thing to you.

What you will have done is establish the deltoid muscle as an "indicator" muscle. You may now ask the body any question you wish regarding its health and well-being, so long as the question can be answered yes or no. Most people soon discover that they can communicate with their body and that their body does not lie. We'll discuss this in greater detail in a later chapter, but for now, be assured that you do have some capabilities you are not aware of.

There have always been those who have exhibited a remarkable capacity to relieve physical suffering. Edgar Cayce demonstrated a remarkable ability to diagnose and prescribe cures for people, many of whom were hundreds of miles away. At least one of his unorthodox prescriptions was later adopted by the medical community.

Using the power of the mind (your own or someone else's) to move energy throughout the body to prevent or overcome illness is a common practice in many Asian countries. The procedure known as acupuncture, practiced for thousands of years in China, is only now gaining acceptance in the West. And with that growing acceptance has come a more tolerant attitude toward such strange-sounding disciplines as kinesiology, radiesthesia, and reiki, all of which claim to use the power of the mind to correct all sorts of manifestations of illness in the body. This will be a fascinating examination.

Art, they say, imitates life. That is certainly true where the strange and unexplainable world of psychic phenomena is concerned. From Shakespeare to Spielberg, art, literature, theater, movies, and television have all found ample grist for their respective mills in the fable and folklore of the metaphysical world. In fact, long before Shakespeare came on the scene, Chaucer was giving credit to the influence of the stars in his monumental work, *The Canterbury Tales.* Today, we can scarcely turn on a television, read a newspaper, or go to a movie without being reminded that the world is full of things we simply do not understand. (Two current television series are titled *Strange Universe* and *The Unexplained.*) But did you know that in addition to the tales told on the silver screen, many of today's producers, directors, and stars have had their own personal and sometimes chilling encounters with the paranormal? You will probably remember George Hamilton's screen role as

Dracula, but you may not be familiar with his real-life run-in with vampires or the agony that dogged the woman who played the voice of the devil in *The Exorcist.* Some of you might remember the story of Joan Rivers's haunted Manhattan apartment and Shirley MacLaine's past lives, but did you know that a ghostly vision of Humphrey Bogart appeared to the real owners of the maltese falcon statue? Or that a spirit voice warned Peter Sellers of his son's riding accident? Then there are the frightening, real-life accounts of famous occult films and the heartbreaking stories of the producers, directors, and stars who dared to work on these strange projects. We'll be sharing some of these stories with you (including my own) in the following pages.

Finally, as the world moves inexorably toward the year 2000, we will examine the prophets and prophecies that have provided humankind with a fearful image of the "last days." Is this the final dispensation of time as we know it? Can we expect an anti-Christ to step onto the world stage and rule with blood and horror? The imagination staggers at the thought of an army of 200 million men or a conflict so horrendous that "blood will flow to the depth of a horse's bridle for 200 miles." But it is no longer "in the future." The clock is now counting down to the final hours of the decade, century, and millennium that has been the subject of prophecy for thousands of years. Are prophets of the apocalypse found only in the Bible? How accurate have they been up to now? And last, but by no means least, is there any way to alter these dreadful images? Someone once defined truth as all things as they are, as they have been, and as they will be. We find it difficult to argue with that definition or its corollary, which is that the truth won't change just because we find it inconvenient, uncomfortable, or contrary to our already cherished belief system.

Information, particularly *new* information, has some fascinating qualities, chief among them the requirement to do something with it. It is one of the principal rules of reason that information must be dealt with. You may choose to ignore it, of course, reject it, or fashion arguments to the contrary, but once the information is at hand, something must be done with it. It has been our experience that the most useful thing to do with new information is to examine it as closely and as meticulously as possible. That is, after all, the way we grow in intellect and understanding and may account for the fact that such great thinkers and philosophers as Plato, St. Augustine, Schopenhauer, Kant, Einstein, Freud, and Jung found the study of clairvoyance and other paranormal events so fascinating.

Much of what you will find in the following pages will be, to many of you, new information. It is by no means exhaustive of what is available on the varied subjects being discussed, but hopefully it is sufficient to excite your interest and open your mind to the infinite possibilities embraced in what we *don't* yet know. In this regard, we will also supply supplemental reading suggestions and pertinent Internet web site information.

All in all, it should prove to be an interesting, informative, and exciting trip through the myth and mystical realms of the paranormal world. You see, we believe that "truth" in all its dimensions does in fact exist. It is simply up to each of us to find it.

For hundreds of years, thousands of people have found their truth in a discipline called astrology. Solidly grounded in the scientifically calculated position of the sun, moon, and planets of the solar system and tied to the mathematics of precise astronomical calculations, astrology is, however, widely regarded as a "pseudoscience" at best. Could it be that after 10,000 years, astrology is still the best combination of the physical and metaphysical yet discovered?

CHAPTER TWO

The Queen of Sciences

O N February 24, 1975, members of the royal families and leading states-men from all over the world gathered in Nepal to attend the coronation of the country's new king. It was an elaborate and glittering affair, filmed for millions of television viewers around the globe. In accordance with Eastern custom, this particular date for the coronation had been chosen by Nepal's official astrologers.

If that sounds superstitious and naive, consider this: The signers of the U.S. Constitution were, for the most part, Europeans and students of the Rosicrucian order, which relies heavily on astrological portents. To many students of American history, the odd hour at which the Constitution was signed—2:17 A.M.—is further proof that the framers of this document were so dedicated that they simply paid no attention to the hour. According to astrologers, just the opposite is true. After months of wrangling and debate, the Constitution was at last ratified. But when to sign it? The location was a given, Philadelphia. That being the case, it was agreed that the signing would take place at precisely 2:17 A.M. That was the precise hour and minute, determined by the astrological portents, that would give the fledgling nation the greatest chance of success.

Nepal, by the way, is not the only modern nation that conducts its affairs according to the astrological clock. Most of the great cities of Asia today are steel and concrete proof that the Orient is on the cutting edge of modern technology; yet, half a billion people in that part of the world consult astrologers daily for advice on everything from getting a haircut to having children or making billion-dollar trade agreements. And before you write that off to Third World superstition, consider the fact that some of America's great financial moguls, including J. P. Morgan and most of New York's famous "400," were zealous clients of astrologer Evangeline Adams (more about her later) and sought her exclusive advice on the stock market.

Astrology is undeniably a popular pastime. But is it a science? Can it be demonstrated that there is any validity to its claims of power to explain who or what we are?

My personal introduction to astrology and astrologers came about in what is probably a rather common fashion. A coworker was telling me of her last visit with Henrietta Harris, an astrologer of some repute who had cast her horoscope and found in her future the promise of a new husband. I laughed and told her I could have made that prediction, whereupon this woman (she was older, with grown children) informed me that if it happened, it would be a big surprise to her, since she had made a firm commitment to herself and her children to leave matrimony in her past.

We talked about astrology for a few moments, but I brushed the whole thing aside, saying, "I don't believe in any of that."

"What's your birth date?" she asked.

"Why?"

"Never mind, just tell me when you were born and where. I want the exact time."

I gave her the information as nearly as I could remember from what my mother had told me and promptly put the whole thing out of my mind. Several days later, my friend came back, this time with two pieces of paper. One was a chart—a completely unfathomable circle divided neatly into twelve pie-shaped wedges and filled with strange squiggles and markings. The other piece of paper contained a handwritten explanation of the pie chart with all the squiggles.

"What's this?" I asked

"It's your horoscope," she replied. "Henrietta did it for me, as a favor."

"Right." I handed the papers back to her. "I told you I don't believe in this stuff."

"This isn't a religion," she replied. "You don't have to believe in it or have faith in it. It's just the way things are." She pushed the papers under my nose. "And things won't change just because you ignore them."

I looked up at her. She was deadly serious. Reluctantly, I took the two sheets of paper, glanced at the first and quickly set it aside. Then I began to read the explanation. I was at first amused, then a little bit nervous, and finally stunned. Henrietta, whoever she was, had written things about me— my personality, my character traits, my likes and dislikes—that only I could know and even some things that I didn't want to admit.

"Did you read this?" I asked my friend.

"Sure," she said, grinning. "Why?"

"There's a lot of stuff here I'd just as soon keep secret."

"You mean the fact that you're egotistical, bullheaded, and think you're smarter than everyone else?"

"Yeah, that too," I confessed.

"Don't worry about it. We've all figured it out."

Like it or not, this astrologer had nailed me. She seemed to have discovered my innermost thoughts, desires, and fears. She knew that I had been seriously injured as a child (I was hit by a car at age three and nearly killed); she knew I had been raised by a stepparent; and she knew that I was traveling a career path that was nothing more than the path of least resistance, something I was reluctant to admit, even to myself.

I did not become an instant advocate for astrology; indeed, that would be too extravagant a statement even today. I did, however, become much more open-minded and receptive to the possibility that there are forces in the world that are much maligned while being little understood. (My coworker did, by the way, get married again.)

Over the next several years, I made an attempt to at least become a bit more understanding. Henrietta Harris, as it turned out, had written one of the first books published in America on astrology. Even though she was already in her seventies I had the pleasure of her acquaintance for nearly fifteen years and spent several enjoyable evenings listening to her somewhat irreverent but always entertaining wisdom. She had learned many years earlier that the public generally would only accept her pronouncements if they were presented tongue in cheek and with just a hint of humor. In private, however, she could be deadly serious and straightforward, as when she told a longtime client and close friend that he would lose his entire fortune as well as his family in the infamous uranium boom of the 1950s. A few years later, he was living in a borrowed room—in Henrietta's house.

Most modern astrologers work with something called an *ephemeris* (Greek for "day book," a precisely calculated manual prepared by astronomers that locates the planets, hour by hour, day by day, month by month. The location is precisely calculated and rendered by sign and degree, up to 100 years in advance. Henrietta is the only astrologer I know of that actually outlived her emphemeris.

There is no arguing the worldwide belief in the influence of the planets and stars on the course of human life (the foundation of the various systems of astrology). It is a prominent philosophy in societies and cultures so profoundly different that they share few other customs. But what exactly is astrology, and how does it differ from astronomy? More importantly, perhaps, what is there about it that would give credence to the label "the queen of sciences"?

Indeed, astrology might be described as the mother of all scientific studies. Astronomy, which is essentially the mapping of the skies, didn't exist as a separate system of knowledge until well after the time of Galileo, (1564–1642). To the first civilizations, the Sumerians and the Babylonians, the effect of the planets on their lives was far more important than their location in the cosmos. Many serious scholars suggest that astrology was an important part of the Babylonian religious system. Whether that is true or not, astrology significantly influenced the minds and attitudes of the people who built their civilizations between the Tigris and the Euphrates, an attitude that prevailed well into the Common Era. In point of fact, for thousands of years, astronomy and astrology were regarded as simply two sides of the same coin. The ancient Greek philosopher and writer Strabo, who died in 24 A.D., left the cryptic note that "Chaldeans were skilled in *astronomy* and the casting of horoscopes." Still, in the popular mind, at least, astrology/ astronomy has had a somewhat perplexing history.

Astrology, according to most historians, was born in the Mesopotamian city of Babylon (though there is some evidence that the Babylonians acquired the knowledge from their conquerors, the Sumerians). The Babylonian priests, without the aid of telescopes, discovered five other planets besides the earth, sun, and moon. By plotting the "workings of the heavenly spheres" and relating them to the plagues, earthquakes, famines, and other disasters that were observable throughout their world, they came to the conclusion that everything was subject to the same set of celestial laws. The first zodiac was drawn up based on the universal application of those laws.

This was no trivial task, however. It took centuries of observation to even approach the orderly arrangement that the Babylonians fashioned into the science of astronomy/astrology. But by the time the Babylonians and Assyrians (collectively referred to as Chaldeans in a later age) had created the fanciful stories and magical tales associated with their observations, their reputation for possessing marvelous powers was revered throughout the known world. In fact, the very name Chaldean became synonymous with "magician." In the fourth century A.D., a Greek writer, Achilles Tatius, reported a tradition among the Egyptians wherein they credited the Chaldeans with mapping the heavens and inscribing their knowledge on pillars. The same tradition held that the Chaldeans claimed the glory for this science.[1]

Of course, all of this very nearly came to a halt somewhere around 600 B.C., when King Nebuchadrezzar threatened to kill all the magicians, soothsayers, and Chaldeans in the kingdom if they did not tell him the content of a particularly vexing dream and give an interpretation. According to the Bible, it was the Hebrew captive Daniel who, by means of direct revelation from God, was able to meet the king's demand and save the soothsayers from certain death.

The astrology of the Chaldeans spread to Egypt, Greece, and eventually the Roman Empire. The widely heralded Claudius Ptolemy, even today revered as a giant among mathematicians and astronomers, wrote a lengthy tome entitled *Four Books on the Influence of the Stars,* which gave the world the Ptolemaic system of the universe and an apologia on astrology that would be the leading text on the subject for fifteen centuries.[2]

During its long and checkered history, astrology has all but disappeared for hundreds of years at a time, but it has always reappeared again somewhere, followed by another worldwide migration. Astrology went from Babylonia to China and the Far East, probably by way of the smuggler's route. The Chinese, however, used a different set of stars and instead of the zodiac developed what is called the Lo King. The Lo King takes the form of a disk on which there are six circles showing the stars, planets, and groups of other symbols. Depending on the exact time and location of a person's birth, the Lo King can reveal everything that will happen to that person on earth and in the world to come.[3]

The Greeks had their own method of looking into the future: cleromancy, or the drawing of lots. Even the great Oracle of Delphi was known to keep a supply of beans that could be used as lots. Surprisingly, it was the Greek philosophers Pythagoras, Plato, and Aristotle who helped swing the Greeks away from the oracles and toward astrology. It was Aristotle, in fact, who, as an avid student of astrology, declared that the earth was governed by the motions of a "far superior world."[4]

Here the line between astrology as a science and as a pseudoscience becomes even more blurred. Johannes Campanus, a mathematician and also the chaplain and physician to Pope Urban IV, is credited with inventing the system of the twelve houses of the zodiac. There was no question as to his scientific credentials or the seriousness of his study of astrology. Two hundred years later, Johann Müller, a professor of astronomy in Vienna who published books on trigonometry, translated the works of Ptolemy, obviously believing them worthy of scientific study. In the sixteenth century, a Danish astronomer/astrologer named Tycho Brahe, working under the patronage of King Frederick II, brought the tables of Copernicus into such precise form and traced the motion of Mars so precisely that one of his assistants, Johannes Kepler, was able to base the three laws of universal gravitation on his research. Kepler, in an address before the University of Copenhagen, defended astrology. "We cannot deny the influence of the stars," he said, "without disbelieving in the wisdom of God. Man is made from the elements and absorbs them as much as food or drink, from which it follows that man must also, like the elements, be subject to the influence of the planets."[5]

Sir Isaac Newton, generally regarded as one of the greatest of all scientists, chose astrology as his life's work. It was only with the greatest reluctance that he took up the study of astronomy. When his colleagues at the Royal Society challenged his belief in astrology, he chided them for being too materialistic and accused them of ignoring the real cause of events. "I do not believe in a universe of accidents," he told them, "and after all, I have studied the subject and you haven't."[6]

During this period spanning several centuries, the scientists, it seems, *were* the astrologers. Or perhaps it was the other way around: The astrologers were the scientists. Newton, of course, went on to prove that gravity is the glue that holds the universe together: the attraction of astral bodies for one another, from galaxies and star systems to human-made satellites. It is a scientific fact that the moon and the sun create predictable tides in our oceans and otherwise substantively affect other natural phenomena on earth. Why, then, the astrologer asks, is it so difficult to believe that this massive gravitational pull can also affect human beings in some clearly predictable way?

The relatively high status enjoyed among scholarly men during the Renaissance was undoubtedly due to the notion that all sciences had a place in the humanistic revival of learning. Science itself was not worshiped as it is today; it was simply another of the many forms that knowledge might take.[7] It is quite likely that the men who signed the U.S. Constitution at 2:17 A.M. to gain an astrological advantage would have been appalled at the ridicule heaped upon President Ronald Reagan when it was revealed that his wife, from time to time, consulted an astrologer.

But as the Renaissance waned, astrology once again slipped into decline. With the discovery in 1781 of the planet Uranus, the skeptics found "proof" that the astrologers' centuries-old system, based on a system that did not include this planet, was just a sham. Some scholars referenced the "Confessions of St. Augustine," in which he carefully detailed the reasons he had lost faith in astrologers. The very different fates of identical twins, St. Augustine said, and of a rich landowner and his slave, who had been born at precisely the same time, made him question the truth of astrological prediction. But then, the charge that astrology was just so much unfounded superstition had always been made and indeed is still being made.[8]

It was another hundred years or so, the beginning of the nineteenth century, before the world saw an upturn in the acceptance of the astrologer's art, but it was a slow revival. In England in 1819, James Wilson published, *A Complete Dictionary of Astrology,* and in 1827, the periodical, *The Prophetic Messenger* began to appear. It was written by Robert Cross Smith, the man considered the father of modern astrology. Smith used the pseudonym Raphael, which turned out to have a lasting effect. The publication has continued to this very day under the title, *Raphael's Almanac, Prophetic Messenger and Weather Guide.*[9] But this was only the beginning, and yet another hundred years went by before astrology was again respectable on both sides of the Atlantic. In 1926, the College of Astrology was founded in San Francisco. It survives today as the American Federation of Astrologers, with headquarters in Washington, D.C.

In 1930, the London *Sunday Express* began running astrological predictions and found their circulation rapidly increasing. By 1941, the August issue of the *New Statesmen* magazine in England could report that "today more people follow their fate (or Hitler's) in the stars, as interpreted by the astrologers, than follow the day-to-day news of God (or Satan) as outlined by his archbishops and vicars."[10] In fact, early in the war years, it became known that Hitler employed a vast array of astrologers to help him determine his strategy and battle plans. Roosevelt and Churchill quickly enlisted the aid of one of Hitler's astrologers who had defected and put him to work analyzing the stars to try and determine what Hitler's next move might be.

It was during the early part of the twentieth century, with astrology once again on the upswing, that Evangeline Adams appeared on the American scene. Her story is a capsule summary of this unique combination of science and metaphysics called astrology.

Evangeline was born in 1872 and was a direct descendant of the sixth president of the United States, John Quincy Adams. She was educated at the exclusive Andover Academy as a genteel young lady. Interestingly, it was a Dr. J. Herbert Smith, a professor of medicine at Boston University, who introduced her to astrology and became her mentor. Not content with what the Boston doctor could teach her, she later studied under the great Indian teacher Vivekananda. Evangeline had found her life's work, and in spite of heated opposition from her family, she moved to New York City and set up practice as a professional astrologer. Her success was instantaneous.

In the mid-1890s, Evangeline, still a young woman, had attracted a number of high-profile clients, among them the owner of the stately Windsor Hotel. On one occasion, she drew up his chart and called on him immediately.

"Your beautiful hotel," she told him, "will be struck by disaster very soon."

The hotelier, a man by the name of Hinscliff, was at first alarmed, but finding such an idea preposterous, thanked Evangeline for her concern and walked away, making light of the whole episode. The very next night, the Windsor Hotel was completely destroyed by fire.

Several such high-profile predictions brought her instant celebrity. By 1914, her client list included most of New York's "400," and J. P. Morgan himself, the most powerful financial baron in the world, was not shy about seeking her exclusive advice on fluctuations in the markets. International stars such as the great operatic tenor Enrico Caruso and America's Sweetheart, Mary Pickford, were both close friends of Evangeline as well as zealous clients.

As any good historian could have predicted, Evangeline also made some powerful and jealous enemies. In 1914, she was arrested on a charge of fortune-telling. Her enemies arranged to have her arraigned before Judge John H. Fresci, known to be particularly hard on those who perpetrated fraud on an unsuspecting public. It was not a small matter. Conviction could result in as much as five years in prison.

Evangeline chose a courageous defense. To prove that astrology was a science and not just a collection of jumbled guesses (which in her case would amount to fraud), she offered to raise a horoscope for the judge's son. The judge agreed, and on the appointed day, Evangeline appeared in court with her charts and papers. Much to his surprise, the horoscope proved to be true in every respect. The judge, obviously impressed, told Evangeline and the court, "The defendant has raised astrology to the dignity of an exact science." The gavel came down with a ring of finality.

King Edward VII made a special pilgrimage to Evangeline's headquarters in Carnegie Hall, as did many other international dignitaries, and in 1930, she began what was to become one of radio's most successful broadcasts. Her show shot to the top of the ratings, and thousands of letters poured in each week. She was, by any measure, as much a celebrity as her most illustrious clients.

At the height of her fame, it was suggested that Evangeline make a lecture tour. She refused. Not even the promise of enormous sums of money, which almost certainly would have resulted from such a venture, could persuade her. Although in perfect health, she predicted that she had only a few months to live, and she did not want to waste them on tour, away from her home and friends. One rainy day the following autumn, Evangeline Adams passed away, exactly as she had predicted.

Does all of this vindicate astrology? Today's scientists, the equivalent of Newton's Royal Society, certainly don't think so. The scientific dictum seems to be, Prophecy cannot be, therefore it isn't. Given the preeminence of the scientific community in today's world, that would seem to be the end of the discussion. The scientists, according to Arthur Prieditis, "think it beneath them even to investigate such phenomena. They believe only in science. And modern authorities have declared—have they not?—prophecy and similar phenomena to be impossible."[11]

Still, the scientists must come to grips with those among them who, like Newton, declare, "I have studied it and you haven't." No less a luminary than Einstein, for example, "in his last book of reminiscences admits that he often had occupied himself with astrology and found it useful."[12]

Does that mean, then, that reading your horoscope in the daily newspaper (there are over 2,000 papers, at last count, that carry such a feature) is going to be useful in your life? In a recent conversation, Sue Apitz Upwall, a nationally known astrologer and member of the American Federation of Astrologers, told me she doesn't think so.

The favorite newspaper feature is based on sun signs. But they are no closer to being a horoscope than the crossword puzzle is to a cookbook. The whole human race is covered by only twelve sun signs, which are really generalizations of our dispositions. Like: People living in Switzerland prefer skiing to tennis. They are too broad to be meaningful, but like fortune cookies, [they] are a lot of fun. But raising a real horoscope is a very complex, mathematical procedure. And a person's sun sign . . . plays only one part.

A good many people resent the idea of fate or destiny. No one likes to think they are being controlled by forces and restrictions they can't do anything about, yet every time we take a trip that is exactly what is happening. Once we enter that dimension, a plane, a ship, a train, we lose a certain amount of control and free will. This earth of ours is a space vehicle. In that regard our "free choice" and "control" options are also limited. We know from very early in our lives there is a certain amount of fate and predestination, which we must accept as part of life: growth, health and sickness, reproduction, maturity, old-age and death. Astrology, at the very least, is a guidebook for our trip through time on the spaceship Earth. At most, as demonstrated by any number of past events, it can provide an incredible window on the future.

Sue may have had her predecessor, Evangeline Adams, in mind when she suggested that past events have demonstrated that astrology has provided a window on the future. Evangeline, in her lifetime, received thousands of endorsements, from the king of England to a poor sharecropper in Mississippi, all attesting to the fact that she was a powerful astrological prophet. And in 1931, she made a two-part prediction that added to her fame and to the nation's consternation. In the first part of her prophecy, she predicted that America would be at war in the early months of 1942. History proved her unerringly correct. In the second part of the prophecy, she warned that the final years of this century, the years we now inhabit, will be the most perilous in the world's history. Coincidentally, this is being written on the fifty-sixth anniversary of the bombing of Pearl Harbor, the event that plunged America into war in the early months of 1942.

But what of the second part of the prophecy? Can we say these are perilous times? Could Evangeline Adams, in 1931, have had any notion of the destructive power of the atomic bomb? Could she have foreseen a national leader who would build up stockpiles of chemical and biological agents to use as weapons against humankind? Was there any way she could have known that earthquakes would increase or that flooding and drought would combine to create the biblical plagues of famine and disease here and in other countries? And could she have known that armies around the world would be facing each other in a constant, if jittery, standoff? It is safe to say that these are perilous times—in fact, the most perilous in the history of the world.

Undoubtedly, there are still those who will find it difficult to give any credence to anything as distant as the sun, moon, and stars, but who would still like to know what's in store for them. Perhaps the answer is right in the palm of your hand.

Chapter Three

In the Palm of Your Hand

Count Louis le Warner de Hamon of Ireland was on his way to the war office in Whitehall, the seat of British government. He had been summoned by no less than Horatio Kitchener, the British army's most respected officer. The count knew Kitchener to be a serious student of literature, language, and music as well as military history and tactics, but he was fairly certain that the field marshal hadn't called him to his office to discuss military strategy.

The count was ushered into a large, mahogany-paneled office where Kitchener was waiting, nervously pacing back and forth in front of his desk. He was solidly built and carried himself ramrod straight, as befitted a soldier.

"Please be seated," he instructed his guest.

The count lowered himself into one of the straight-backed chairs near the center of the room and waited. He took note of the seemingly endless energy exhibited by Kitchener as the officer continued to move about the room, straightening a picture, staring out the window momentarily, and then turning back straightaway. Almost anything to keep from sitting down. The count concluded that here was a man of limitless energy and courage and probably at least as strong in intellect.

Abruptly, Kitchener stopped pacing and turned toward Count Hamon. "I wonder," he said and then paused, twirling his large handlebar moustache. "I wonder if you could . . ."—and again he paused. "I want to know about my future," he blurted out at last.

The count was unflustered. He had expected as much. Count Louis le Warner de Hamon was born William Warner near Dublin, Ireland, in 1866. As a young man, he had traced an obscure family line back to the petit Norman nobility, and, as was the fashion of the day, he renamed himself a count. Still more recently he had taken the name Cheiro, from the Greek word *cheir,* meaning "hand." It was not Count Hamon, but Cheiro, who had been summoned by Kitchener. The field marshal wanted his palm read.

"Let me see your right hand," Cheiro said.

Kitchener stiffly proffered his hand. Cheiro looked up at him. "This may take a moment," he said. "You will probably be more comfortable if you are seated. I'm sure I will be."

Kitchener harrumphed and pulled up a chair. This was a man trained for leadership and accustomed to being in charge. It was, in fact, probably due to someone else's power of persuasion that he even considered the idea of something as ridiculous as "fate." Nevertheless, he extended his hand once again, palm upward.

Cheiro carefully examined the palm of Kitchener's right hand for several moments. Then he took the left hand and examined it as well. Finally, he looked up at the man himself and smiled. "I can see nothing but success and honors for you over the next twenty years. You will become one of the most illustrious men in the land, perhaps in the world. But after that your life is at great risk. I see disaster at sea taking place in your sixty-sixth year. It does not mean, however, that you will necessarily die. If you do not travel by water in the year 1916, you will live to reap even more fame and riches."

Kitchener withdrew his hand, looked at it momentarily, closed it into a fist, and opened it again. "You can tell all of that," Kitchener asked, "just by looking at my hand?"

"Everything you are sir, or will be, is written in the palm of your hand."

Cheiro proved to be correct in every detail. Four years after his reading, Kitchener gained worldwide fame by taking Khartoum. He distinguished himself further in South Africa against the Boers. At the beginning of World War I, it was Kitchener, now Lord Kitchener, who was named England's war minister. But in 1916, Lord Kitchener either forgot or ignored Cheiro's advice and at the czar's invitation, sailed for Russia to discuss that country's role in the war against Germany. Kitchener was aboard the cruiser HMS *Hampshire* and still in British waters when the ship struck a German mine and went down with the loss of most of her hands—and Lord Kitchener. His body was never found.

Cheiro later gave the world his own interpretation of his interview with Kitchener. "The line of Life," he said, "gave the expectation of a long life under ordinary conditions, but my prediction was based on the cross at the end of the travel line opposite the age of sixty-six."[1]

The process by which Cheiro made his determinations was called *scrying*, and at the end of the nineteenth century, scrying (and divination of all kinds) was not only respectable but quite fashionable. Unquestionably, Cheiro was the foremost palmist of his time, and he is still regarded as one of the leading experts on palmistry the world has ever known. In his best-selling books, he theorized that the palm print revealed the psychological nature of the subject, but in Cheiro's day, police agencies were still scoffing at Bertillon's theory of fingerprints as a physical form of identification. The idea that palm prints were personality identifiers had even less appeal, with a few notable exceptions. The great German psychiatrist Sigmund Freud became quite interested in Cheiro's theories. Carl Jung, a student and contemporary of Freud, actually tested the concept on some of his most difficult patients.

By and large, Cheiro followed the time-honored rules of palmistry that had been set down long before he came on the scene. He would ask no personal questions of the subject but would first classify the entire hand according to the seven main classes determined by the French palmist Casimir D'Arpentigny. From there, the shape, length, and thickness of palm and fingers were noted, as well as coloration, all before a single line in the palm was scryed.

But palmistry, like astrology, had a long and checkered history. Cheiro was aware of this and often remarked that had he lived in an earlier time, he might well have been executed for trafficking with the devil. References to palmistry and related arts can be traced back to 1000 B.C., where mention of the practice is made in the Vedic writings of ancient India. The oldest known manuscript on palmistry in England dates back to 1440, and the first book to be published in Europe on the subject is dated 1475. It was called, *The Art of Chiromancy* and was written by John Hartlieb.

By 1530, however, the art of palmistry was under attack. King Henry VIII himself launched the offensive. Singling out the gypsies, who were then scattered throughout Europe, King Henry made no secret of his disapproval of not only the gypsies in general but the practice of palm reading in particular:

> [The gypsies are] an outlandish people calling themselves Egyptians . . . who have come to this realm and gone from shire to shire in great companies and used great subtle and crafty means to deceive people, bearing them in hand that they, by palmistry, could tell men's and women's fortune, and so . . . have deceived the people of their money and have also committed many heinous felonies and robberies.[2]

Needless to say, the art of reading palms quickly went out of fashion. When James I came to the throne, he added his own brand of contempt and attacked those who persisted in the practice as "devil-dealers." In 1664, the English writer Richard Saunders could blast the palmists of London with impunity, accusing them of nonsense and impudence.[3]

For the next 250 years, palmistry was practiced in secret and only by those who dared to risk official censure from both the government and the church. But by the early nineteenth century, palmistry began to stage a comeback. Royalty was less strident in their denunciations, the church seemingly more broad-minded. In Paris, Madame Adele Moreau had so many clients she was forced to turn them away. Her male counterpart was the same Casimir D'Arpentigny mentioned earlier. Almost single-handedly rescuing palmistry from centuries of disrepute, these two French practitioners laid the foundation for those who would take the art of palmistry into the twentieth century. One of their most ardent and gifted followers was Cheiro.

Still, in the early 1900s, the attitude was more one of tolerance than of acceptance. The level of skepticism was still high on both sides of the Atlantic. On his first visit to New York City, Cheiro's fame had preceded him and he was challenged by the *New York World*, one of the city's leading newspapers, to prove his abilities. In an attempt to test his powers, the publisher presented Cheiro with the handprint of five persons, all completely unknown to him. Among the handprints was that of a Dr. Meyer, an infamous physician who had recently been convicted of several murders.

Cheiro examined the prints and provided the *New York World* with what amounted to "life readings" of four of the five people. The *World* published Cheiro's commentaries, all of which were chilling in their accuracy. Cheiro was an instant celebrity. These readings alone would have more than proved his unique ability, but there was still one more handprint, that of Dr. Meyer.

When the *New York World* published Cheiro's profile of this man, readers were stunned. His evaluation of Dr. Meyer was astonishing in both its accuracy and its detail:

> Whether this man has committed one crime or twenty is not the question. As he enters his 44th year he will be tried for murder and condemned to death. It will then be found that he has used his intelligence and whatever profession he has followed, to obtain money by crime, and he has stopped at nothing to achieve his ends. He will be sentenced to death. Yet his hands show he will not end in this manner. He will live for years, but in prison.

The infamous serial killer, a trusted family physician, had poisoned at least a dozen patients for profit. He was on death row awaiting execution in the electric chair. Cheiro had identified his characteristics perfectly, even the term of his sentence, except for that business of the death penalty not being carried out. On this point, the press and the public were skeptical. There didn't seem to be any chance that Meyer would escape the chair.

A week before his scheduled execution, Meyer pleaded to be given the opportunity to speak with Cheiro. Permission was granted, and Cheiro made the trip to Sing Sing prison to speak with the murderer. By this time, Meyer was reduced to a quivering mass of fear. His only thought was whether he would die or escape death as Cheiro had predicted.

"Let me see your hands," Cheiro said.

Meyer quickly extended his hands. "Could you . . . could you see the ghastly thing?" he asked, referring to the electric chair that was to be the instrument of his death.

"No, it's not visible." Cheiro was clearly taken aback by what he was looking at. "Dear Lord, such evil in these hands."

"I don't need you to tell me that," Meyer snapped.

"Are you afraid, Meyer?" Cheiro wanted to know.

"This is a living nightmare. There are no words for the horror I feel."

"But not for your victims."

"They never knew," Meyer replied. "They died quickly, almost painlessly, but this is grotesque, inhuman."

Cheiro stood up and walked to the cell door. "What a thoroughly evil animal you are, Dr. Meyer."

"Think what you like," Meyer snapped, "but do you still believe what it said in the paper, that I shall escape the chair?"

The guard opened the cell door and Cheiro stepped out into the long, empty corridor. He paused briefly, then turned back to the terrified prisoner. "You won't be executed, Meyer, but there will be times when you wish you had been. The rest of your days in a cage will be most unpleasant. The nights, I assure you, will be even worse."

Cheiro returned to his apartment. The story of his conversation with Meyer had been published, but as the number of days to the execution counted down to one and then turned into the agonizing hourly countdown to midnight, at least one of the reporters for the *New York World* let it be known that he didn't believe Cheiro's prediction. He left the paper early to take up a position near Cheiro's apartment, so he could be the first to get the palmist's embarrassed comments when Meyer died. At approximately 10:00 P.M. on the evening of the execution, Cheiro's doorbell rang. He opened the door to find the reporter standing on the stoop, pencil and pad in hand.

"Can I help you?" Cheiro asked politely.

"I came to gloat," the reporter said tersely. "Meyer dies at midnight."

"I see. Well, what would you have me say?"

"That you're a fraud. That you made some lucky guesses but that you blew the big one."

Cheiro looked at his watch. "There are still two hours," he said.

Before the reporter could reply, they were interrupted by the sound of a newsboy shouting in the street.

"Extra, extra, read all about it! Meyer escapes the chair! Supreme Court finds a flaw! Read all about it!"

The reporter hailed the newsboy, who quickly brought him a paper. "I don't believe this," growled the reporter.

"Of course not," Cheiro replied, and added, "how very sad for you."

In spite of his successes, Cheiro's path to fame and riches was not always a smooth one. "I had not been in London a month," he wrote, "before a Catholic priest refused to give absolution to an entire family because they consulted me against his wishes." And during his first year in America, two clergymen visited him, both trying to persuade him that his success was solely due to the agency of the devil. One of them offered him a clergyship, at a small salary, if he would just recant his association with the evil one.

But it was not a supposed alliance with the devil that got him into the most trouble with the church, but rather a dispute over an interpretation of a passage in the Bible. In the standard King James version, Job 37:7 reads: "He sealeth up the hand of every man: that all men may know his work." Cheiro and the palmists insisted that the original Hebrew read: "God placed signs and marks in the hands of all the sons of men that all men might know their works." Cheiro's thousands of clients, of course, accepted his version, eagerly maintaining that the church was simply too obstinate to admit that palmistry was divinely inspired.

Whether divinely inspired or not, Cheiro's record of predictions is truly amazing. He foretold the Boer War two years in advance, as well as the death of Queen Victoria. He predicted an assassination attempt on the Shah of Persia in Paris that was thwarted and the assassination of King Umberto of Italy that was not. His list of consultations reads like a "who's who" of the times. He advised the greatest and most famous names of his day, from Mark Twain to President Grover Cleveland and the czar of Russia. He was twice a war correspondent and a British intelligence agent and, surprisingly, a lover of the famous German war spy Mata Hari. It almost seems fitting that Cheiro would migrate to Hollywood and become an advisor to the movie screen's biggest stars. He died there in 1936. His home, on a quiet side street, still draws the curious, even after sixty years.

Cheiro did leave behind one interesting bit of insight into what one would need to take up the vocation (or perhaps avocation) of palmistry. "The most important quality a responsible palmist can have," he said, "is humility. The humility to know when it is kinder and more Christian not to speak."

But is it just the palms of the hands that can be read? According to some people, the bumps on your head can reveal your future (*phrenology*); and there are others who believe that character can be determined by the shape and contours of the face (*physiognomy*). All in all, it would seem that to the practiced eye, each of us is an open book.

About the time of the American Revolution, a clergyman and mystic from Zurich named Johann Kaspar Lavater shifted his emphasis from palmistry to a new "science," which ultimately became known as physiognomy. While all paranormal practices deal in some way with the future, Lavater was most interested in defining character. One's character, he thought, was the most likely key to one's future endeavors.

By 1770, Lavater had refined his process and wrote and published a book that he hoped would elevate his process to the level of an exact science. The book, *Physiognomical Fragments,* was an immediate success with the public but failed to get physiognomy accepted by the scientific community. Lavater's ideas were nevertheless a forerunner of modern forensic science. He wrote that "the hands of man are equally diverse and dissimilar as their faces . . . just as it is impossible to find two faces perfectly alike, so it is impossible to find two people whose hands resemble each other perfectly." Nearly 200 years later, Bertillon's fingerprinting notions would prove him 100 percent correct.

Lavater went far beyond the obvious, however. He believed that even the deepest human traits could be discovered from the human face. He boldly declared that certain facial characteristics denoted strength of mind or a lack thereof. He would proclaim one person to be resolute, industrious, and sincere, while proclaiming another to be powerful, daring, and eloquent but devoid of grace. Such qualities as sincerity, fortitude, humor, perseverance, perception, and even poetic genius were all apparent to Lavater, and even though his work never achieved the status of "true science," many of his views were expounded by scientists of the nineteenth century and became the foundation of today's character analysis. Charles Darwin, the great naturalist, in his book, *Expression of the Emotions in Men and Animals,* found Lavater's concepts to be quite useful. The Italian anthropologist Paolo Mantegazza went so far as to divide the face into three sections: the forehead, the nose, and the area from the base of the nose to the tip of the chin. From this he arrived at some interesting generalizations, many of which are still with us today. The longer the forehead, he stated, the brainier the person; the longer the nose, the more energetic and forceful; the longer the mouth and chin, the more determined and dogged the person is likely to be.[4]

Coming from a mystic like Lavater, such conclusions were greeted with skepticism, but in the mouth of an anthropologist, they could inspire criminologists to declare that criminals fall into clearly identifiable physical types. Eventually, such notions as a thief's "handle-shaped" ears or a murderer's "thumb" were ridiculed out of existence, but the residue of Lavater's concept is still around and occasionally sneaks up on us.

A friend recently told me that a mutual acquaintance was a hunter of considerable prowess. I knew the man in question to be a fierce competitor, but I was genuinely surprised at this revelation. He looked like someone that central casting would choose for one of Santa's elves. He had a sparkling personality and intelligent demeanor, and furthermore, I knew him to be a deeply spiritual man.

"You're kidding," I said, "he doesn't look like a hunter."

"What do you have to look like to be a hunter?" my friend asked. I knew I had been caught in a stereotype trap that was set over 200 years ago.

The practice of phrenology was started by a physician. That is not too surprising, perhaps, considering that not many people, other than your doctor, are likely to take much notice of any bumps you might have on your head. Franz Joseph Gall was born in Baden, Germany, in 1758, studied medicine in Strassburg, and began his medical practice in Vienna. An admirer of Lavater, he was nevertheless a scientist by training and advanced his theories of phrenology based on extensive research.

The reading of character by a careful examination of bumps on the head made perfect sense to Gall, who noticed as a schoolboy that the most outstanding scholars were those with "peculiarities" in the shape of the head. These shapes, he thought, must be the result of variations in the development of certain surface areas of the brain. Later, as a student of Lavater (and in keeping with the medical practices of the day), he applied the same rationalizations to his theories as Lavater had to physiognomy. With physiognomy, facial appearance or formations were checked against the traits they seemed to represent. With phrenology, Gall divided the skull into three major regions, then subdivided those regions into a number of others, all identified by specific enlargements. Gall listed twenty-six of these enlargements and checked them against the characteristics of persons having the same noticeable bumps.

Another Viennese physician by the name of Johann Kaspar Spurzheim, a disciple of Gall, increased these "irregular" areas to something in the neighborhood of forty-one separate sections. Unlike Gall, who stayed fairly close to home and worked from his own patients or skulls that were sent to him, Spurzheim took his show on the road, so to speak, and lectured widely on the benefits of phrenology. While in Scotland, a lawyer by the name of George Combe heard one of Spurzheim's lectures and was so impressed that he became instrumental in bringing the practice to America.

Gall often referred to phrenology as "a scientific form of divination," and he and Spurzheim might have made the practice at least somewhat acceptable to the larger scientific community. Unfortunately, the system was so badly abused by a host of quacks and charlatans in central Europe that the whole concept was largely buried under a barrage of unfavorable press. Gall himself was attacked and ridiculed by fellow doctors and priests. His lectures in Vienna were often shouted down by an ever-growing cadre of opponents.

Given the temper of the times, that might have been the end of Gall's noble experiment; but as we will see, any of the psychic sciences that promise to tell us who we are, what we might become, and when and how it will all take place are very hard to put down. Phrenology, like palmistry, began to make a slow comeback in the early part of the nineteenth century, and today phrenology ranks as one of the most popular of all the psychic sciences.

Add to that the study of moles on the body for purposes of divining the future, taking into account their size, shape, color, and location on the body, and the interpretation of the lines of the forehead according to certain zodiac designations, and we apparently have bodies that are like pamphlets to be read by whomever has the psychic skills.

Donald Campbell, at one time the holder of both the land speed record and the water speed record, was known worldwide as a man of immense courage and skill. On the morning of January 4, 1967, he took his famous speedboat, *Bluebird*, to Coniston Water in the Lake District of England. Campbell was determined to keep the water speed record on his side of the Atlantic, and one way to do that was to improve on the record he still held. American challengers were already lining up in an attempt to bring the water speed record back to the United States. This was to be the run that would discourage all would-be competitors.

Coniston Water was smooth as glass when Campbell fired up the supercharged engines in *Bluebird*. There was not the slightest hint of a breeze. Conditions were perfect for what he hoped would be a preemptive run. The big boat eased out onto the lake and maneuvered into starting position. A moment later, *Bluebird* was streaking across the water, the speedometer inching up toward the magic mark of 300 miles an hour.

Millions of speed boating fans around the world have seen the film of what happened next. Just short of the 300-mile-per-hour mark, the bow of *Bluebird* lifted into the air. In a horrifying ballet of death, the boat did a complete backward somersault and plunged into the lake, coming apart in the process as if it were made of matchsticks. It sank in seconds, quickly dropping 140 feet to the bottom. Divers were able to recover parts of the hull, but Donald Campbell's body was never found.

Everyone knew that Campbell would go all out on this run, pushing his boat and himself to the very limit. What only his closest associates knew was that he was a man who believed in "signs," and just two hours before the ill-fated run, Campbell had decided to seek his fortune in the cards. He spread the deck of cards and withdrew two and turned them over. He glanced down at the queen and the ace of spades.

"Interesting," he said to friends who were watching, "these are the two cards that Mary, Queen of Scots, drew the night before her execution." He slipped the two cards back into the deck and tossed it into the boat. "I fear someone in my family will die very soon."

If Campbell was concerned that the cards indicated him, he gave no sign of it. Yet, it's doubtful that even Campbell knew that the standard 52-card deck of playing cards he used to cast his fortune was based on the 78 cards of the tarot. Had he been aware of their origins, he might have heeded the cards and may even be alive today.

The origin of the tarot cards has never been fully explained, but they do have a long history. Some experts believe that they evolved from Chinese divining sticks; others claim that they were adapted from the pages of the legendary Book of Thoth used by the ancient Egyptians. Whatever their source, they seem to have been devised specifically for the purpose of fore-telling the future.

Their appearance in Europe can be dated back to around A.D. 1300 and is usually credited to wandering tribes of gypsies who, perhaps to give them-selves status, claimed to have come from "Little Egypt." No one knows what wag shortened "Egyptian" to "gypsy," but the name stuck and became a syn-onym for soothsayer and, rightly or wrongly, thief. As noted earlier, the gyp-sies incurred the wrath of King Henry VIII because of their skill in palmistry, but it's a safe bet that, then as now, there is not a self-respecting band of gyp-sies anywhere in the world that does not have its deck of tarot cards and someone in the camp skilled in their interpretation.

It appears that the cards themselves were not referred to as "tarot" until their emergence in Europe. Each deck, or pack, consists of 78 cards, of which 56 are "suit" cards, not unlike a modern playing deck, the difference being that the suits were originally swords, cups, coins, and batons. Each suit also contained 4 cards representing the court (as opposed to 3): the king, queen, knight, and knave (jack). The rest of the deck ran down from 10 to 1, the latter being the ace. The additional 22 cards all bore symbolic pictures.

It should be pointed out that the 22 additional cards of the tarot in a modern deck are not always the same. Certain cultural differences seem to have crept in over the centuries, but a typical list might be as follows:

1. The Juggler
2. The High Priestess
3. The Empress
4. The Emperor
5. The Hierophant
6. The Lovers (very big in the Bond film)
7. The Chariot
8. Justice
9. The Hermit
10. Fortune
11. Strength
12. The Hanged Man
13. Death
14. Temperance
15. The Devil
16. Lightning
17. The Stars
18. The Moon
19. The Sun
20. Judgement
21. The World
22. The Fool[5]

These cards, known as the "greater arcana," have a special significance in the process of divination. Sometimes, when dealing the cards, they come out upside down, in which case the divination is changed, usually for the worse. The remainder of the deck, or the suit cards, are known as the "lesser arcana" and have their own interpretations.[6]

Originally, the cards were strictly for fortune-telling, but the French changed the suits to the now familiar hearts, clubs, spades, and diamonds, with spades replacing swords, clubs replacing batons, hearts replacing cups, and diamonds replacing coins. It was perhaps inevitable that card games would develop, but that presented a few problems. Original tarot cards were all printed one way—that is, there was a top and a bottom to each card. As mentioned earlier, whether or not the card was dealt right side up or upside down had a different meaning in the divination. This had no significance at all with reference to games, so the reversible, or "top-top," style familiar today was adopted. The knight was dropped, and the Fool became the joker. The remainder of the greater arcana was eliminated, reducing the deck to 52 "playing" cards, and the transformation was complete.

The tarot as a means of divination has remained pretty much intact, however. Devotees see in its structure an entire system of symbols that provides the "key to the mysteries" and "holds the secret of the true nature of man, the universe and God."[7] Like virtually all of the psychic sciences, however, the rise in popularity of the tarot meant an almost inevitable confrontation with the church. The first salvo in the conflict was fired by a Swiss monk in 1377. His problem was not only with tarot cards but with playing cards in general. The monk's displeasure notwithstanding, the denunciation seems to have had little effect on the growth of the use of either playing cards or the tarot. The tarot appeared in royal courts all over Europe and were a fixture in the castles of the nobles. King Charles VI of France actually commissioned the painting of three packs of cards that became famous as works of art.

Some of these cards appeared as an integral part of the plot of the popular James Bond movie *Live and Let Die*. Set in New Orleans and the Caribbean, the story revolves around the ability of a young priestess who has the power to tell the future from the cards. It is an effective, if somewhat simplistic, view of the hold that the tarot can have on true believers.

But the church was not about to throw in the towel. In 1423, St. Bernadin of Siena leveled an attack on the tarot that actually resulted in the burning of untold numbers of packs of the cards. This time, the battle seemed to go in favor of the religious point of view. The political and religious leaders of Europe attempted to stifle the use of cards in general. For a time, importation of the cards was banned by both the Viennese and English kings.

But just as with the other psychic sciences, the tarot made a comeback, due in large part to the efforts of the highly respected French writer Antoine Court de Gebelin. In volume eight of a monumental work that compared the Old and New Worlds, published between 1773 and 1784, Gebelin included a section entitled "The Fame of the Tarot." His enthusiasm for the tarot seemed boundless, regarding it as "a work of ancient Egypt [concerning] their most pure and interesting doctrines." It was Gebelin, perhaps, who was responsible for giving credit for the tarot to the Egyptian Book of Thoth. Gebelin believed the tarot to be a source of magical learning and wisdom that everyone should be eager to obtain, because "what had validity and was in force (in ancient times) is also present in our modern times."[8] At least one great French leader apparently agreed. Napoleon Bonaparte is said to have employed Marie Lenormand (shades of James Bond) to advise him before each of his battles. Even though he threw her into the dungeon on two occasions for predicting things contrary to his designs, he and Josephine both seem to have relied on her reading of the cards with an almost religious conviction. Unfortunately, he ignored her prophecy that he would die by either a rope or a bullet.

The use of the tarot continued to expand well into the nineteenth century and even began to take on new and unforeseen characteristics. In 1856, a Frenchman who called himself Eliphas L`evi linked the tarot with the Kabbala, an occult system of thought originated by Jewish mystics in the second or third century. In 1887, in London, the Hermitic Order of the Golden Dawn was founded. This group followed some of L`evi's teachings but added their own twist. The 22 cards of the greater arcana were linked with the 22 paths of the Sacred Tree of the Kabbala and the 22 letters of the Hebrew alphabet in an attempt to show a direct relationship between God, humankind, and the universe. The Hermitic Order still has its adherents.

Coming down to our own day, the various designs and conflicting interpretations of the cards can make the study of the tarot an arduous and time-consuming effort. Only truly devoted practitioners have the stamina for the task. A French barber and wig maker named Aliette wrote a series of very popular books about the tarot. In his text, he warned: "I have studied the mysteries of the cards for more than thirty years and it is only now that I am beginning to understand them at their truest and deepest level."[9]

The study of the cards, or the palm, or the shape of the face and head is only one aspect of the particular discipline one chooses to follow. Implicit in all of these activities is the intuitive nature of the person doing the reading. We can easily understand Cheiro's explanation of the lines that crossed the "travel line" in Lord Kitchener's palm and even see how a scale of sorts could lead him to the age of sixty-six years. But what was there in the field marshal's palm that told Cheiro he must avoid travel on the sea? On the other hand (no pun intended), Donald Campbell, a novice with the cards, was not sensitive enough to realize it was his own doom the cards predicted.

In every case, it seems that the psychic mind is the key to giving credence to the psychic science. In the next chapter, we will meet perhaps the greatest of all the psychic intellects and try to discover what, if anything, he had to say about the time in which we live.

Section Two

PSYCHIC PATTERNS

The Chessboard is the world,
the pieces are the phenomena of the universe,
the rules of the game are what we call the laws of nature.
The player on the other side is hidden from us.
THOMAS HENRY HUXLEY, *Collected Essays*

IT WAS A BRIGHT SUNDAY MORNING. Outside, the splendid fall colors were made even brighter by a brilliant Indian summer sun. Inside the modest home, a typical middle-class husband was getting everything in position for a leisurely afternoon of football and his favorite snacks. His wife (we'll call her Gayle) would be home from church shortly, and after dinner, he didn't want any delays in getting to the game.

Suddenly the front door opened and closed. He looked at his watch. She shouldn't be home for another hour, and the kids couldn't have come home without her. He hurried from the den into the living room and saw his wife, her coat still on, sitting on the couch and crying softly.

"Honey," he said, as he hurried to her side, "what is it? What's wrong?"

Somewhere in the back of his mind was the suspicion that someone in the neighborhood had become aware of his wife's "sensitive" abilities and had said something to upset her. He was wrong.

Wiping the tears from her eyes, she looked up at him. "Stephanie," she whispered, "something is terribly wrong with Stephanie."

Stephanie was the-twelve-year-old daughter of one of the church officials. She was a bright and talented little girl who played piano for the smaller children and generally brightened everyone's day just by being in the room.

"Stephanie?" he echoed. "What's wrong . . . I mean, how do you know something's wrong? Is she ill? Did her father . . . ?"

"No, no," she said, waving her hand in frustration. Then she looked up at him, gravely serious. "I don't know how I know," she said, "but something is terribly wrong in that little girl's stomach."

"Oh, I see," he said, patting his wife gently on the shoulder. "Here, let me take your coat."

He really didn't see at all, but they had been married long enough that he knew when to back off and leave her to struggle with what she called "her problem." But deep inside, he felt a little sick. He had never known his wife to be wrong when she got these "impressions."

Two weeks later, little Stephanie began to complain of terrible stomach cramps. Her parents, after trying all of the usual home remedies, rushed her to the hospital. Exploratory surgery revealed a huge tumor in the child's stomach that had already involved most of her internal organs. By the end of the following month, she was dead.

Gayle was almost as devastated as the parents. Why, she wondered, if there was nothing that could be done to save the child, did she have to know of the coming agony? Worse, could she somehow be responsible? The image of the dark mass in the little girl's stomach had come to her completely unbidden. It had thrust itself into her mind, and the sudden awareness had left her weak and trembling with a sudden wave of sadness, as if Stephanie were already dead. Terrified and angry, she had turned and fled from the church. There was nothing she could do but await the inevitable and go through the suffering a second time.

A few weeks after Stephanie's death, Gayle came home from church, again in a state of emotional disarray. Bill, a young father in the neighborhood, had been in church that morning with his wife and two daughters.

Bill's wife was expecting, and she had just been told to expect twins. They were both beaming, eager to share the good news with everyone.

Gayle had smiled and congratulated them, but then she hurried home to tell her husband that a feeling of dread had come over her as she shook hands with Bill. "I just wanted to take him by the shoulders and tell him to be very, very careful."

The following week, Bill, an officer in the air guard, left home for a two-week training mission. He never returned. Two days into the training program, Bill's crew had taken off on a routine overwater flight. Something went wrong, and the plane powered into the ocean, killing everyone on board.

In many ways, this experience was even more agonizing. "Why didn't I tell him?" she asked her husband.

"Tell him what?"

"I don't know . . . something."

She might have told him, of course, but history is filled with examples of psychics who tried to warn friends, relatives, patrons, even strangers of impending disaster, only to have their warnings ignored.

Gayle was, at the time, what the experts call an *accidental seer*. She was one of the many psychics who only occasionally—and sometimes only once in their lifetime—experience some kind of psychic awareness. Like all accidental seers, she had no control over when the impressions would come or what they were likely to be about. Deeply troubled that they always seemed to bring with them some dark tragedy (and almost always death), Gayle began a lifelong study of the phenomenon.

Ultimately, Gayle became convinced that what she had was not a "problem," but rather a "gift," one that she was obligated to use for the benefit of others. The more she studied, the more she realized that her abilities went far beyond simply recognizing "death." As an event that can be, and often is, detected by psychics, dying is probably the most profound of all of life's phenomena. But the death impressions were only the beginning. As both her study and the awareness of her capabilities increased, she became what is referred to as an *incidental seer*. A much smaller group, these individuals are able to exercise some control over their gift. Still, most of these psychics use it sparingly. It was at her husband's insistence, for example, that Gayle had agreed to "read" jewelry during a break in the activities at a broadcasters convention. That event, however, served to sharpen her understanding even more.

Gayle continued to study the history and processes of psychics of all kinds and eventually achieved "membership" in the smallest psychic club of all, the *intentional seers,* a tiny group of men and women who, throughout history, have demonstrated that they have considerable control over their abilities. We have already introduced a few of the psychics in this latter group. Cheiro, and Evangeline Adams, for example, were intentional seers who recognized their abilities early on and made their psychic gifts their life's work. Gayle is a more modern example, and we'll get to know her better later on. But now it's time to meet the most famous and most remarkable of all the intentional seers.

Chapter Four

Physician, Poet, Prophet

THE VERY NAME NOSTRADAMUS CONJURES UP thoughts of prophetic images, impossible flights into the future, and word puzzles that an anxious world has been unable to solve. Nearly a third of all of Nostradamus's quatrains are still complete mysteries to even the most astute expert on his writings. But we're getting ahead of ourselves.

Nostradamus was much more than just a prophet with incredible foresight. He was also a true Renaissance man, a physician of such courage and consummate skill that the city of Salon settled upon him a pension for life in gratitude for his work among the sufferers of the great plague in that city. Other physicians, seeing no hope of curing the deadly disease, simply left with those who had not yet contracted it. Nostradamus stayed on, trying new and innovative ways to restore his patients to health. Many of his ideas worked. As a result, the citizens of Salon bestowed upon him their trust and gratitude, and the city became his home. The house in which he lived and wrote his prophecies still stands and is a major tourist attraction.

Nostradamus also demonstrated that even the intentional psychic can be deeply involved with every aspect of not just his own life, but the lives of all those around him. Not only was Nostradamus an innovator in his own field—medicine—but he was also an inventor in seemingly unrelated fields. In addition to his medical skills, he gained fame as an herbalist, a creator of cosmetics, and an expert in preserving fruit. He was a poet and what many have called a "celestial" scientist. He argued in favor of the Copernican theory that the sun

was the center of the solar system a hundred years before Galileo was perse-
cuted for advancing the same concept. Yet, in the final analysis, Nostradamus
set all of this aside and devoted himself almost entirely to the strange, and one
suspects often frightening, inner world of prophecy. Ashe tells us in his preface
to *Centuries,* it was a world that "lifted him above finiteness and showed him
the course of history as one continuous, coherent spectacle."[1]

It is that spectacle that engages us. No study of psychic ability can be
complete without some analysis of the patterns of prophecy employed by
Nostradamus. They were, by any standard of measure, unique.

It is well documented that Nostradamus had an abiding interest in astrology from a very early age. Some experts have even suggested that his quatrains
are, in fact, astrological forecasts. While it is probably true that Nostradamus
"used" astrology, his own words tell us that the source of his vision was quite
something else indeed. He was, perhaps, the ultimate clairvoyant.

Our dictionary defines clairvoyance as "the paranormal power of seeing
objects or actions beyond the range of natural vision" and also the "quick,
intuitive knowledge of things and people; sagacity." As we shall see, Nostradamus was all those things. Yet, even the best clairvoyants have some
notable difficulties. Their visions do not always provide a clear sense of
where events will occur or in what chronological order. Astrologers, on the
other hand, can fix times and places quite precisely, but many of them lack
the intuitive power to fully understand their forecasts. Nostradamus, it
seems, had the best of both worlds. He used astrology, much as a carpenter
uses a level and a tape measure, to try and fix his clairvoyant visions in a specific time and place. As to the source of those visions, Nostradamus wrote:

> Sitting alone at night in a secret study;
> it is placed on the brass tripod.
> A slight flame comes out of the emptiness
> and prophesies that which *should not be believed in vain.*

It is clear that Nostradamus used some device. Most experts believe that
"it" refers to a brass bowl filled with water that was placed upon the tripod.

Some have found evidence that a certain plant or plants were used to condition the water to help make the vision even clearer. There is, as you might expect, an enormous amount of conjecture when it comes to ascertaining whatever it was that gave Nostradamus such incredible foresight. What can be stated with certainty, however, is that he worked with his device and with astrological signs and devoted himself to the subsequent writing of his *Centuries* to the exclusion of almost everything else.

Perhaps we should take a moment here and define some of the terms by which the Nostradamus predictions can be identified.

Centuries refers to the collections of prophetic writings created by Nostradamus. The intent, apparently, was to include 100 quatrains in each book—hence the name *Centuries*. The term, however, is a bit misleading. Not all of the *Centuries* contain precisely 100 quatrains. The first book, in fact, contains 354 of the cryptic messages and is usually referred to as the *True Centuries*. Thereafter, the mathematics become more precise, although some of the later volumes contain fewer than 100 verses.

The *quatrains* are themselves the descriptions of Nostradamus's prophetic visions. They derive their name from the fact that each was written in a cryptic, four-line verse form, a format that permitted Nostradamus to employ several devices for obscuring the meaning of the vision without completely obliterating it. For example, quatrains written in sequence and relating to a single event could be separated and dropped in randomly in other *Centuries*. What's more, Nostradamus could use both the number of the quatrain and its position in a particular volume to add meaning to the verse itself. Some experts believe that he would also juxtapose certain quatrains, putting the last first and vice versa. Clearly, the effort was to make the meaning of the verses as obscure as possible. But why?

Again, Nostradamus himself provides the answer. He was keenly aware that the kings, princes, and potentates of his day could easily do away with him if his predictions were not to their liking.

He also knew that as surely as the rain falls on the just and unjust alike, there would always be those who would find his forecasts highly disagreeable. He wrote:

For this reason, I have withheld my tongue from the vulgar and my pen from paper. But afterwards I was willing, for the common good, to enlarge myself in dark and abstruse sentences, declaring the future events, chiefly the most urgent and those which I foresaw, (whatever human mutations happened), would not offend the hearers.

Clearly, Nostradamus knew that he was taking risks, but his sense of "the common good," compelled him to declare the future as he saw it.

Let's consider for a moment what kind of man we're dealing with here. Nostradamus was, by any standard, supremely intelligent and one of the most enlightened physicians of his time. He had settled upon him a lifetime annuity sufficient to care for himself and his family to the end of his days, and he enjoyed the trust and admiration of all his neighbors, commoner and nobleman alike. His association with the church, likewise, was never put in question. Yet, he was willing to put all of this at risk for what he deemed to be "the common good." Whatever the force that moved him, it must have been powerful indeed. Once again, it is Nostradamus who gives us a hint of what that force might be:

The wand in the hand is placed in the middle
of the legs of the tripod. He sprinkles both the hem
and his foot with water. A voice. Fear: he trembles
in his robes.
Divine splendor. The God sits beside him.

What a remarkable description of both the process and his feelings about it. Alone at night, filled with trepidation and trembling at the prospect of what was about to take place, yet knowing he must take another journey into an unknown and fearful future, he prepares to accept whatever comes. One wonders if we are brave enough to take that journey with him.

The next question, of course, is, Was he right? Did his predictions actually prove to be accurate enough to draw attention to himself? In many cases the record is clear, so let's take a look, not at the history of the man (we'll do that later), but at the history of the prophecies themselves.

Upon publication of the first volumes of *Centuries,* and much to the surprise of Nostradamus, he became the darling of the court. Catherine de Médicis, in particular, was one of his most ardent and loyal fans. She would often consult him, going in secret late at night and climbing the narrow stairway to the small upstairs room that served Nostradamus as both study and bedchamber. Her husband, King Henry II, did not share her fascination with Nostradamus, but he fully understood that the queen believed his every word. He was persuaded, therefore, to promise the queen that he would refrain from individual combat on the strength of one of Nostradamus's dire predictions:

> The young lion will overcome the old one on the battlefield
> in single combat.
> In a cage of gold his eyes will be put out.
> Two wounds one. Then to die a cruel death.

Nostradamus assured the queen that this terrible fate predicted for her husband could be avoided if the king would simply decline any further attempts at single combat. But this was rather like telling Michael Jordan that he could avoid injury by simply not playing basketball. It might be the wise thing to do, but the instincts of a lifetime often overshadow reason.

Three years later, Henry threw a gigantic party to celebrate the weddings of his daughter and his sister in a huge double ceremony. Trial at the lists, as always, was an important part of the entertainment. The king, ignoring the pleas of his wife, insisted on a joust with the young Count de Montgomery. Even the young count, who was well aware of the prophecy, tried his best to desist, all to no avail.

Everyone gathered at the lists, most of them mindful of what Nostradamus had predicted, and watched as the king put on his gold helmet and dropped into place a special visor that had been added for the specific purpose of protecting the king's eyes. Surely now he would avoid the consequences of the dreadful prophecy.

Seated in the place of honor, the queen gasped and clutched her breast. How like a golden cage the helmet with its strange visor looked. Her small cry of fear went unheeded by the king. There was nothing she could do but watch.

Taking their respective places at each end of the list, the combatants eyed each other carefully, then lowered lances and spurred their horses forward. In the first charge, Henry's lance caught the young count a glancing blow that nearly unhorsed him, but Montgomery managed to stay in the saddle. Now more confident than ever, the king gathered himself for the second charge. The two riders thundered past each other, and again Henry's lance found a weakness that sent Montgomery's lance clattering to the ground. The king turned to face his young opponent. He lifted the visor to let the count see the confidence in his eyes. He was certain now that the third pass would drop young Montgomery unceremoniously to the ground. A groom handed Montgomery a new lance, the king slammed the visor down once again, and two great war horses pounded toward each other for the final charge. This time, Montgomery aimed his lance squarely at the center of Henry's shield. He was young and inexperienced, but he was a knight, and if he was to be unhorsed, it would take a perfect hit to do it.

It required only a matter of seconds for the two horses to close the gap between them. Montgomery's lance found its mark, but it shattered on impact, sending the point directly into the helmet of the king. Somehow it found the eye space in the king's visor and penetrated his right eye. With a scream of pain, Henry fell to the ground, the splintered lance point protruding awkwardly from the "golden cage."

The queen and the physicians, in all likelihood Nostradamus among them, rushed to the king's side. But there was nothing they could do. The splintered lance had pierced the king's eye and continued on into his brain. Two wounds in one, just as Nostradamus had foretold, and remaining absolutely true to the prophecy, the king lingered on in agony for ten days before dying.

From this single event, the name of Nostradamus spread throughout Europe. But that fame was not entirely favorable, and Nostradamus proved to be a prophet in his own behalf. Just as he had anticipated, many people, hearing of his uncanny ability to see into the future, responded in fear. The night the king died, an angry mob gathered and demanded that the church burn Nostradamus at the stake. He was, in fact, burned in effigy. The dreaded inquisition was in its heyday, and just the mention of heresy was enough to get anyone, great or small, consigned to the flames. His enemies accused him of witchcraft, but being unable to decipher his quatrains, their efforts proved fruitless. If anyone doubted the wisdom of Nostradamus in couching his prophecies in obscure verses, that doubt was forever erased.

Nostradamus was, according to most experts, very much a man of his own time. At least 200 of his predictions were fulfilled while he lived. But more than anything, he was a visionary of the future. Much of what he saw and wrote about could not even have been imagined in his own time. For example, all the nations of Europe were ruled by kings who ruled by what was believed to be "divine right." No one had questioned that concept in hundreds of years. A revolution to overthrow a king was unheard of and the idea of an "elected" king simply incomprehensible. Yet, with the storming of the Bastille still two centuries away, Nostradamus wrote:

By night through the forest of Reims
two partners by a roundabout route.
The monk king dressed in gray at Varennes.
The elected Capet causes tempest, fire and bloody slicing.

Here, in these four lines, Nostradamus paints a startling scene of the future in which he names names and identifies locations with unerring accuracy. Recorded history, in fact, provides a template by which we can measure every line. Louis XVI and his partner, Marie Antoinette, did in fact escape from the castle in Paris by means of a secret door. They were trying to get to Varennes through the forest of Reims, but lost their way and had to take a "roundabout route." The king was disguised in a simple gray monk's robe, which fits the quatrain perfectly. But now comes the truly astonishing part. Louis was a Capet and the first *elected* king of France. Then, just as the last line predicts, the mobs terrorized the city, burning and looting, and with the world as witness, they put to use that most gruesome device, the guillotine. Louis XVI and Marie Antoinette were among the first victims of its "bloody slicing."

Somehow Nostradamus was "tuned in" to some of the most devastating events in history, almost as if he had acquired a television of the future and was watching a CNN News broadcast. And his vision stretched much further into the future than just the French Revolution. Consider the following quatrain:

An Emperor will be born near Italy,
one who will cost his empire dearly.
They will say that with such people as rally round him
he will be found less prince than butcher.

Once again the pinpoint accuracy of Nostradamus is truly astonishing. Napoleon was not born in France but on Corsica, an island near Italy. The wars of Napoleon took the lives of his best and brightest young men, so much so that the height of the average Frenchman was reduced by three-quarters of an inch. He bled both the treasury and the populace of France and littered Europe, from the tip of the Italian boot to the gates of Moscow, with corpses. Certainly, in retrospect, but even to historians of the day, Napolean was more of a butcher than a prince.

Experts agree that seventeen quatrains scattered through five different volumes of *Centuries* refer specifically to Napoleon. And yet, it is almost impossible to understand the amazing reach and pinpoint accuracy of the Nostradamus prophecies.

Imagine one of the first settlers in what was to become Virginia, stepping forth one day and prophesying that in the distant future a great city would be built on this land, and in that city there would be a theater where a great leader would attend a performance and there be assassinated. Just for good measure, this prophet would throw in the names of Lincoln and Booth. Today we would acclaim that person as a prophet of uncanny ability and foresight.

Nostradamus apparently accomplished precisely that sort of thing with astonishing regularity, and yet he continues to suffer the slings and arrows of skeptics and debunkers. Clairvoyance, fortune-telling, or seership of any kind, according to those who insist on the more "rational" approach, is simply a matter of stating generalities and providing simple statements of probabilities.

For the garden-variety fortune-teller on a typical carnival midway, that may indeed be the case. Nostradamus, however, continues to startle us by naming names and places right into the modern era. Consider this quatrain, which most experts agree refers to the Spanish civil war of 1936:

> From Castille, Franco will bring out the assembly.
> The ambassadors will not agree and cause a schism.
> The people of the Riviera will be in the crowd.
> The great man will be denied entrance to the gulf.

There exists within these four lines an almost unbelievable amount of detail and a truly remarkable coupling of names. Primo de Rivera was the dictator of Spain. Franco exposed him to the people, and the "ambassadors," who could not agree on what should be done, did indeed cause a great schism in the government. Franco, one of the great men of modern Spanish history, was banished to Morocco, thus being denied access to the Gulf.

Generalities? Simple statements of probabilities?

This kind of specificity in many of the quatrains has earned Nostradamus the grudging admiration of some of the staunchest critics of prophecy. What's more, his predictions were not all confined to the workings of government and the fate of nations. His marvelous insight can, and does, focus on individuals who have made unique contributions to the world. Here is one stunning example:

> The lost thing is discovered.
> Pasteur will be celebrated almost as a god.
> This when the moon completes her great cycle.
> But he will be dishonored by other rumors.

Here Nostradamus demonstrates his use of astrology to fix a time in the future. In astrological terms, the great cycle of the moon ran from 1535, in Nostradamus's lifetime, to 1889, the year the Pasteur Institute was founded. As for Louis Pasteur, his contributions to medical science are almost incalculable. He discovered vaccines and was the first to use them to halt the spread of disease. The term *pasteurization,* of course, takes its name from his discovery of a method of destroying disease-causing bacteria. At one point there was a movement to propose him for sainthood. But the rest of the prediction is also true. Certain factions in the French Academy of Science, motivated by jealousy or ignorance (or perhaps both), attacked him continually and viciously in an attempt to ridicule his use of vaccines. Who, what, when, and where could not have been more precisely named; yet it was an event some 350 years in Nostradamus's future.

But the prophecies of Nostradamus creep even closer to our own time. Some experts believe that his most impressive predictions have to do with events in the twentieth century, specifically Hitler's rise to power and the Second World War. There are, in fact, some twenty-two quatrains that deal specifically with Hitler (three in which he is mentioned by name). Consider this example of Nostradamus's prophetic insight:

> From the deepest part of Western Europe, a child will be born
> of a poor family, who will entice many with his oratory.
> His reputation will grow even greater
> In the kingdom of the East.

Hitler was born in the Austrian Alps, the deepest part of western Europe. His father held a low-level civil service job and was by any standard poor. There can be little argument that Hitler won many fanatical adherents with his now-famous oratory. Whatever else he was, Hitler proved to be a spellbinding speaker. But it was in the kingdom of the East, the USSR, that his reputation was taken most seriously. Joseph Stalin, the Communist dictator, considered Hitler his number one enemy long before the rest of the world began to take notice.

Perhaps the world would have taken Hitler more seriously if they had taken Nostradamus more seriously. After all, in some forty quatrains that have been translated and interpreted, Nostradamus foresaw not only aircraft but actual battles in the sky. He wrote of submarines and the mining of shipping lanes. He saw tanks and rockets and the people of London fleeing to subway tunnels for shelter. And while he did not name Mussolini directly, he did say that his name was "lowly." The name Mussolini means "muslin maker," a trade considered by Italian craftspeople to be the lowest of the low.

As we proceed through the quatrains to our own time, Nostradamus becomes no less enigmatic and no less accurate. His description of events that are still burned into the hearts and brains of most American adults instantly ignites a memory of those awful moments:

> The great man will be struck down in the daytime by a thunderbolt.
> An evil deed foretold by the bearer of a petition.
> Another is struck at night.
> Conflict in Reims, London and pestilence in Tuscany.

What better way would a man in the sixteenth century have of describing the impact of the high-powered rifle that "struck down" John Fitzgerald Kennedy on a sun-filled afternoon in Dallas, Texas? And not only did Jeane Dixon, a well-known American psychic also foretell this disaster, she actually sent a warning to Kennedy, pleading with him to forgo his trip to Dallas. A few years later, his brother Robert was also struck down—and at night, just as Nostradamus predicted. The last line expresses the sense of shock and confusion felt in capitals around the world when they heard the news of the assassinations.

The Nostradamus prophecies, of course, don't end there. In fact, there are quatrains that speak of things still well into *our* future. Many experts believe that his predictions concerning our day are some of the most volatile and most useful of all time if we can just decipher them properly. What Nostradamus has to say about events surrounding the "end time" will be discussed in a later chapter dealing specifically with those events. You can be sure, however, that his attention to detail and the specifics of his predictions are no less startling than those we have seen so far.

Perhaps there is a lesson to be learned in all of this. The question is, Have we learned it?

Coming up next, another of the remarkable intentional seers, who, like Nostradamus, was a healer. This man, however, discovered the gift of prophecy while asleep. He is a man of our own century whose patterns of discerning the future were quite different from those of his illustrious predecessor but in some ways even more startling.

CHAPTER FIVE

THE SLEEPING PROPHET

EDGAR CAYCE WAS BORN ON MARCH 18, 1877, the only son of Kentucky farmers. According to Edgar's late son, Hugh Lynn Cayce, it would be more appropriate to say that Edgar Cayce came into the world *this time* on March 18, 1877, "in order to bring psychic ability to the age."[1]

The young Edgar was very close to his mother, Carrie Cayce, and he developed a bond with his grandfather Cayce that, according to Edgar, lasted even beyond the grave. The eldest Cayce was the county's dowser, a man skilled in the process of locating water underneath the ground by using a forked stick, usually from a fresh-cut sapling. The forked end would be held in the hands of the dowser, with the end of the "dowsing rod" held horizontal to the ground. When water was present, the rod would dip toward the earth. Some witnesses report that the forked stick would turn so violently in the dowser's hands that the bark would be stripped from the sapling. This was undoubtedly Edgar's first association with the paranormal, although in the late nineteenth and early twentieth centuries, dowsing was an accepted occupation in many communities and would not have been considered paranormal at all.

Edgar's father, Leslie Cayce, was an elected justice of the peace, which afforded him the title of "squire," but left him little time to spend with his son. Nevertheless, Squire Cayce made every effort to see to it that his son's education would be of value to him. Edgar wasn't a particularly good student, but he submitted to his father's demands and suffered through some grueling tutoring sessions with his father. It was during one of these sessions, a torturous drill on spelling, that Edgar had his first personal encounter with the paranormal. During a break in the studies, Edgar fell asleep with his head resting on the spelling manual. When his father returned to resume the lessons, Edgar realized he had absorbed the contents of the book while sleeping on it. To his delight, he discovered that was also the case with other texts, and thereafter, his grades in school showed a marked improvement. Here Edgar Cayce provides us with another insight into the world of the psychic. His was a "chosen" gift, something fairly unique even among intentional seers.

By all accounts a very religious young man, Edgar always accompanied his mother to church and read the Bible daily. While still in his teens, so the story goes, Edgar came out of church one Sunday and went by himself into some nearby woods. He had been particularly impressed by the sermon he had just heard, and he was seeking solitude in which to read his Bible and pray for the gift of healing the sick. While still engrossed in his prayers, Edgar was visited by what he described as a "radiance" that told him that his prayers had been heard and that he would indeed have the opportunity to heal the sick if he remained faithful to those prayers. So far as can be determined, Edgar Cayce, throughout his entire life, remained true to the promise he made that Sunday afternoon in the woods.

To the serious student of the paranormal, this presents two problems. The first is the notion that psychic gifts can be "requested," if you will, and that the request can apparently be granted. The second is the source that grants the request. Typically, the orthodox Christian church has been skeptical of almost all psychic gifts; yet clearly, Edgar Cayce was praying to God and asking that he be granted the ability to heal the sick. The "radiance" he described spoke either to his ears or his heart (or perhaps both) and left no doubt in his young mind that his prayers had been answered and that they had been answered by God. To just about everyone except Edgar Cayce and his followers, those two problems remain unresolved.

Edgar did not immediately begin using his psychic gift to heal the sick. Indeed, there is some question as to whether he was even aware of just how he would go about it. Interestingly, he would discover the power of his healing gift by first having to use it to heal himself. Shortly after his experience in the woods, he was playing baseball with friends and was struck in the spine by the ball. He was fifteen at the time, and many students of Cayce's psychic gift have suggested that it was this event that triggered his healing abilities. In a sense that may be true. It was certainly this event that made him *aware* of his gift.

Following the accident, Edgar, normally a quiet, reserved young man, inexplicably became noisy and quarrelsome and seemingly lacked the ability to control his emotions generally. The squire found his son's antics intolerable and ordered him to bed. Edgar obeyed and fell into a kind of semicoma, during which he began to give his astonished parents very specific instructions. He told them to prepare a poultice of certain herbs and chopped raw onions and apply it to the base of his brain. The squire hesitated, but Edgar assured him that if he was ever to be normal again, the poultice must be applied and just as he prescribed. The special herbs were gathered and the poultice mixed and applied as per Edgar's instructions, after which he drifted off into a deep, untroubled sleep. The following morning he awoke, completely cured and back to his quiet, reserved self again.

In spite of these brief encounters with the paranormal as a boy, Edgar Cayce grew to manhood not much noticed by the rest of the world. He took a job as a salesman, an occupation that kept him in contact with people of all kinds. It is not known whether he particularly liked the job, but he seemed to be quite good at it. Then one day his throat constricted to the point that he could hardly breathe. Talking was an impossibility. The condition seemed to worsen with each passing day, and Edgar knew that if he couldn't find a solution to the problem, his days as a salesman were over.

Physicians of the early twentieth century were of no help. None of them could even diagnose the problem, let alone suggest a cure. Cayce consulted a hypnotist and asked that he be put in a trance. In this state he was able to correctly diagnose his problem. Coming out of the hypnotic trance, Cayce told the hypnotist that nervous stress was forcing a tightening of the muscles and a constriction of the nerves throughout his body. Cayce asked the hypnotist to put him in a trance once again, only this time he was to give Cayce's body a command, while still in the hypnotic state, to increase the circulation in the area of his vocal cords. The hypnotist did as he was instructed, then watched as Cayce's neck began to flush red as the blood circulation steadily increased in that area. Upon being awakened, the stiffness was gone and Cayce could speak normally once again.

Following this experience, Cayce made two important discoveries. The first was that he could put himself into a trancelike state without the help of a hypnotist, and the second was that while in this state, he could diagnose and prescribe remedies, not just for himself, but for others as well. He now knew how he could keep the promise made that Sunday afternoon in the woods so many years before. Throughout the remainder of his life, he would always go into a sleeplike trance before giving a reading. The press dubbed him "the sleeping prophet," and the name stuck.

Edgar Cayce is easily the most prolific of all the intentional seers. By comparison, Nostradamus looks like a piker. On file today at the Association for Research and Enlightenment (ARE), the foundation established by Cayce in Virginia Beach, Virginia, there are over 14,000 readings given by Cayce. Of those readings, 8,976 are devoted to medical subjects. These readings amount to 900,000 pages of notes, roughly 14 million words carefully transcribed during each session by his wife, Gertrude, or his secretary, Gladys Davis Turner. The sheer volume of effort is staggering; yet Cayce, true to his promise, would give of his marvelous talent almost upon request. Nor was an inability to pay any barrier to receiving his help. Edgar Cayce, it appears, truly believed that his remarkable gift was not given *to* him for his own benefit, but rather *through* him for the benefit of others.

Cayce's amazing insight into the cause and cure of various medical problems seems to have been limitless. He required nothing more than a name and address. He never laid eyes on the vast majority of his "patients," except perhaps in a photograph, and he personally knew very few of them. Even more amazing, providing him with an account of their illness was not something that was required. A name was brought to him with a request for his help. He would arrange himself comfortably on a couch in his modest home, and in a few moments, he would slip into his familiar, sleeplike trance. One of his two stenographers was always nearby to take down every word. Then, like Daniel in the Old Testament, he would describe the illness, pronounce his diagnosis, and suggest a remedy. The records indicate that he made virtually no errors. In fact, Cayce told the world that if he ever did any harm to anyone through his pronouncements, he would cease prescribing forever. No complaints were ever lodged, but thousands of people credited him with giving them the means to a new and healthier life. Some of his remedies actually predated the discovery of the same cure sometime later by medical science.

But there were some 5,000 readings given by Cayce that had nothing to do with medical problems and their cure. As his fame spread and his confidence in his own ability grew, Cayce began to give readings on a number of issues that captivated the interest of those around him. Unlike Nostradamus, however, Cayce ignored the skeptics and delivered his readings in clear, unambiguous terms.

As with all prophets, the true test of their ability lies in their record of accuracy. Apart from his uncanny success as a healer, Cayce's record as a genuine seer is also quite remarkable. For example, at a time when the Russian Communists were turning that nation into a bloody battleground, Cayce predicted the *end* of Communism in Russia and indicated that nation would become the hope of the world. At least part of that prophecy seems to have come true.

It seems only fair that we submit the prophecies and predictions of Edgar Cayce to the same test as those of Nostradamus. Simply put, was he right? But in making that analysis, let's not lose sight of the kind of man he was. To demonstrate the scope of his psychic ability, let's take a few examples directly from some of his health readings. Keep in mind that all he had to work with in his trance state was the name of the person involved and a general location, such as the name of a city or town. Furthermore, that location was frequently hundreds of miles away and, since he traveled very little, virtually unknown to Cayce personally. ". . . Jacksonville. Looks like rain." And for a man in Chicago: ". . . Creiger Avenue. Yes—where the trees are."

Sometimes there was a street address, but since most of these readings were done for people he had never met, living in places he had never been, the street address was meaningless, although he frequently verified or corrected it. "Yes—something wrong about the address here, but we have a body—for she is praying." Or, as in the case of a man whose address was given as 418: "Yes. That's where he was yesterday. He's at 419 now."

Present were the stenographer and the person who had brought him the patient's name. Such petitioners were free to ask questions during the session:

Q. Where is the body at the present time?
A. He is here at this address, you see, right at present. Just came in.

Q. Where did you first locate him?
A. At the street here. Union.

Each of these examples is a literal quote from one of Cayce's health readings. In each instance, the accuracy of his statements about who the "body" was (that was, after all, what he was dealing with), where it was, and what it was doing at the time of the reading were later verified. What's more, this astonishing clairvoyant accuracy was repeated thousands of times.

Once the "body" was located, he would then diagnose the ailment. "Yes, we have the body here. And the body is experiencing one of the little attacks it has with the nerves."

The final step, of course, was to prescribe a remedy. For example, in a long and very comprehensive response to a question about the common cold, Cayce dropped the information that "the use of an abundant supply of vitamins is beneficial, of all characters, A, B, D, B_1, E, G, and K." Today, the idea that we should load up on vitamins when getting a cold is old news. In 1936, it was a groundbreaking notion. In fact, the enormous benefits of vitamin E are still being discovered.

These, then, were the psychic gifts Edgar Cayce was to employ when asked to discuss important issues of the day or events that might impact the future. Before his death in 1945, he had "seen" laser beams, predicted the discovery of the Dead Sea Scrolls (which occurred almost within his lifetime), and forecast the great Wall Street crash of 1929. While still a young man, he accurately predicted the California earthquake, the hurricanes that struck Japan, and tidal waves that inundated the Philippines in rapid succession in 1926.

But of all of Edgar Cayce's predictions, he is probably best known for his comprehensive prophecies regarding the ancient continent of Atlantis. According to Cayce, Atlantis was the original Garden of Eden, and he even suggested to some of his healing clients that they were reincarnated Atlanteans. Cayce believed that Atlantis had been destroyed on three different occasions, a notion that differs markedly from the original version written by Plato. Cayce's Atlantis was destroyed in 50,000 B.C., again in 28,000 B.C., and most recently about 12,000 years ago in 10,000 B.C., the latter coinciding more closely with Plato's tale.

Cayce's contention was that most Atlanteans escaped the disaster because their highly advanced technology permitted them to know in advance what was coming. Given that advance warning they spread out to other regions— to Greece, Egypt (from whence the original story was passed down to Plato), Sumer, Mexico, Peru, and the Americas. According to Cayce, all the survivors of Atlantis have one thing in common: an intense grasp of things technological. Coinciding with the last part of the Plato story, Cayce believed that it was in fact their own technology that destroyed Atlantis through arrogance and misuse.

With regard to Cayce's extensive writings about Atlantis, some experts have wondered if perhaps his visions were more of a premonition of things to come. They wonder if rather than looking at some remote past, he might not have been seeing the imminent future of industrialized America. In fact, Edgar Cayce does have some very interesting things to say about what is to come at the end of the second millenium, A.D., which we will review in some detail a little later on. But Edgar Cayce also gave us a definition of psychic awareness that we think is worth sharing. During one of Cayce's trance states, a participant requested the prophet define "psychic phenomena." Cayce replied:

> Psychic means of the *spirit* or *soul* . . . in the broader sense meaning spirit,
> soul or the imagination of the mind when attuned to the various phases of
> either of these two portions of the entity of an individual, or from the entity
> of others who are passed into planes other than the physical or material; yet

in a broader sense, the phenomena of psychic forces is a material, as the forces that become visible to the material or physical plane.

Psychic forces cover many various conditions, depending upon the development of the individual or how far distant the entity is from the plane of spirit and soul forces.

Psychic means not understood from the physical or material or conscious mind. . . . Hence in the truest sense, Psychic [means] the expression to the material world of the latent or hidden sense of the soul and spirit forces, whether manifested from behind, or in and through the material plane."[2]

According to Edgar Cayce, psychic phenomena come about through the activity of the soul or spirit, and these are as "material" as anything on the physical plane. He also seems to be suggesting that the phenomena varies from individual to individual, depending on a number of factors, including distance. This is a bit surprising, since distance seemed to be no barrier at all to Cayce himself.

Miracle healer and clairvoyant, Edgar Cayce amassed a record of psychic events unmatched in either the ancient or the recent past. He is easily one of the most renowned psychic figures of all time, and yet skeptics abound, all of whom seem willing to dismiss the mountain of evidence supporting his psychic gifts with such axioms as, "circumstantial," "coincidence," and (my personal favorite), "lucky guesses."

Many of Cayce's critics pounced on his indisputable belief in the prior existence of Atlantis as proof that his trance statements were all just part of the show. In the early 1940s, however, Cayce predicted that some part of Atlantis would be discovered in 1968. As it turns out, the Bimini wall, obviously human-made and submerged for centuries under the sea off the island of North Bimini, was discovered in 1968. Scientists have yet to explain its origins.

Edgar Cayce wandered into the woods that Sabbath day when he was fifteen years old. Already predisposed to accept the unexplainable through his close relationship with his grandfather, the young Edgar seems to have been completely open to the voice of the "radiance" when it spoke to him. Yet, his growth as a prophet appears to have evolved in stages. His early experience with healing was born of desperation and the fear of losing his ability to work as a salesman. And significantly, perhaps, the gift was first used to heal himself. It's not clear whether his decision to seek the help of a hypnotist was instinctive or just a "lucky guess," but the result seems to have set the pattern for the thousands of healing experiences that followed.

The question is, Can one *learn* to be a clairvoyant? There are those who maintain that we are all composed of the same "material" and therefore we all start out with the same potential. Does that mean that we can overcome the preachments that tell us that such things are impossible and, at the very least, enhance our metaphysical skills?

It is sometimes a chilling prospect. While still a young couple, Gayle and her husband lived on a quiet suburban street corner in a home with a large bay window overlooking the intersection. One morning, just as the first streaks of light began to filter through the shades in the bedroom, Gayle's husband was startled into full consciousness by strange sounds coming from the living room. It sounded vaguely like steam escaping, but with odd "explosive" noises that occasionally interrupted the "whooshing" sound. He jumped out of bed and hurried into the living room to find his three-year-old daughter standing on the couch staring out the window at the intersection. The sounds were coming from her as she moved her finger in a sweeping circular motion with each whoosh and ended it with a crash.

"What are you doing, honey?" he asked.

She looked at him with a patient smile and said emphatically, "I'm watching the cars crash and go around in a circle." Once again she moved her hand and arm in a circular motion, staring intently out the window.

He looked out onto the intersection. Everything was quite. The occasional car that drove by did so without incident. He shrugged and picked her up and carried her into his bedroom. He chalked up the whole thing to a childish imagination and began getting ready for work.

"What was that all about?" Gayle wanted to know.

"Ask her," he said, pointing to their young daughter, who had found something fascinating about the bedspread.

A short time later, Gayle's husband pulled out of the driveway and headed down the street toward his office. Just prior to getting on the freeway there was a service station, and since his daughter had managed to give him an earlier start than usual, he decided to stop and get gas. He had barely gotten the pump in place when he heard the crash. He looked up, and there in the intersection was a car turning in a circle. Another car had run the light and struck this car on the passenger side. The impact had knocked the driver partially out of the car, and she was desperately clinging to the steering wheel, unable to reach the brake and hanging on for dear life. The car was necessarily pulled into a tight, uncontrolled circle, barely missing other cars as it went around the intersection, finally coming to rest, with another small crash, against the car that had hit it. A chill ran through him as his daughter's words echoed in his mind: "I'm watching the cars crash and go around in a circle."

Later that evening, he repeated the whole series of events to Gayle. They thought briefly about questioning their daughter, but decided that they were too far removed from the actual event to have a meaningful discussion. It's not quite clear how meaningful the discussion could be with a three-year-old under any circumstances, but she had certainly appeared impatient with him when he questioned her that morning.

"I am certain she thought it ridiculous for me to be asking what she saw when it was right there, at least to her, as plain as could be," he told us, and added, "I had another thought. What if I hadn't stopped to get gas? Would it have been my car in that intersection?"

The next question that comes to mind is, How would you know if you have any psychic skills? There is no straight answer to that question, but there might be a couple of things you can try to help determine whether or not you have an affinity for these things. Dowsing, for example, though not quite as acceptable as an occupation as it once was, is still highly regarded in many areas of the United States and in many nations around the world as a legitimate means of finding not only water but various minerals and even oil. Someone who can produce consistent results in this field of endeavor is usually (although not always) sensitive in other areas as well.

You can determine whether or not you have any ability as a dowser without even leaving your own backyard. Simply take two wire clothes hangers from your closet—the kind the dry cleaner gives you free. (Actually, any stiff wire of a similar gauge will work, but wire hangers are usually easy to come by.) What you want to wind up with is two L-shaped pieces of wire. Think of the L tipped up on its foot, as opposed to lying on its back, and cut the hangers accordingly. (The hangers are essentially triangles. Cut away the hook and one side of the triangle, and discard the piece with the hook.) What you are left with is a sort of V-shaped piece of wire with one side longer than the other. With a pair of pliers, bend the angle of the V until the sides are at right angles to each other. A carpenter's square is a good guide, but failing that, bending the wire until it fits neatly into the corner of a cupboard or cabinet will work just as well.

When you have the two pieces of wire cut and bent, take the shortest side of each and hold one firmly in each hand. You will be making a fist, and you will find it virtually impossible to hold the wire tight enough to control its movement. Now bring your arms up to right angles with your body, which should bring the long side of the wires just long enough to protrude from the bottom of the hand to the ground. Keep them at an even height, about a foot apart, and as level as possible. You now have your very own dowsing rods.

To see if they will work with your energy field, go out into the backyard (or wherever the main water line comes into your house) and walk slowly back and forth across the terrain. At the point where you cross the water line, the two metal rods will slowly swing toward each other, crossing at the point where an active water source is found. Once you walk past, the rods will separate once again. It is important to move slowly so that the rods have enough time to react to what is normally a rather small water line. Moving back over the same spot should cause the two rods to cross each other once again.

My father-in-law put me onto this kind of dowsing. While living in an isolated farming community in northern Idaho, he had tried unsuccessfully to find a spot to dig a well. Several dry holes had just about convinced him that there wasn't any water on his property. But then one day, a neighbor and longtime resident of the valley stopped by and made the dowsing rods out of two wire hangers as described here. My father-in-law had expected him to do the dowsing as well, but the neighbor insisted that the wires didn't work for him but they might for my father-in-law. Anyway, it was worth a try.

Slowly, the two men began to crisscross the property. It was a lengthy process, since my father-in-law was situated on roughly five acres of land. Eventually, his arms got tired and the muscles in his forearms began to cramp up. He would have to stop, mark his spot, go do something else for a while, and then come back and start again. My father-in-law didn't have the foggiest notion whether or not the rods would work for him any more than they would for his neighbor, but he was determined to give it his best shot.

The process was ongoing for several days. Finally, just as he was about to give up, the two rods suddenly crossed. He looked around. He was near the north boundary of the property and not far from the house. He put a stake in the ground at that spot, checked to make sure he had not somehow managed to manipulate the rods, then walked back and forth across the same piece of ground. Approximately five yards on either side of the stake the rods would separate. Going toward the house, they actually turned back 180 degrees and pointed back toward the stake.

Puzzled, curious, and delighted all at the same time, my father-in-law hooked up the power auger and began to punch a hole in the ground at the precise spot he had placed the stake. This was good for only a limited depth, but if he could find any moisture at all it would be worth calling in the local drilling rig. Barely 10 feet beneath the surface, water began to bubble up into the hole.

A few years later, he was visiting my home when I mentioned that a main sprinkler line had burst and I didn't have a clue as to where the feeder line came into my property. I had had to turn off the entire system to repair the broken line, and I thought that if I could just find the feeder, I could put a valve on it and not have to shut off water to the house in order to fix the sprinkling system.

"No problem," he said. A few minutes later, he had fashioned the dowsing rods. (I still have them and use them.) It took us less than five minutes to find the line, and a couple of shovelfuls of dirt and sod soon verified that the line was in fact there. The most astonishing thing to me, however, was that I was the one using the rods. My father-in-law was there for backup, just in case. I do not, however—at least not yet—have visions of the future.

According to Edgar Cayce, "the phenomena of psychic forces is a material." It is quite likely that all of us have a certain amount of whatever that material is. My own view is that he is referring to the energy that flows from both the physical and the spiritual components of the body. We all know that energy is expendable in any number of ways, and we also know that everyone has the same amount of it. But wouldn't it be interesting if, like a body-builder who expends enormous amounts of energy to build up his strength and muscle tone, we could build up our "psychic bodies" using similar methods—namely, practice, repetition, and ever-increasing challenges to our psychic energy?

Can the future be seen in a crystal ball? If it can, why don't all clairvoyants use one? If not, why have some of the world's most famous psychics used them? And what of the famous crystal "skulls"? Do they, in fact, have strange psychic powers?

CHAPTER SIX

CRYSTAL CLEAR

ONE OF THE MORE INTERESTING FACETS of any study of the paranormal is how often the seemingly disparate disciplines seem to converge at some point. Edgar Cayce was only one of a number of psychics who believed that the only thing wrong with Plato's story of the lost continent of Atlantis was that he didn't finish it. Well, others have had nearly 2,500 years to devise an ending of their own. According to some of them (Cayce included), that end is rapidly coming upon us.

It was the ancient Greek philosopher Socrates who told us that we can only learn those things that we have forgotten. Socrates seems to be suggesting that the only worthwhile study is the study of what has gone on before. If that is true, then all the knowledge of our future is hidden somewhere in the past. There is some question, however, as to whether he was referring to things forgotten in our own lifetime, things forgotten from past lives, or forgotten knowledge from some plane of existence before we came here.

Let's assume for a moment that Socrates was really onto something. Apart from the minuscule amounts of information that can be gathered by archaeologists, what methods, devices, or knowledge exists today that can help us uncover this past knowledge of the future? One group of psychics believes that the answer can be found in that amazing substance that powers virtually all of our modern communications systems—quartz crystal.

It begins with water dripping steadily onto silica in deep volcanic caves. Eventually, the heat and pressure of volcanic activity causes the quartz to crystallize at the extremely high temperatures of molten magma. Yet this marvelous material can also be deposited on the seafloor in water just a few degrees above freezing. Of the nearly 2,000 known types of minerals, none even comes close to quartz in its diversity of origin or its abundant variety. Highly prized as a gemstone, it is nevertheless often separated from other ores and discarded as worthless, nothing more than sand to be used as a binder in concrete or scattered on highways in the dead of winter.

At one time, quartz was believed to be ice frozen so hard that it could not be melted. One legend held that it was the tears of God, who wept for a wayward world. And while modern geologists know that the specific gravity of quartz is more than 2½ times too heavy to be water of any kind, quartz crystals do grow by crystallization from watery solutions. Perhaps there is merit in the legends after all.

It is the process of "growing" that gives quartz crystal some of its unique and captivating properties. Typically, quartz crystal grows in hexagonal bars, and in 1678, Dutch physicist Christian Huygens suggested that "in general the regularity which occurs in these productions comes from the arrangement of the small invisible equal particles of which they are composed."[1] Huygens noted that in viewing the flame of a candle through a polished prism of crystal, everything appeared double, with the images quite close together, and he quite correctly concluded that it was the internal structure that produced the external form.

A hundred years later, a Frenchman, Romé de Lisle, made precise measurements of the angles of quartz crystal and determined that the angles did not vary with the changing shape and size of the crystal. Another Frenchman, René Just Haüy, often referred to as the father of cyrstallography, discovered that the pyramidlike terminations really consisted of two sets of three faces at both the top and bottom ends of the crystal. Haüy also found that quartz crystals were of two kinds, corresponding to each other as the right hand does to the left. He was closing in on one of the more interesting characteristics of quartz, the rotation of the plane of polarization of light. In 1821, Sir John Herschel discovered that quartz crystals with left-handed beveling faces rotated the plane of polarization to the left, while right-handed crystals rotated the plane of polarization to the right. Little by little, science was beginning to unravel the age-old mystery of this amazing rock.

Finally, in 1882, Jacques Curie and his brother Pierre, the famous codis-coverers of radium, hit upon the one characteristic of quartz that affects all of our lives today. In attempting to measure the electrical conductivity of quartz plates, they found that applying pressure on the plates produced a deflection of the current. They had discovered the property known as *piezoelectricity* (*piezon*, from the Greek, meaning "pressure"). They found that oriented slices of quartz, properly mounted, would vibrate mechanically at specific radio frequencies and thereby stabilize the frequency of a radio transmitter. Every time you tune into a favorite radio station, you can be sure that the reason you find it at exactly the same place on the dial every time is that there is a small quartz wafer keeping the transmitted signal on that precise frequency.

It is this same characteristic that keeps the digital watch on your wrist (and even some analog watches) ticking away in perfect time. More recently, the manufacturers of computer chips have found ways of enhancing the characteristics of quartz crystal to the point where billions of precise calculations can be made in fractions of a second. In fact, virtually all of our modern communications depend to some degree on nature's formula of water and silica.

Interestingly, and perhaps significantly, the most amazing discoveries with regard to these crystals have come from outer space. An experiment was undertaken recently to grow crystals in a weightless environment. The result was that free from the pull of gravity, there were no striations on the finished product. What that meant was that the scientists now had a "perfect" crystal. According to David Adair, a technology transfer consultant speaking at a 1997 conference in Laughlin, Nevada, the scientists knew what they had, they just didn't know what it would do. A wafer was prepared and put into an ordinary computer chip, the kind of chip that is "common as dirt." The chip was then sent to the Cray Computer Center in Silicon Valley for testing. Here, virtually all the accumulated knowledge of humankind is stored on the huge Cray computers—computers capable of so many calculations that their processors must be nitrogen cooled to protect the machines from meltdown.

The Cray engineers were instructed to put the chip in a "test" bed and report their findings. A short time later, the stunned and breathless engineers reported back. The chip had performed at a level so far above anything in their experience that they had no way of measuring it. Quartz crystal—*pure* quartz crystal, that is—has put humankind on the threshold of a communications and knowledge revolution the likes of which no one has ever dared to dream.

Or is all of this old news? Could it be that the scientists are simply proving Socrates correct and *learning what had been forgotten*? Long before scientists were studying the properties of quartz, long before the characteristics of light and frequency were discovered, psychics were using crystal in a variety of forms to help them discover the knowledge of both the future and the past. We are all familiar with the caricature of the gypsy fortune-teller staring into a crystal ball. But that is only one of its many incarnations. There are crystal wands, some highly polished, some in the natural state; crystal amulets; and just plain old chunks of crystal carried from place to place by psychics who claim that various powers emanate from the rock. A current television commercial touts crystal pendants that can be worn to put you in touch with your own psychic abilities. (More about that later.) But easily the most intriguing of all the crystal artifacts are the crystal skulls.

You may be surprised to learn that there are several of these beautifully carved and highly polished skulls in existence, at least one of which forms the base for a reliquary cross that is also made of highly polished crystal. The origins of both the skull and the cross are somewhat obscure, but that is the case with all of these relics. You see, there is another characteristic of crystal that we haven't mentioned: It cannot be carbon dated. Therefore, the age (or relative age) of any of the skulls can only be inferred from the archaeology of its surroundings at the time and place of its discovery.

One of the more famous crystal skulls resides in the British Museum of Mankind in London. This skull was supposedly found in Mexico by a soldier of fortune during the reign of Maximilian and Carlota (mid-1800s), but its origins are shrouded in mystery. It was apparently purchased by the museum from Tiffany's of New York, who acquired it from a Mr. Sissons of that city. Sissons is believed to have been a partner of the French adventurer M. E. Boban, who obtained the skull from the aforementioned soldier of fortune just before the man died. In the 1960s, the skull was removed from view in the museum because the flower children of that era would gather around the skull and just sort of camp out. The museum found this kind of attention embarrassing and withdrew the skull, placing it in a box in the basement. The Mexican government has tried to have the skull returned, but without success. They believe it to be of Mixtec origin.

The Paris Museum is home to yet another authenticated crystal skull. This one is believed to be of Aztec origin and is thought to represent Mictlantecutli, the Aztec god of death. If, indeed, it was made to represent the god of death, its almost grotesque appearance is most appropriate. Of all the crystal skulls, this one is the least attractive. Adding to the notion that this skull represents the god of death is a groove and a retaining ring carved into the skull for the purpose of affixing it to the priest's staff. The skull would have topped the priest's staff on the Aztec observance of the day of "skinning alive." On this day, the priest, representing the god Xipe, would wear the skin of a freshly killed captive while dancing in celebration of a successful springtime. The grisly ritual was supposed to ensure a fruitful crop and harvest.

Another crystal skull of unknown origin can be found in a most unlikely place: a quiet neighborhood in a suburb of Houston, Texas. Several years ago, the family that now owns the skull was frantically trying to find help for their twelve-year-old daughter, dying of bone cancer. The doctors gave her only two to three months to live. Having exhausted all the conventional options open to them, the family sought out a "healer" who owned this particular crystal skull. The healer, according to the family, was able to extend their daughter's life and give her three additional quiet years. A few years later, in 1980, the healer himself died, and upon his death, "gifted" the skull to the family, telling them that when the time came, they would know what to do with it.

According to the mother, the skull had sat on a shelf in a box for seven years when she began having dreams about it. She would go to the box in the closet, remove the skull, and talk to it. The thought did occur to her that it was probably ridiculous to be talking to a rock, but the messages she received seemed clear. His name, the skull told her, was Max, and he was to be used for the benefit of humankind.

Since coming out of the closet and participating in many ceremonies at the family home, the skull has revealed a number of things. Amerindian and Mayan mystics who have attended these ceremonies believe that the skull came from the Pleiades, a distant star system, and somehow wound up on the continent of Atlantis. They believe it to be encoded with the entire past history of the earth and of humankind—a kind of prehistoric computer. Given what we now know about the capacity of pure crystal and the fact that this particular artifact is about the size of an average adult human head, the capacity to store that much information certainly would not be a problem.

Another crystal skull has been literally unearthed in the valleys of central Mexico within the past half century. A psychic, employed by a group of archaeologists to help them determine where to dig, was instrumental in finding a terra cotta basket. In the basket was a crystal skull the psychic calls Shinera,[sic]. The psychic claims to "see" within the skull a record of its entire history, but more importantly, it has given him the gift of healing. Like Edgar Cayce, he now "works" on patients all over the world. They do not have to be in his presence for the healing to work, and it is Shinera, he says, who "always shows up" and is one of several healers that speaks to him through the skull.

It is no accident that the crystal skulls all seem to be found amid the ruins of the ancient Aztec or Mayan cultures. The skull, as a symbol, was featured throughout their carvings, painting, and sculpture. It appears to have been important in all aspects of their lives, including their religion. Actual human skulls numbering in the hundreds of thousands were discovered by the early Spanish conquerors.

The fascination seems to have rubbed off on some of the Spanish religious orders as well. A small, crystal skull formed the base of a reliquary cross (mentioned earlier) that was used by the Franciscans in Mexico City. The cross, with its unique base, came into the hands of the Redo family during the last century when the government began to confiscate church property. To avoid such confiscation, many church treasures were put into private hands. This particular skull is much smaller than the others (roughly the size of a baseball), but it exhibits a high degree of craftsmanship, and according to the present owner, it does have certain magical qualities that help control emotions and promote clarity of thought.

Easily the most impressive of all the crystal skulls, however, is what has become known as the Mitchell-Hedges crystal skull. Anatomically correct in every detail, even to the hinged lower jaw, and polished to a breathtaking clarity, the M-H crystal skull has fascinated scientists and psychics alike ever since its discovery in the 1920s. All who touch this amazing artifact report immediate and unusual changes within themselves. Could this striking piece of quartz actually have some strange, transcendental power?

F. A. Mitchell-Hedges, a famed British explorer (his listing in Britain's *Who's Who* is longer than Winston Churchill's!), was on an archaeological expedition to British Honduras, where Mitchell-Hedges hoped to find some evidence of the lost continent of Atlantis. He had taken his adopted step-daughter, Anna, in honor of her approaching seventeenth birthday. Anna, whose nickname was Sammy, often accompanied her famous father on his travels and seemed to be as filled with the spirit of adventure as he was.

This particular expedition, however, was proving to be more frustrating than fruitful. Then one day, Sammy was climbing about the ruins of an ancient Mayan temple near Lubaantun when she spotted something shiny just out of reach under the ruins. Being experienced with the rules of this kind of archaeological exploration, she made no attempt to recover whatever it was until it had been photographed and its precise location carefully mapped. But there was a certain excitement in her voice when she told her father that *something* was lying just beneath the surface near the temple.

Earthquakes had toppled many of the giant rock slabs that made up the temple walls, and it took the workers several days to carefully remove them. On Anna's seventeenth birthday, the last stone was reverently moved out of the way, making it possible to reach the shiny object. It turned out to be a clear, beautifully carved crystal skull.

The local Mayan natives reacted with astonishing joy. It was as if they recognized the skull, and they began dancing about the object and paying homage to it. Within a matter of hours, an altar had been raised upon which the skull was placed and worshiped. This presented something of a problem for Mitchell-Hedges, since he wanted the locals back at work. Finally, a compromise was struck. He would put the skull in the keeping of the native chief if they would return to the dig. They readily agreed, and by the next day, the natives were back excavating. Several months passed, however, before the detachable lower jaw was found. It, too, was in perfect condition.

At this point, the full impact of the find hit Mitchell-Hedges. Mitchell-Hedges was a great believer in the story of Atlantis. He had, remember, mounted this entire expedition to British Honduras in the hope of finding some clue to the existence of the lost city. Suddenly it seemed as if he had found it—and purely by accident. Could ancient Mayan cultures have fashioned something as anatomically correct and artistically sophisticated as this? He didn't believe it was possible, but he would never get a definitive answer, even though the skull was in his possession for the rest of his life.

The skull is now in the possession of Anna, and she has been quite willing, during her lifetime, to permit the skull to be submitted to a number of tests, both psychic and scientific. Various experts place the age of the artifact at around 12,000 years. Others are sure that it is far older than that. But since carbon dating is impossible, not even the scientists at Hewlett-Packard, one of the world's leading communications companies, could confirm an actual date of origin.

Carol Wilson, a psychic from Toronto, Canada, who gained fame by helping detectives in that city solve a grisly murder, was granted permission to "channel" using the skull. Channeling is the process whereby a psychic becomes a voice, or "channel," for a spirit. The voice that spoke through her indicated, among other things, that the skull was 100,000 years old and had been polished to its brilliant luster using a combination of human hair and *sound*. (This latter revelation is interesting in view of another of the discoveries made by space scientists working with molten metal in a weightless environment. They have discovered that sound is the only way the alloys can be shaped.)

Another psychic to whom Anna gave access to the skull concluded that the spirit that resides within the skull is female and that the skull is a replica of the skull of a people who, unlike modern humans, lived for hundreds of years. Modern science does, in fact, support the notion that it is a skull representing a female. Using the skull to re-create what the person looked like, forensic scientists have determined that it was indeed most likely the skull of a woman.

While all of this is interesting, it doesn't begin to explore all the fantastic characteristics of this particular skull. It took a team of internationally known art conservators nearly ten years to discover the full range of the skull's amazing construction.

In 1964, Anna brought the skull to New York and turned it over to Frank and Mabel Dorland. They had heard of the skull from a neighbor, Frances Fowler III, who owned the Southern Comfort distillery. Fowler collected famous drinking cups and had made purchases from F. A. Mitchell-Hedges; he was therefore acquainted with this famous world traveler and explorer. The Dorlands had, in fact, been in touch with Anna and her father since 1950. When F. A. Mitchell-Hedges died in 1959, leaving all his treasures in the care of Anna, it became her decision as to whether or not the Dorlands should take possession of the artifact. Anna decided to let them work with it under very strict rules and procedures. One of those rules had to do with its enormous monetary value. The skull, she insisted, when not being tested, was to be kept in a velvet-lined box in a bank vault.

Dorland was soon totally intrigued by the crystal skull. Other artifacts could be weighed, measured, and authenticated as belonging to some identifiable period, but the skull was a new kind of challenge. It could be photographed but not analyzed. It didn't fit any of the known patterns. Then one evening, having worked with the skull until it was too late to return it to the bank, Dorland placed it on a coffee table in front of the fire. Relaxing in his easy chair, he glanced over at the skull and noticed something odd. The eyes of the skull were reflecting the fire *exactly*, without any distortion.

The next day, Dorland had the skull under his microscope. There were, he discovered, incredible optics carved into the skull, the sophistication of which should put it well beyond any ancient civilization. Halfway back in the roof of the mouth, a broad, flat plane is carved, similar to a 45-degree prism. This surface directs the light from beneath the skull into the eye sockets. A thin, ribbonlike surface carved next to this plane acts as a magnifying reading glass. Next to the 45-degree prism is a natural ribbon prism. Extending through the more than 6 inches of solid quartz crystal, this channel is free from veils and inclusions. Items viewed through this prism are not only legible; they are slightly magnified and completely undistorted.

And there's more. Behind this prism, and this could only have been carved intentionally, is a concave and a convex surface that acts as a gatherer of light, bouncing the light to the 45-degree prism and then out to the eye sockets. The back of the skull itself is as beautifully formed as a camera lens, gathering light from everywhere and, again, reflecting it to the eye sockets. But probably the most significant indication of the skill of whoever carved the skull is in the delineation of the zygomatic arches, the arches formed by the bone just below the eye in the human face. They are carved in relief, beside the cheekbones, just as they would be in a human skull. This is a sculptural device that has never been used in any statue anywhere in the known world.

The device provides for a narrow channel that is actually an air space that makes it possible for light from either the back of the skull or underneath to flow through these arches. At their end is a hollow depression that acts as a lens and scatters light into the sockets. Light from the rear of the skull will therefore show the same as light from underneath. Amazingly, this piece of intricately carved crystal exhibits a technology only discovered in relatively recent years. What could possibly account for such precision in view of its unquestioned antiquity?

Edgar Cayce believed Atlantis to be the cradle of civilization, believing that several geological upheavals destroyed the island repeatedly. Cayce also said, in a 1933 reading (#440-5), that "initiates" of Atlantis engineered and manipulated precious power crystals for the production of galvanic and spiritual energy. These crystals were so potent that they were responsible, in large part, for the advanced civilization of the Atlanteans. Unfortunately, according to Cayce, the crystals were improperly used and actually contributed to the final destruction of the great island empire.

Cayce also believed that the crystals' function could be understood either literally or symbolically. Atlas, the principal figure in the mythology of Atlantis, is credited with being the founder of astrology. Possession of the crystals, therefore, might have been a symbolic representation of possession of the stars themselves. Of course, there are those who scoff at the idea that any of the crystal skulls came from Atlantis or were by-products of their advanced technology. But we are left with the nagging realization that someone had to produce them, and neither the Mayan nor the Aztec cultures seem to be very good candidates for the job.

Historically, crystal has been used for any number of purposes. It could dispel sorcery, divert the evil eye, and bestow divine power on those who possessed it. In the Old Testament, several references are made to the Urim and Thummim as being devices by which revelation could be given to humans by God. These objects are believed by many scholars to be quartz crystal. Some credence is given this observation by virtue of the fact that the twelve semi-precious stones representing the twelve tribes of Israel, inscribed into the breastplate of Aaron, did not include crystal. The Urim and Thummim was, however, attached to the breastplate (Lev. 8:9). It seems logical that stones of such renowned power and beauty would almost certainly have been included.

Apollonius, the famous Roman sorcerer, is said to have discovered the remarkable ability of quartz crystal to make opaque objects, including the body, invisible. Summoned before Caesar Dominicus to answer charges of sorcery, Apollonius, according to the legend, suddenly appeared before the emperor even though he was many miles away. He was tried and found guilty, but dematerialized and reappeared a short time later near Mt. Vesuvius. Tradition holds that it was Apollonius's understanding of the uses of quartz crystal that made such feats possible.

The Chinese called quartz crystal the "living stone." The Egyptians used crystals in the mummification process and always placed a quartz crystal in the west wall of a pyramid to protect it from evil. In the Celtic literature, Merlin is said to have full command of the power generated in the "crystal cave." The stone also appears in the ancient Vedas of India, and the Latin epic poet Claudius Claudianus wrote the following:

Pass not the shapeless lump of crystal by,
Nor view the icy mass with careless eye.
All royal pomp its value far exceeds,

And all the pearls the Red Sea's bosom breeds.
This rough and unformed stone, without a grace,
Midst rarest treasures holds the chiefest place.[2]

In more modern times, the quartz crystal still holds "the chiefest place," although its use and power has been more broadly defined. Some mystics use a crystal wand, many of them elaborately constructed; others use just a piece of raw crystal, polished to a high sheen. The color can be anything from a smoky gray to perfectly clear, and in some cases, the source of the stone is said to have great meaning. Essentially, modern crystal can be used to accomplish whatever the psychic using it wishes to accomplish.

Then, of course, there is the ever-present crystal ball, which perhaps should not be dismissed lightly simply because those who use them are frequently carnival midway fortune-tellers. Jeane Dixon, probably America's most famous psychic and clairvoyant, often used a large, perfectly clear and highly polished crystal ball to help her discover future events. The crystal ball may actually have been a holdover from her first psychic experience. At the age of eight, while living in California, Jeane's mother took her to see an old gypsy. The woman was the very stereotype of the itinerant gypsy fortune-teller. She lived in a canvas-covered wagon along with a brood of chickens and was the talk of Santa Rosa. Local residents often stopped by to have their palms read, their fortune told in the cards, or their future seen in the crystal ball. To both her mother's and Jeane's surprise, when the old woman looked at Jeane's palm, she dropped the famous gypsy stoicism and became quite excited.

"This little girl is going to be world famous," the gypsy exclaimed. "She will be able to foresee worldwide changes because she has the gift of prophecy."

Apparently, there were several lines on Jeane's palm that excited the gypsy. Breathlessly, she explained their significance to Jeane's mother. "They mean that this child will grow mightily in wisdom," she said with great solemnity. "The lines in the left hand are the blueprint of one's dreams and potential. Those in the right hand signify what you do with what God has given you. She is already developing fast." Sometime later, a Hindu mystic said that markings like Jeane's occurred no more than once in a thousand years.[3]

As Jeane grew older, her awareness of her abilities also grew. Tests of her extrasensory perception (ESP) demonstrated an almost unheard of 90 to 97 percent accuracy. Most people are lucky if they test at 3 to 4 percent. Mindful of the old gypsy's prompting that her gift came from God, Jeane was eager to use these gifts for the benefit of others. She learned astrology from a Jesuit priest at Loyola University in Los Angeles, and though she preferred to give her personal readings by means of a crystal ball, it wasn't long until "Jeane Dixon's Horoscope" became a popular newspaper column, syndicated in more than 300 newspapers nationwide. Her obvious sincerity and a record of amazing accuracy brought her to the attention of people at the highest levels of society and politics.

By the time World War II was drawing to a close, Jeane Dixon had become one of the leading seers of the twentieth century. Late in 1944, President Franklin Delano Roosevelt asked her to come to the White House. Always direct and to the point, FDR asked the prophetess just how long he had to complete his "mission for mankind." Mrs. Dixon reportedly asked the aging president if he really wanted to know the truth. He assured her that he did, whereupon Mrs. Dixon told him, "You have no more than six months." FDR died on April 12, 1945, not quite six months from the day of their meeting.

While Jeane was famous for her astrological forecasts and preferred to give personal readings by means of a crystal ball, neither was necessary for her to pronounce future events. At a Washington party in 1945, she told Winston Churchill that he would lose the upcoming election. Angered by what he considered an effrontery, Churchill assured her that the people of England would never let him down. Much to his and the world's surprise, the great World War II leader was indeed dumped by the British voters the following July.

She also foresaw the deaths of U.N. Secretary-General Dag Hammarskjöld and Mahatma Gandhi and the suicide of Marilyn Monroe. She predicted the launching of Sputnik, the first satellite in space, placed there by the Russians much to the embarrassment of the American government. She also "saw" the "uncontrollable blaze" that killed three young astronauts on the launchpad at Cape Kennedy in 1967.

Jeane Dixon was not shy about making her visions known, and she frequently announced some future event at large gatherings. At a reception in Washington in 1945, she told an Indian military attaché that she had seen in her crystal ball that his country would be partitioned on June 2, 1947. Her prediction proved correct. At a luncheon at a Washington hotel in 1968, a discussion came up at her table concerning the imminent march on Washington by Martin Luther King and his followers. Leaning over to the person sitting next to her, she told him not to fret about that. "Martin Luther King will not get to Washington," she told him. "He will be shot before he can get here. He will be shot in the neck. He will be shot first . . . and Robert Kennedy will be next."[4] Once again, her predictions proved to be only too true. Martin Luther King was shot in the neck with a high-powered rifle on May 28, 1968. He never made it to Washington for the planned march. Robert Kennedy died at the hands of an assassin just ten months later!

Before she died, Jeane Dixon left us her vision of our immediate future. It was, in fact, Mrs. Dixon who, more than any other psychic, defined the one essential event that will usher in the "last days." This vision, we know, did not come through the crystal, and we will examine it thoroughly in a later chapter.

Some psychics claim to actually see visions of the future appear in the crystal ball as they gaze into its depths. Others use the crystal merely as a means of focusing their attention, relying on their own intuitiveness for the actual vision. But however it is used, there does appear to be some amazing power that resides in this beautiful and mysterious rock. Scientifically, we know that it refracts light in specific ways and that it is the most critical component in just about every communications device known today. Radio, television, sonar, radar, watches, computers, and telephones all rely on the properties of quartz crystal in some form or another. Can it be that this fantastic rock has the same power of communication in the metaphysical world as well?

There is a way to test your own ability to communicate through the crystal, and it will not require the purchase of a crystal ball. All that is necessary is a small crystal pendulum, probably just an ounce or two (the size is not terribly important), affixed to the end of a small chain or ribbon not more than 2 inches in length. On the other end of the chain a small ring, about the size of a dime, is preferable. This allows you to suspend the pendulum between your thumb and forefinger without actually touching the chain.

Take the pendulum in your right hand (or left if you are left-handed). Allow it to hang freely on the chain. The flesh of the tip of the thumb and the tip of the forefinger should be felt through the ring. Now move the crystal pendulum directly over the center of the palm of your left (right) hand approximately 2 inches above the palm.

Using only your mind, ask a question that can be easily answered with a yes or no. It should be a question for which you already know the answer. For example: Is my name_____? If you ask the question using your correct name, the crystal pendulum will begin to rotate to the right, or clockwise. If the name you use is false, the pendulum will rotate to the left, or counterclockwise. (Some people have found that their energy causes the crystal to respond in exactly the reverse. That isn't important. Just make certain you determine which movement denotes truth and which denotes falsehood before you proceed.) It is very important that you hold the pendulum as steady as possible, making every effort not to influence the rotation by any physical motion. A neutral response will result in the pendulum moving in a side-to-side rather than a rotating motion.

The crystal will not respond to everyone, of course, but it is amazing how many people will discover that they have at least some ESP power. Don't be impatient. Like anything else being attempted for the first time, it requires practice to achieve the necessary concentration. Psychics who use the pendulum frequently find that they can ask questions about virtually anything. It is for many of them another form of dowsing. I have personally witnessed a pendulum in the hands of a gifted psychic moving with such energy and force that its rotation was virtually horizontal. Try it. You have nothing to lose but your skepticism.

In the next section, we will deal with some of the most active and most controversial of all the psychics: those who have followed in the footsteps of Edgar Cayce and developed their own methods of psychic healing.

THE PSYCHIC HEALERS

*The fairest thing we can experience
is the mysterious.
It is the source of all true art and science.*
Albert Einstein

We have already established that Gayle's husband was in the broadcast industry, and like so many who work in radio and television, his first experience was as a disc jockey. During the early years of their marriage, while he was finishing school and they were busy having a family, it was his work as a nighttime DJ that put bread on the table.

By the time Gayle became pregnant with their fourth child, the routine was well established. Her husband would go into the radio station about noon and get home around 2:00 A.M., following his last on-air stint and setting up the broadcast logs and commercials for the following day. This meant that Gayle was always up and about every morning long before her husband even began to stir.

She was in her seventh month when it happened. Her husband rolled over in bed and discovered that Gayle was still there. He woke up immediately, sensing that something was wrong. As a waking awareness began to push the sleep from his mind, he discovered that not only was Gayle still in bed, she was also wringing wet. Her nightgown clung to her like a wet T-shirt. The bedsheets and pillow were likewise soaked.

Still not fully awake but fearing the worst, he threw back the covers. It was not blood, thank God! His wife was usually a light sleeper, easily awakened by the slightest moan from one of her children. But she had not responded to his frantic movements, and without thinking, he grabbed her by the shoulders and began to gently shake her.

"Gayle, honey, is something wrong?"

The hair around her face was plastered to her forehead and cheeks. He brushed it back away from her tightly closed eyes. Sweat, he wondered? Could this be sweat? He placed his hand on her forehead. It seemed cool enough, but what in the world . . . ?

"Gayle," he became more insistent, "Gayle, wake up. Are you all right?"

She moaned slightly and reached for the covers he had thrown back. When she pulled them back up around her shoulders, the dampness, now cooled from evaporation, gave her a jolt, and she pushed the sheets and blankets back. Slowly and with great difficulty, she forced her eyes to open.

"I'm cold," she said.

Her husband quickly moved her over to his side of the bed and tucked the blanket up under her chin. Gayle was still fighting her way out of an exhausted sleep, but gradually she began to focus on the worried face of her husband. She reached up and touched his cheek.

"I'm fine," she said.

"The hell you are," he replied. "What's happening here?" He held up her wet pillow and placed her hand on it.

"Oh!" She reached over and ran her hand over the damp sheet where she had been lying, then fell back once again, her eyes closed. "I guess it was harder work than I thought."

Her husband could tell she was struggling to stay awake and would have much preferred that he just leave her alone, but the combination of fear and curiosity was now firmly in charge, and he was not about to go anywhere without some kind of an explanation.

"Hey," he said roughly, "you can go back to sleep in a minute. Right now you have to tell me if there's something you need . . . something I should do?"

She opened one eye and looked at him, one arm across her forehead. "No, there's nothing you need to do except maybe see if the kids got off to school."

"Oh jeez!" He looked at the clock on the sideboard. It was nearly 10:30 in the morning. He jumped up and ran into the kitchen. There were three bowls that had obviously held Cheerios or some other kind of cereal, a half-filled glass of milk, some orange juice spilled on the table, and a half slice of bread stuck to a knife with peanut butter. He checked their rooms. Their coats were gone, along with their school books. They must have managed on their own.

By the time he got back to his own bedroom, Gayle was up and trying to push a brush through her long, dark hair. "I can't believe this," she said, looking at him in the mirror.

"You can't believe it? I don't even know what not to believe!"

She put the brush down and turned to him, tears touching the brim of her eyes. He rushed over to her and put his arms around her, the firm protrusion of her belly still something of a surprise to him.

"What is it?" he asked again. "What's the matter?"

"Let's go in the other room and sit down," she whispered, kissing him on the cheek, "but I better get out of this wet nightgown."

That made sense. He let her go and turned and walked into the living room. He sat in his favorite chair and waited. A few minutes later, Gayle came in and seated herself on the couch next to the chair.

"Last night," she said, taking his hand in hers, "just before I went to sleep, but while I was not really awake—you know, that kind of in-between state—my mind was filled with an image . . . an image of the inside of the baby's mouth, the roof of the mouth actually."

"You mean this baby?" he said, pointing toward her stomach.

"Yes, this baby."

He was suddenly filled with a sense of familiarity. His wife had obviously had another of her psychic experiences, but this was different, there was something very physical about whatever had happened.

"How do you know it was the roof of the baby's mouth?" he asked.

She just looked at him. "How do I know any of this?" she answered, "I just know."

"Okay, okay. Go on."

"It was open."

"Open?"

"You know, split, from front to back." Tears began to well up again and she squeezed his hand.

"So what did you do?" he asked in a tone he hoped sounded like this was just another routine event.

Gayle looked at him to make sure he wasn't making fun of her. Satisfied that he was taking this all as seriously as she was, she went on.

"I locked onto the image with my mind and I made it close. It was so hard. I kept wanting to go to sleep but I knew I couldn't. I had to make it close. Little by little, it started to come together, and I knew that if I could get the two sides to meet, they would stay together."

Gayle stopped. Even the memory seemed tiring. Her husband got up and moved over next to her on the couch. "Did you get it done?" he asked quietly.

She leaned her head on his shoulder and nodded, "All but just a little tiny bit right at the back." Gayle sat up and looked at him, "But she'll be all right, I know it."

"She?" he said, smiling.

"Yes, it's a girl," she said matter-of-factly, "and just before I gave out and went to sleep, I had this feeling of calm come over me, a feeling of assurance that everything would be okay."

They sat on the couch for a long time in silence. Once again, Gayle was opening new territory. Experiences she neither wanted nor understood were being thrust upon her while her family could do nothing but go along for the ride. One thing was certain. Whatever had happened that night required enormous physical and mental concentration. Not even prizefighters work up that kind of a sweat.

Two months later, Gayle went into labor. At the hospital it was discovered that the baby was breached. It was a long and difficult delivery, but a little baby girl finally arrived and was, to all outward appearances, perfectly healthy.

The earlier experience was still very much with them, however, and Gayle watched with a certain amount of anxiety as the doctor ran a finger inside the baby's mouth, then opened it wide for a closer look. He ran practiced hands all over the infant's body, checked the ears and nose and eyes, then handed her over to the nurse to be bathed and wrapped.

"Is she . . . is she all right?" Gayle asked.

"She's perfect," the doctor replied, then added, "she has just a bit of a split uvula, that's right at the very back of the upper palate," he explained. "She may have a little trouble learning to talk, but it's nothing to worry about."

Gayle smiled, "No, she won't have any trouble," she said, "she'll be just fine."

Three years later, this same child would tell her father that she was "watching the cars crash and go around" as she looked out the window onto an empty street.

What brought about this remarkable healing occurrence? Could it have been the baby itself warning the mother that something was wrong? Was it just the natural tie between mother and child that forced the image into the mother's mind? Whatever the genesis of the event, there can be no doubt that it was the power of the mind that corrected what could have been one of nature's tragic mistakes. We are also reminded that even psychic healing sometimes requires enormous physical stamina.

CHAPTER SEVEN

THE HEALING MIND

A S WE MENTIONED EARLIER, there can be no doubt that through the sheer weight of numbers alone, Edgar Cayce is by far the most famous and most successful of all the psychic healers. His method was well defined, and he never varied the application of that method. He relied solely on his intuitive abilities and what we call today "long-distance, or remote, viewing" to first acquaint himself with his "patient." He would then diagnose the problem and prescribe the cure. It was unquestionably the power of his mind that permitted him to accomplish thousands of successful readings.

Cayce's method, however, is not the only one. Behavioral kinesiology uses the power of the patient's mind to find and diagnose illness. This discipline, in fact, has been embraced by many practitioners of such traditional specialties as psychosomatic medicine, allergies, sports medicine, psychiatry, nutrition, dentistry, and osteopathy.

Reiki (pronounced "ray-key") is an oriental word that means "universal life energy." It is a term that currently applies to a specific technique for restoring and balancing our natural life-force energy. Reiki, according to its adherents, is an effective technique for prevention of disease and energy imbalance at all levels of our being. It is a discipline that has its roots in the 4,500-year-old Chinese philosophy of the life-sustaining energy called Chi that circulates throughout the body.

Some modern healers have actually combined some of these ancient practices with scientific techniques in a logical attempt to get the best of both worlds. In *Anatomy of the Spirit,* by Caroline Myss, we are treated to the idea that "your biography becomes your biology." According to this philosophy,

"The Divine is locked into our biological system in seven stages of power that lead us to become more refined and transcendent in our personal power."[1] Caroline Myss describes herself as a "medical intuitive."

In *Biogram Therapy: A Quantum Leap in Mind/Body Healing,* Richard L. Johnson, Ph.D., has transformed over a decade of clinical study of biofeedback into a process that helps us understand the molecular code of the chemical transmitters in the body. Some believe that this may be the breakthrough that will lead to the discovery of the blueprint of the mind, just as DNA is the biological code and the blueprint for the construction of the body. The term *biogram* is derived from two words: *biology* (the physical) and *telegram* (the electronic message). The theory is that the mind is capable of sending healing messages to various parts of the body to correct, overcome, or even prevent some malady. The power of the mind in this case is not Dr. Johnson's. It is the power of your own mind. Is such a notion rational? The crucible in which Dr. Johnson tested his theory will amaze you, but the results are even more startling.

Then there are the psychic surgeons. These practitioners do their work without using instruments of any kind. Only the healer's bare hands touch the patient. The body is apparently opened and the surgery performed without the use of anesthetics, antiseptics, or sanitary precautions of any kind. The patient is awake throughout the entire operation, yet feels no pain, and no case of "postoperative" infection has yet been reported. The diagnosis that precedes the operation is done psychically and is unfailingly accurate.

We will look at each of these healing possibilities in some detail in this chapter and the next. But since we have most recently been discussing crystals, let's continue in that vein and discuss them specifically as a healing power. For untold generations and in virtually all cultures, stories have been passed down from generation to generation telling of the great healing power of crystals— not just quartz crystals, though they are undoubtedly the most prominent, but many other gemstones as well. Have our modern medical schools overlooked some of these "forgotten" cures? There are many who believe so.

It doesn't necessarily follow, by the way, that psychic healers have no respect for modern methods. Psychics simply believe that the scientific approach is too narrow and confining. By rejecting any but their own scientific conclusions and having the power to enforce their judgments, the American medical establishment often sees to it that alternative healing practices are routinely consigned to the trash heap by either legal declaration or public discourse or both.

While the *holistic* approach to health (the idea that treating individual symptoms of disease is secondary to one's *total physical and psychological state*) does seem to be gaining ground, it is still the physician, frequently unfamiliar with any of the practices he or she is condemning, who is in control of things. Perhaps *we* can learn what they have forgotten.

Crystals, according to those who work with them, have long been used to see into the "hidden dimensions" that permeate physical reality. In a very real sense, a crystal is a focus for knowledge that helps to magnify and transmit psychic energy and healing power.[2] The mind, it has recently been discovered by Dr. Johnson and others, can activate the immune system. And while it is the mind that is the actual healer, the crystal, according to these practitioners, amplifies the effect of the individual's effort. But care should be taken. The crystals will amplify negative as well as positive thought transference.

There are those who believe that of all the ways of employing quartz crystal, it is their propensity for healing that is the best and highest use. In the introduction to her book, Phyllis Galde says:

> They [crystals] have long been known for their curative effects when used in the preparation of tinctures; for their protective characteristics when worn as amulets and talismans; and for their ability to enhance the energy field of the body as they emit uniform vibrations in harmony with the natural vibrations of the human body. . . . Crystals do actually hold an electrical charge as such (like a battery) and they do have a memory. They act as if they're charged when held in the hand and "turned on" by direct contact with the human body."[3]

We should point out here that your own mind holds the power on which you should rely. The crystals do not demand a specific healer in order to make them work. Quite the contrary. No one knows as much about your body as you do. After all, you're the one living in it. What is required is a high degree of honesty and concentration. Beyond that, it is a question of suspending the rational mind and setting aside all of your preconceived notions that "it can't be done" or "this is ridiculous" or, the universal favorite, "this will make me look silly." Once that has been accomplished, it is simply a matter of focusing on solving the problem.

That sounds easy, but most of us find it difficult to do. After all, the institutions we have been taught to trust—education, medicine, even family—have told us that such things can't be done. The really nice thing about these "alternatives," however, is that in most cases, it costs nothing to try, and as some wise person once said, "It can't hurt."

In terms of what kind of crystal to try, just about any kind will do, but quartz, polished to a smooth luster and of a size that easily fits in the palm of your hand, is probably preferable. Just as a laser is a highly organized state of light, the quartz crystal is used because it is the most perfectly organized state of matter that exists in nature. Interestingly, it works in much the same way as a laser; but instead of focusing light, it takes scattered rays of energy and focuses them, providing an energy field that is coherent and going in one direction. The result is a vastly amplified energy force. When used with love, the energy of the mind is added to the energy of the person's life force, and both are amplified for the specific purpose of healing.

Just as there is no perfect crystal for healing, there is likewise no perfect method. Most psychic healers would probably tell you to simply go with your own intuition. The crystal may be placed on the spot where the difficulty or discomfort is most apparent. Or the crystal may be brought into close proximity with the body without actually touching it. The best idea is to practice on yourself and on those close to you. Meditate and try to discover the method that will work best for you. Some people use specially carved crystals with a gently pointed end that can be used for acupressure (being applied at specific acupuncture points). The other end is often rounded and used as part of a healing massage. But regardless of the size, shape, or type of crystal used, always remember that it is the mind that must be focused. Properly applying the power of the mind is what makes everything work; the crystal can only amplify and focus what your mind does. That is the true healing energy.

But what if you're not sure just what the ailment is? Is there any way to discover what might be causing your "dis-ease"? Or more importantly, is the symptom sufficient to determine the source of the problem? This is where kinesiology comes in. Dr. John Diamond, author of *Your Body Doesn't Lie,* believes that our "life energy is the source of all physical and mental well being, of glowing health, of the joy of living." In that context, he quotes from a health book published in 1853, in which Dr. T. L. Nichols declares:

> HEALTH in a human being is the perfection of bodily organization, intellectual energy and moral power.

> HEALTH is the fullest expression of all the faculties and passions of man, acting together in perfect harmony.

> HEALTH is entire freedom from pain of body and discordance of mind.

> HEALTH is beauty, energy, purity, holiness, happiness.

> HEALTH is that condition in which man is the highest known expression of the power and goodness of his Maker.

> When a man is perfect in his own nature, body, and soul, perfect in their harmonious adaptations and action, and living in perfect harmony with nature, with his fellow man and with God, he may be said to be in a state of HEALTH.[4]

Assuming it is the life force energy that makes such abundant health possible, how do we know when we have achieved that state? Certainly, we know when we are not healthy. There are symptoms aplenty to tell us when something is wrong. These symptoms are the body's way of letting us know that we are not "in perfect harmony with nature." But what exactly is wrong? Are a runny nose and itchy eyes the symptoms of a cold or an allergic reaction? Is nausea the result of the flu or a bad combination of choices at the dinner table? Likewise, aches and pains can be deceptive when it comes to determining their cause. Before my friend Jim was diagnosed with a tumor on his spine, the only pain he complained of was in his right leg.

If the body doesn't lie, then we obviously need to learn how to ask the right questions and be able to interpret the answers correctly. This is the purpose of kinesiology, and as it turns out you already know how to do it. Remember the exercise we gave you in Chapter One? That was an expression of kinesiology. No, don't turn back and try to find the page; we'll repeat it for you here and add another small test you can perform to discover your own level of vitality. Vitality, by the way, does not necessarily mean activity. The two may frequently run together, but a truly vital person will exhibit true vitality even while resting.

All right, here's the exercise once again, but this time in context. Let's say you have a friend or relative who hasn't been feeling well. She would like you to use your newfound psychic abilities to help her discover what is wrong. Proceed in the following manner:

1. Have your friend stand in front of you, with one arm relaxed at her side, the other extended out from the shoulder, parallel to the floor. The elbow should be kept straight.

2. Face your friend and place one hand on the shoulder of the arm that is hanging at rest. Place your other hand on her extended arm, just above the wrist. Place only the first and second fingers of your hand on your friend's arm.

3. Tell your friend that you are going to try and push her arm down, and instruct her to resist with all her strength.

4. Now ask your friend a question relative to the problem at hand that can be answered with a simple yes or no. (Example: Is this a problem with your heart?) Your friend should verbalize the answer out loud. It doesn't matter whether she knows the answer intellectually or not. The body, remember, doesn't lie.

5. When your friend answers, press down firmly on the extended arm. Push hard enough to "test" the resistance in the arm, but not so hard that it will fatigue the muscle. This is not a test of strength. You want to push just hard enough to be sure that the muscle *can* lock the shoulder joint against the push.

6. Examine the result. For example, if the problem is indeed related to the heart, the arm will have stayed firm, with hardly any perceivable "give." If, on the other hand, the problem is not related to the heart, the arm will have dropped precipitously.

7. To confirm the result, ask your friend the same question, but tell her to change her answer. The response (unless your friend is a very skilled liar) will be the opposite.

Ask as many questions as you like or as is necessary to pinpoint the problem. Then use the same process to determine the proper "cure." Let's say, for example, that you finally get to the question, "Is this condition being caused by a bacterial infection?" Your friend responds with a firm no, but her arm falls away under your pressure, indicating that that is a wrong answer. You might then ask, "Would antibiotics be appropriate?" If the answer is yes and the test confirms that answer, it would probably be a good idea to call a doctor who can write a prescription.

In all matters of healing, let common sense be your guide. Kinesiology can be a great help in discovering that what you think is a sprained ankle is actually a hairline fracture, but if a bone is obviously broken, it makes little sense to ask the body what to do about it. But if you are looking for the best place to apply a crystal massage, for example, you will find this process enormously helpful.

We promised you a test for vitality. In the procedure just outlined, the deltoid muscle is designated the "indicator" muscle. You and the person working with you can test each other in precisely the same manner. In almost every case, the results will not vary. Now we are going to suggest a method by which the indicator muscle can tell you about specific points on your body, one of the most important being the spot immediately over the thymus gland. This is the spot where the second rib joins the breastbone (the ster-nomandibular joint). Now, with your partner touching this spot with his or her free hand, do the muscle test just as before. Since a strong and active thymus has been found to be an excellent indicator of overall vitality, the result of this test is an excellent indicator of your own vitality. According to Dr. Diamond, testing the thymus can tell us several other things as well:

> Suppose your subject's thymus gland point tested strong. . . . Test again to confirm the result. Now have him think of some catastrophe, such as being in an automobile accident. Test again. . . . Usually, if not invariably, the thymus gland will test weak. Next, ask your subject to think of someone he hates. The thymus will probably continue to test weak. But now ask him to think of someone he loves. Instantly the gland will test strong. You can see how quickly we can learn significant things abut the mind and the body by [kinesiology] testing.[5]

Like virtually all psychic healing processes, kinesiology is primarily concerned with maintaining a healthy energy flow throughout the body. This is also the focus of the crystal and another of the more modern methods based firmly in ancient knowledge: Reiki.

According to Barbara Ray, Ph.D., author of, *The Reiki Factor,* the first and (so far as we know), the *only* book on the subject:

> Life is made of energy and energy is in perpetual motion, moving in swirling spirals. Each moment in your life is a new part of the unfolding spiral of your own life's process. The very essence of life is motion—nothing is status quo. Movement and change are basic, natural laws of energy—and life.[6]

"Reiki," according to Ray, means "universal life-force energy." In essence, the Reiki technique is a method for activating and amplifying the natural life-force energy within the body through the precise use of light energy to restore balance as well as physical, emotional, and mental vitality.[7]

Virtually anyone of any age can learn this technique. Just about the only requirement is to be alive. And if you are alive and using energy, you can use Reiki—not just when you are feeling ill or out of sorts, but when you are healthy and want to stay that way.

This concept of energy flow, by the way, is almost universal. Over 4,000 years ago, the Chinese concluded that there was a life-sustaining force circulating through the body, and they called it *Chi*. The Hindus came to the same conclusion, but they called it *prana*. Hippocrates called it *nature's life force*. The Hawaiian Kahunas call it *mana* and the Russians refer to it as *bioplasmic* energy. Christ, the greatest healer of all, said it was *light*. (As in most things, the modern world is just beginning to catch up. French physicist Jean Caron reported recently that "matter broken down is energy and energy examined is transparent—is *light* [therefore] spirit is within the field of physics now!")[8] Regardless of what it is called, the amount and balance of this energy is essential to the proper functioning of the living body.

Reiki, we should point out, is a commercial enterprise. Entire families will frequently sign up to take Reiki seminars, and the techniques can easily be learned by people from five to ninety-five years of age. It is also promoted as a "scientific" methodology (which may seem a little incongruous in a book on the paranormal), but even though the techniques are repeatable and therefore provide knowledge through experience, the actual practice is not likely to be found among practitioners of traditional healing methods.

In general, the twelve steps associated with Reiki treatments address all of the major organs, glands, and veins with natural energy, i.e., only the body's own energy. The treatment begins at the top of the head and progresses through to the lower back and spinal cord. In the seminars, complete details are given regarding the use of Reiki for specific diseases and disorders. As an ongoing process, it is recommended that treatment of the entire body be done routinely. The idea is to correct the cause as well as deal with symptoms.

Once again, according to Barbara Ray, "The essence of Reiki is light-energy that transforms us—each according to an individual unfolding process."[9] And having experienced these treatments, we can tell you that at no time does the person giving the treatment touch or manipulate the body in any way. The work is entirely with the "energy body." Scientific or not, some form of remarkable extrasensory ability is being employed. That anyone can do it is perhaps the most enlightening aspect of the entire process.

Next we will encounter the psychic surgeons of the Philippines and explore the remarkable story of a man who became the world's only fully recovered quadriplegic—using only the power of his mind.

CHAPTER EIGHT

MEDICAL MYSTERIES

THE PERSON SPEAKING IS IRENE PRZBYCIEN. She is describing a surgical procedure she had recently undergone in the Philippines:

> His hands broke right through my skin, as if it were no thicker than water, and he poked around inside me with his fingers. I didn't feel any pain. I was wide awake: I could raise my head up and look right at his hands squishing my blood around, but I didn't feel a thing. Then he pulled this big hunk of tissue out of me—right before my eyes. He grinned and showed it to me, then casually tossed it into a wastebasket.[1]

You can imagine the reaction that a practicing surgeon in the United States would have to that statement. Admittedly, it is tough to accept at face value. And the reality is that a host of skeptics and members of the medical profession ferociously maintain that the whole concept of psychic surgery is a gigantic hoax. There is only one problem: No one has yet been able to explain the healings that have resulted from this procedure.

The "surgeon" in the case just described was Antonio C. Agpaoa, or Tony, as he has come to be known. Tony is, in fact, the most famous of the Filipino spiritualist healers. But he is just one of many such healers who have demonstrated the ability to open the human body without any instruments—just their bare hands. Neither antiseptics nor anesthetics are used, and the patient remains awake and alert throughout the procedure. In spite of such unsanitary conditions, no case of infection incurred during the "operation" has ever been reported. In one instance, the patient indicated that he was hungry, so the surgeon stopped what he was doing and waited while the patient ate an orange.

Irene, by the way, is a native of Chicago, where at least 200 home videos of psychic surgeries can be found. Most of them, as you might expect, are quite amateurish. But what is taking place before the lens is astonishing nevertheless.

In his investigation of the psychic surgeons of the Philippines, Tom Valentine cites a number of well-documented cases that seem to defy modern "scientific" explanation. But as someone once pointed out, it only takes one white crow to prove that all crows are not black. One of the most fascinating "white crows" involves twenty-three ophthalmologists from Los Angeles who took three blind patients to the Philippines. The patients suffered from glaucoma and cataracts and were far beyond the skill of the ophthalmologists. Tony Agpaoa's bare-handed surgery was performed before the unbelieving eyes of the medical doctors, who watched intently. Tony cured all three patients. Upon their return, the ophthalmologists allegedly wrote to their medical association, recommending further study. They were told to forget it.

Tony, by the way, is a fugitive in America. During a visit to the United States in the fall of 1968, he was arrested and charged with fraud. After four months of waiting to be brought to trial in Detroit, he finally jumped bail and returned home, where he was welcomed with open arms. In the Philippines, Tony is not just another psychic healer; he is also head of the church that he founded, the Philippine Church of Science and Revelation, which has a small mission in Chicago. It is not too surprising, then, that Tony approaches his work with religious conviction. One colorful story, perhaps apocryphal, demonstrates how seriously he regards his healing gift.

While attending a gathering of Asian mystics, fakirs, swamis, and assorted miracle workers in Tokyo, Tony was asked to "perform" for the group. He refused, telling them that he didn't demonstrate his abilities for the sake of a show. One of the delegates challenged him, suggesting that his refusal was tantamount to an admission that he was a fraud. The man attempted to embarrass Tony into a performance by defying him to pull a tooth and proffered one of his own front teeth. Tony reached out, pulled the tooth, and handed it to his stunned antagonist. Then he turned and left the room. What the poor fellow didn't know was that pulling teeth was an almost daily routine for the psychic surgeons of the Philippines.

In this country, however, getting any kind of official recognition for his work is about as likely as pulling hens' teeth. Otherwise objective scientists, doctors, and surgeons continue to condemn, without any investigation, this amazing phenomenon. In spite of the many firsthand testimonies, photographs, and videotapes and the hundreds, perhaps thousands of otherwise unexplainable healing events, the scientific mind remains firmly closed on the matter. Happily, the other subjects of this chapter have fared a little better.

I first met Dr. Richard Johnson at dinner in a restaurant near his office in Ventura, California. At the time, he was just completing a decade of study on biofeedback in the human body and had made what he thought were some startling discoveries. A respected clinical psychologist, he was on the threshold of putting his considerable reputation at risk by suggesting that, "anything that can go wrong with the body, the mind can fix." The term *biogram* was still a couple of years into the future, since some aspects of his theory were not yet fully in place. But there was no mistaking the excitement in his voice as he tried to explain the importance of his discovery to someone who was far removed from his area of expertise. I didn't understand any of it beyond the "bumper sticker" level, but even the little I could comprehend was intriguing.

Within two years of that first meeting, Johnson had shut down his biofeedback laboratory and moved from Ventura to Yuba City, on the California-Nevada border. He was, he said, devoting all of his time and considerable energy to refining his "biogram" theory and getting it all down in a book. The bare bones of his original research was finally getting fleshed out, and he seemed more confident than ever that he was on the right track. Then the unthinkable happened.

While recovering from a cold, Richard Johnson picked up the wrong bottle, and instead of his cold medication, downed a large dose of hydrogen peroxide. The effect was almost instantaneous. He slipped into a coma. Doctors told his wife, Eileen, that it was very similar to the "bends" and was almost sure to be fatal. But Eileen knew something about the bends and knew that its effects can sometimes be reversed with decompression. Thinking only of saving his life, she rushed him to the nearest facility with a decompression chamber. Doctors assured her that she was only wasting time and money. Even if he survived, he would probably be a vegetable. But Eileen persisted, and the decompression worked, at least to the degree that Johnson came out of the coma with his mind fully intact.

That was the good news. The bad news was that there had been nerve damage: He was now a quadriplegic. From the neck down, nothing worked. Once again, the doctors told Eillen that she had had her miracle: Her husband was alive with his mind intact, but to expect his condition to ever change was foolhardy. The entire body of medical knowledge asserts that damaged nerves cannot be repaired. On the other hand, Johnson assured his wife that he would be just fine. "I know how to fix it," he said with a smile.

Although it had never been his intention to use himself as a laboratory animal, Johnson now had the perfect opportunity to put all of his theories to the test. He was not happy about this strange turn of events, but of all the people in the world for this to happen to, Richard Johnson was probably the one man who did not see it as the end of his active life. Johnson is absolutely convinced that there is a self-healing mechanism in all of us, a mechanism as old as Creation. He often quoted Dr. Albert Schweitzer, who said: "Each patient carries his own doctor inside him. They come to us not knowing that truth. We are at our best when we give the doctor who resides within each patient a chance to go to work."[2]

This was the ultimate case of "Physician, heal thyself." According to Johnson, it is an indisputable fact that there is an intercommunication between the mind and the body. It is how that communication takes place that is the basis of biogram therapy. The theory was born in September of 1979, when after a particularly difficult day struggling with the problem of how the mind directs the behavior of the body, Johnson finally drifted off to sleep. We'll let him tell it in his own words:

> I was sleeping when it felt like I was being awakened by someone. In this transitional state between sleeping and waking, I felt as though I was being taken into the inside of my brain by someone else. I was an ordained minister before entering the mental health field and so intuitively, I knew that it was God. As I watched my thoughts, I could see them becoming liquid in form and flowing in a narrow stream out in front of me. The brain was creating a chemical process from those thoughts. Then, at a more microscopic level, I could see tiny particles coming from many different directions. Selected particles were brought forward and linked together to form a chain. I knew at once that these particles were amino acids and that the chain being forged in this manner was a peptide. My thoughts had become living things, living words, biological symbols—biograms.[3]

According to the biogram theory, then, a peptide chain is a chemical record of a thought that becomes solid in form. A communication system as tangible as that, Johnson was certain, would have to be measurable. The intervening years had confirmed that hypothesis. Unfortunately, he hadn't yet discovered exactly how to control the process.

Given his current situation, the immediate problem was to discover some method of forming and controlling the transmission of appropriate biograms to specific parts of the body. Years earlier, he had searched the literature and discovered that there was nothing written on how the mind communicates with the body. He knew that he was on his own.

Alone at night and unable to move without assistance, Johnson began to experiment with communications procedures. Direct commands, he quickly discovered, didn't work. Asking or even pleading produced no result whatsoever. Night after night, he focused all of his mental energy on trying to send healing messages to his numbed body. He knew that it should work. He knew that it *could* work. But for some reason, nothing was happening. Finally, late one night, in the quiet of his hospital room and on the verge of giving up, he surrendered all control to his mind. "You have my permission," he murmured silently, "to do whatever is necessary to correct my condition."

There was an almost immediate reaction—a slight tingling sensation in scattered locations throughout his body. How beautifully simple, he thought. All I really have to do is get out of the way. But the reaction was too general. Over the next few weeks, he began formulating specific ways of granting his mind *permission* to do the healing work by focusing on well-defined areas of the body. The results became more pronounced as feeling and motor capability began to return. Nurses who had gone to great lengths to teach him how to use certain self-help devices were astonished when they returned the next day to find that he no longer needed them. Within three months, he was ambulatory with the help of a wheelchair and already beginning to train an amazed hospital staff in the applications of his therapy.

Once he had opened the door of understanding, he began to make other discoveries. He found that he could utilize the mind's "alpha" state, that state of mind between sleep and wakefulness, to ask questions regarding his general level of physical, spiritual, or mental health. The answers would come in a dream, which he schooled himself to always write down. A pad and pencil is a permanent fixture on his nightstand even today.

Initially skeptical, the doctors and staff of the hospital soon grew to appreciate the miracle they were witnessing. Johnson's progress was duly monitored, recorded, and eventually applauded.

Much of the information reported here was given to me in personal conversations with Richard Johnson during breaks in a three-day seminar he conducted just a little over a year from the date of what he refers to as his "accident." Fully recovered, except for a slight weakness in his left ankle, he was on his feet for most of the eight-hour sessions—certainly the most agile "vegetable" in medical history.

It was another year before his book, *The Biogram Theory and the Healing Mind,* was released. In it he forcefully states the premise on which his theory (and later his actual experience) was based:

> The mind has access to the most complete information about the symptoms from inside the body. It is equipped to select the most appropriate repair techniques and isolate those areas from other responses to prevent harmful side effects. The mind alone is fully equipped to coordinate those responses

Uri Geller often demonstrated his mind-boggling powers by bending an ordinary key borrowed from someone in his audience. This key is similar to the one described by the author.

The twelve signs of the zodiac are depicted in a highly stylized version of the symbols used to represent the corresponding planets in their heavenly sphere.

Known as the "Sleeping Prophet," Edgar Cayce helped thousands of people suffering from sometimes undiagnosed ailments. His writings are also cited by modern researchers looking into prophecies of future events.

The early twentieth-century clairvoyant Edgar Cayce predicted that the western portion of the continent of Atlantis would rise from the sea in 1968 or 1969. The Bimini Road, seen here, was discovered in 1968. Some believe this could be the lost continent of Atlantis.

Jeane Dixon, Washington, D.C.-based astrologer and clairvoyant, predicted the assassination of both President Kennedy and his brother, Robert. Her efforts to warn both men were ignored.

Some claim that during the now-famous "Philadelphia Experiment," the USS *Eldridge,* became invisible, disappeared from its berth in Philadelphia, and reappeared in Norfolk (some 400 miles away) within minutes.

Five World War II Avenger bombers similar to this one disappeared over the Bermuda Triangle on a routine training flight. The flight, led by an experienced World War II pilot, was never heard from again. No trace of any of the planes was ever found.

A Hindu fakir (Holy Man), in the process of levitating, or making his body float in mid-air in defiance of gravity. In India this activity is accepted with hardly a murmur by onlookers.

This photograph of "Nessy," the Loch Ness monster, launched a search that began over sixty years ago and continues to this day. Everything from sonar to submarines has been used to locate this elusive monster.

The great biblical city of Babylon has withered away over the centuries. Efforts are currently under way to restore the city to its former splendor.

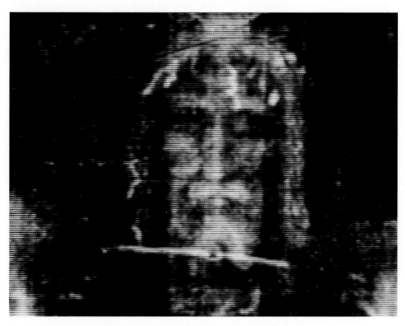

Is this the face of Jesus Christ? The Shroud of Turin has undergone tens of thousands scientific studies by international and interdenominational teams to try and determine if it is, in fact, the shroud of Jesus Christ.

Native Americans of the Southwestern United States left behind a vast array of petroglyphs that offer insight into their tribal ancestry, their wars, and their prophetic warnings. Newspaper Rock in Arizona is a stunning example of their art and wisdom.

with the total psychological and biological changes required to produce healing. Where and how to begin, or when the total job of healing is complete, is something only the mind and body, working together, can know.[4]

Richard Johnson does not consider himself a psychic healer. So far as biogram therapy is concerned, he regards it as every bit as scientific as DNA. According to Johnson, DNA is a

living form of literature that comprises the specifications, the very blueprint of the body. It seemed reasonable to me that if this molecular system of literature worked so well for the body, it was a proven technique that could be used with equal effectiveness for the mind.[5]

It is true, however, that it is the "alternative" practitioners who have welcomed biogram therapy with the greatest appreciation. Perhaps that is because hypnotherapists, chiropractors, and even acupuncturists have long held a reverence for the power of the mind as a participant in the process of healing. To be fair, there are some traditionalists who have the courage to raise their voices in support of the notion that the mind cannot only cause bodily disorders but cure them as well.

Norman Cousins, in his book, *Anatomy of an Illness*, said:

The human mind has a role to play in control of pain, just as it has a key role in combating illness. . . . Both on the conscious and subconscious level, the mind can order the body to react or respond in certain ways. Such response involves body chemistry and not just psychological reactions.[6]

The research of Candace Pert, a neurobiologist, seems to support Johnson's theories almost to the letter. According to Pert, neuropeptides, the chemicals triggered by emotion, are *thoughts converted to matter*. Furthermore, the body's emotional responses may trigger the manufacture of emotional chemicals even *before* the brain registers the problem. Could this be a form of precognition?

The question is, Can everybody do this? The answer Johnson gives in every seminar is "Of course." No special equipment or level of education is required. Your mind and your body function as a single unit, and the mind, not the body, is in charge. Dr. Johnson made several efforts to contact actor Christopher Reeve who was paralyzed in a riding accident. He hoped to be able to share this information with both Reeve and his doctors. He was unsuccessful. A polite note expressing appreciation for his interest was the only response.

That is not too surprising. As with all things new, and particularly those of a paranormal nature, doubt is the greatest barrier. One wonders why, since there is nothing to lose—absolutely no cost or risk. The only expenditure is time and mental energy, and as Johnson has demonstrated, even there, much can be accomplished while you sleep.

If you are harboring doubts, try your own version of Dr. Johnson's "dream diagnosis." Place a pencil and a pad of paper on your nightstand when you get ready to go to bed. Know in advance what question you would like answered, and then just before falling asleep, when you are not quite awake but still not asleep, ask the question of your inner self and request that the answer be given to you in a dream. Whatever the nature of the dream that comes, write it down as soon as you awaken. Dream memories are fleeting. When you are fully awake, analyze the dream with specific reference to the question you asked.

Not every question will generate (or even deserve) an immediate dream response. This is a learning process. You learn to communicate with the sub-conscious mind, and it learns to respond in a manner appropriate to your requirements. The ability to become attuned to your inner self will increase with practice.

Probably no individual healer since Edgar Cayce has created such a storm of interest as Caroline Myss. Myss calls herself a medical intuitive and makes a strong case for her particular brand of "energy medicine." Like Cayce, Myss diagnoses illness through intuitive means, and like Cayce, her view of the mind-body connection also includes the spirit. In fact, as far as Myss is concerned, it is the spirit that takes the principal role in energy healing.

Caroline Myss has a rather unique background for the role she has assumed as a medical intuitive. A newspaper journalist with a master's degree in theology, she put both of those careers aside to go into the publishing business. The publishing firm called Stillpoint specializes in books about alternative healing methods. Yet, despite her professional interest in alternatives to established medical practices, she claims to have had no interest in participating in any of them—hardly a candidate, it would seem, for any sort of metaphysical encounter.

But an accidental seer, you'll remember, does not choose to be psychic or intuitive; rather, they seem to be chosen. Caroline Myss, by her own account, grew into an awareness of what seemed to be an ever-increasing perceptual ability: "A friend would mention that someone he knew was not feeling well and an insight into the cause of the problem would pop into my head. I was uncannily accurate and word of it spread through the local community."[7]

In that respect, at least, Caroline Myss came to an understanding of her gifts in a manner quite common in the world of the paranormal. In just a matter of months, she had gone from a reporter with no interest in alternative healing to giving readings for people on a variety of health crises "from depression to cancer." But as we have seen, this can be a confusing, even frightening experience:

> I felt as if I were suddenly responsible for explaining the will of God to dozens of sad, frightened people, without any training. Ironically, the more these folks wanted insight into what God was doing to them, the more I wanted insight into what God was doing to me.[8]

Unlike Edgar Cayce, whose abilities seem to have burst upon him through the intervention of an ethereal voice, Myss's intuitive skills simply unfolded within as she continued to deal with the problems of others. Myss was probably unaware of it at the time, but she was following a fairly typical pattern: first a simple awareness that something about her association with people was different, then a willingness to use this "gift" for the benefit of others, and finally total commitment to the process. Ultimately, there was the realization that her gift was immensely beneficial to the people around her, even though she had no clue as to where her uncanny ability came from.

What is different in Caroline Myss's story is her absorption of religious principles into the matrix that produces her visions. The great spiritual traditions of the Hindu chakras, the Christian sacraments, and the Kabbalah's tree of life are all woven into the fabric of her understanding of the way the body and the spirit unite. The concept is quite remarkable, since the church has almost always been a foe of anyone claiming any kind of spiritual insight. But Dr. Myss throws a whole new light on the subject. "By learning to see your body and spirit in a way that draws on old truths," she says, "you can begin to develop your own intuition and to understand and manage your own spirit."[9]

Some of those "old truths" suggest much the same thing: Unfortunately, intuitive gifts cannot be transferred. They can, however, be learned. Myss and C. Norman Shealy, a Harvard-trained neurosurgeon and founder of the American Holistic Medical Association, are already planning "medical intuitive residency" programs at holistic health centers all across the country. They envision a time when medical intuitives will be essential members of health care teams.

None of this would be possible, however, if the work being done by Caroline Myss did not demonstrate a high degree of reliability—which of course it does. One case in particular is noteworthy, since her diagnosis and subsequent follow-up program led to a healing of what is easily the world's most dreaded (and officially incurable) disease: AIDS.

The young man in question was already past the HIV positive stage before Myss was called in for an evaluation. He knew he was HIV positive, but he didn't know that the disease had already taken hold in his lungs. When Myss told him he had AIDS, he had several choices: he could just give up; he could fall into a state of self-pity; or he could get angry and shake his fist at a medical profession that had let him down. Instead, he took a positive attitude toward the recovery program outlined by Myss and Shealy. Rather than throw in the towel, he followed their recommendations to the letter. These recommendations included, but were not limited to: quitting smoking, eating a near-vegetarian diet, getting plenty of aerobic exercise, getting into psychotherapy, and putting castor oil packs on his abdomen for forty-five minutes a day. In six weeks, subsequent HIV tests came back negative. As of the last we heard, still negative.

Myss is different in another respect. She firmly believes that "intuitive or symbolic sight" is not a gift but a skill. She suggests that it is a matter of learning to interpret the language of energy, or, more specifically, the body's energy field. The idea of working on the energy body, of course, is in accord with virtually all psychic healing disciplines. Reiki, kinesiology, therapeutic touching, and acupuncture (though in recent years the latter has become more acceptable medical practice) all work with the energy body, or energy field. Some psychic healers insist that anything that doesn't deal with the body's energy field is only dealing with symptoms and is bound to fail as a cure.

How to acquire this skill is the subject of Myss's book, but it is interesting how the various concepts of psychic healing seem to support one another. For example, behavioral kinesiology is predicated on the notion that the body cannot lie. Myss confirms in her studies that "if we tell a lie our energy field will communicate to the other person the 'energy fact' that we are not telling the truth. Energy does not and cannot lie."[10] Kinesiology, of course, provides a physical mechanism for determining that fact. And another striking example, already noted, is the mutual support of the work of Dr. Johnson and Dr. Pert.

Several interesting questions arise from our brief overview of the psychic healers but by far the most intriguing is, Are the psychic and the physician finally getting together? Myss and Dr. Shealy apparently find their working relationship very satisfying. The neurobiologist seems to have confirmed Johnson's findings, and even some general practitioners and chiropractors routinely use kinesiology as part of the diagnostic process. News stories, articles, and television programs hailing the advent of the mind-body connection have become routine. If the trend continues, we may yet see the day our first step to better health will be a visit to a medical intuitive. And if Caroline Myss and Richard Johnson are right, it may be as simple as standing in front of your own mirror.

We met a psychic detective in Chapter One. In the next section, we'll meet the most famous psychic detective of them all. Also, find out what the government is doing in the world of the paranormal, and discover that truth is stranger than fiction, even in Hollywood.

Section Four

A PSYCHIC POTPOURRI

*We are not human beings
having a spiritual experience,
but spiritual beings having a human one.*
GEORGES I. GURDJIEFF

By THE TIME GAYLE'S YOUNGEST DAUGHTER was grown and out on her own, Gayle had become a certified hypnotherapist and a teacher of yoga and the ancient Chinese "moving meditation" called *T'ai Chi*. She had read dozens of books on virtually every aspect of the paranormal and had, on several occasions, provided readings for friends, friends of friends, and a fair number of relatives, though most of her family, those who had grown up with her, couldn't imagine that she could possibly do anything out of the ordinary. In truth, hardly anything in her life *was* ordinary, but for the most part, she managed to keep it to herself. There were times, however, when some unspoken sense of duty called, and always in a clear and unmistakable voice.

She had spent most of the morning doing her marketing and running the errands she could no longer put off, and each time she got into her car, she somehow managed to hear the same news story. A young girl who lived in the area had been kidnapped. Police, the radio said, were stumped. There were no clues. Each time she heard the story, Gayle had the unmistakable feeling that she could help, but she shook it off. Common sense told her that if the police could do nothing, there would be nothing she could do either.

That worked the first three times. The fourth time she heard the news story, she received a different message. Clearly she heard someone say, "Go to the police station."

By now she had enough experience in these matters to know that ignoring these impressions was futile. There was just one problem. She didn't have the foggiest idea where the police station was. She did, however, know where Main Street was, and that's always a good bet. A short time later, she found the building and pulled up in front. Sitting there in the car, she almost changed her mind. These people are not going to listen to some middle-aged housewife, she reasoned. Besides she didn't as yet have any notion of how she might help.

"Go in!"

Well, there was no mistaking that. Gayle got out of the car and walked into the building. She spotted a desk sporting a sign that said "Information" and went directly to it.

"I'd like to speak to the officer in charge of the kidnapping investigation," she said.

The officer behind the desk pointed down the corridor. "Last door on the right," he replied.

Gayle walked down a narrow corridor lined on both sides with small cubicles. Each cubicle was wood framed from the floor up to about 4 feet and then glass panels above that. The wood partition between cubicles was barely chair height, and again, a glass plate finished the partition and provided what little privacy this kind of arrangement afforded. It appeared that the plan was to make it easy for the detectives to see each other. Each cubicle had a door but none of them were closed.

Gayle reached the last door on the right and waited. The detective was on the phone. He glanced over and saw her standing there and quickly cut the conversation short. Middle-aged housewife or not, she was still a very striking woman.

"May I help you?" he asked.

"I may be able to help you," she replied. "May I come in?"

"Yes, of course." The detective stood and pulled out a dingy office chair for her.

Gayle seated herself, trying to look as confident as possible. When the detective sat back down, she wasted no time in getting to the point.

"I am a practicing clairvoyant," she said, "and I've been listening to the news about the kidnapping. I thought I might be able to help."

The detective put both hands in back of his head and leaned back in his chair. He stared at her for a moment, then looked across the partition at his partner in the next cubicle. The smile on his face went from ear to ear.

"I'm sorry," Gayle said, starting to get up, "but this is very serious to me."

"No please, sit down." The detective leaned forward. "I was smiling because just ten minutes ago I said to my partner"—he jerked his thumb toward the next cubicle—"I wish we had a psychic to help us with this one, but they don't advertise in the yellow pages."

From that point on, Gayle knew she was in friendly company. Whether or not she could be of any help was yet to be determined, but at least they would take her seriously.

After a brief discussion of the details of the case, Gayle asked if she could have something that belonged to the kidnap victim with which to work. The detective picked up the phone, and a short time later, the girl's mother showed up with several items of clothing, a favorite toy, and a photograph of her daughter. Gayle took each item and held it in her hands. The energy was still strong and vibrant.

"She's still alive," she told them. "In fact, I would say, to this point at least, she's in good condition."

"Thank God," the mother whispered.

"Do you have any idea where she is?" the detective asked.

Gayle brought the toy to her bosom and held it tightly for a long moment. "No, I get no sense of location, but I can tell you that you should be looking for a car with out-of-state license plates."

The detective looked up at his partner, who had joined them in the small cubicle.

"I'll take care of it," the partner said and disappeared.

Gayle didn't know it, but until that moment, the police had assumed that the kidnapper was someone local. Neighboring states had not been notified.

If the child turned up anywhere else, authorities wouldn't know to call here. Within moments, an "all-points" was sent out.

"I'm sorry," Gayle said, "that's all I get right now."

She handed the items back to the girl's mother and started to leave, but the mother held onto her arm. "I don't pretend to know what you're doing or how you're doing it," she said quietly, "but thank you for the hope."

Gayle returned home, but the plight of the little girl was never far from her mind. Several times over the next two days, she tried to "lock on" to the image in the photograph but without success. Then, toward evening of the second day, Gayle seated herself on the couch and began to prepare for her regular evening meditation. She had barely begun to meditate when the image of the girl popped into her mind. It came with such suddenness and force that she cried out. The little girl was trying to make her way up a staircase, but she was wobbling badly, as if she had been drugged. Near the top of the stairs another image appeared. It was indistinct except for thick glasses, but Gayle sensed it was a woman. The woman, Gayle said later, screamed at the little girl, "What are you doing in my house? Get out! Get out!"

At this point, Gayle decided to take things into her own hands. Locking onto the image of the little girl, she began to project a message: *Go to a police station. Hurry!* She continued to send the message over and over, focusing all of her considerable mental energy on the task. She saw the little girl stumble out of the house, and the image was lost.

The following day, Gayle called the detective and told him what had transpired. "Have you heard anything from any other police departments?" she asked.

"No nothing," the detective replied, "we'll let you know if we do."

The hours dragged by. Another evening meditation, but this time there were no images. The following day, just before noon, the phone rang.

"Gayle?" It was the detective.

"Yes, what's happened?"

"Just thought you'd like to know, the girl wandered into a police station a couple of states away from here. She had apparently been drugged and couldn't tell them anything, and just as they were about to ship her over to social services, one of their guys remembered the 'all-points' we sent out the other day." The detective paused. Gayle could almost hear his smile over the phone. "I thought you'd like to know, the girl's on her way home." There was another pause. "Thanks," he said.

"Sure, anytime."

The police in Gayle's hometown remembered that last remark and took her up on the offer on several other occasions, but none engaged her interest as did this particular kidnapping. After all, she had not been called into it by the detective. Someone or *something* else had directed her to get involved. Perhaps that was what made the difference.

Of course, it could all have been just a string of eerie coincidences. There are those who insist that all psychic phenomena are at best coincidence and at worst outright fraud. But remember, it only takes one white crow to prove that all crows are not black.

CHAPTER NINE

THE PSYCHIC DETECTIVES

THE LOS ANGELES POLICE DEPARTMENT had very quietly been using psychics for some time before I called and asked them if we could film one of their psychic detectives in action. To my surprise, they were cordial and accommodating. My surprise stemmed from the fact that they knew we were making a motion picture, and I would have thought that their use of psychics would be something they would want to keep secret.

What the police knew that I didn't was that we would be filming the work of a young man by the name of Peter Hurkos, whose stunning accuracy had been proven several times before. They were confident that Peter would come through for them again, even with the cameras rolling.

Peter Hurkos is today the world's most famous psychic detective. Indeed, the term may originally have been coined to describe him. At the time of our meeting, however, he was just one of several psychics that the LAPD used, although he was their most accurate in terms of crime-solving success.

We were invited to go to Peter's home. The arrangement was that we could set up our equipment, lights, sound, cameras, everything, just like a regular shoot, but we had to remain quiet and in the background. We were instructed to do nothing to attract attention to ourselves. The case that Peter would be working on was a multiple murder, and the police had only one clue for him to work with.

When everything was set up and ready to go, I moved to the background and settled in to watch. My earlier experience with Uri Geller had taught me not to prejudge these people, but I was not prepared for what happened next.

A police officer came into the room. In his hands he was carrying something wrapped in a scarf. Peter was sitting in a large, overstuffed chair, still trying to get comfortable with the lights and equipment even though it was well back and out of the way. As the officer approached, Peter suddenly became very agitated. The officer had not yet unwrapped whatever he was carrying, but it was clear that Peter found it disturbing.

"You're carrying a bloody knife," he said, pointing at the scarf.

The officer nodded silently and handed the knife, still completely wrapped, to Peter. Hurkos stiffened, almost as if he had been struck with an electric shock. Sweat began to pour from his face and forehead. His hands shook as he opened up the scarf and revealed the bloody knife.

At this point, the words began to rush from his mouth, and as the information poured forth, his whole body seemed to get involved. First he described, in great detail, the room where the knife had been found. He told the officers (and our cameras) where the windows were, where every chair was in the room, even what could be seen from the windows. Then he began to describe each person who had been in the room when the murders took place. He gave a detailed description not only of what they looked like, but how they were killed. All of this, we were assured by the police, was in complete agreement with what they already knew, even though Peter had been given no information about the case beforehand and in fact didn't even know the nature of the crime until he was handed the bloody knife.

Then the really remarkable portion of the session began. Peter began describing the *feelings* of the killer. Hurkos seemed to be able to insinuate himself into the murderer's mind. He told the police what the killer was thinking at the moment of the crime and how he felt inside when the deed was done. But he didn't stop there. Peter gave the officers considerable detail about the place where they might find the killer, and finally, he gave them a physical description of the man.

I stood in open-mouthed amazement as the information poured out. It was almost as if he were reading from a book. There were few hesitations and no equivocation about anything. Three weeks later, the LAPD made an arrest in the case. The killer matched Peter's description in every important detail.

Following the arrest, we went back and interviewed one of the officers. He admitted that the reason they had gone to Hurkos in the first place was because, other than the murder weapon, they had no leads at all: no fingerprints, no witnesses; they literally didn't have a clue. Somehow, by simply holding the murder weapon, Peter had been able to lead them to the killer. The officer, who had worked with Hurkos before, seemed almost blasé about it, but to me it was one of the most impressive exhibitions of psychic power I had ever seen.

In the years that followed, Peter Hurkos's fame spread worldwide, helped in no small way, I'm sure, by our film. We had opened the door just a crack on something that police departments had been doing for some time (the LAPD was by no means the only police department using psychics). The secrecy was not due to any lack of success, but rather to an understanding of human nature. Even now, there are those of you reading this book who are saying to yourself, "I don't believe it." Unfortunately, for a significant number of criminals, many police departments did and still do "believe."

Peter Hurkos was an intentional seer and went on to not only fame, but a certain degree of fortune as well. That is not always the case, of course, and some psychic detectives have come to regret even one vision of a crime.

Approximately twenty years ago, Judy Jones (not her real name) was jolted awake one night by a dream so real that every detail remained with her long after she was awake. She tried desperately to make it go away, but to no avail. What she had seen was the body of a young woman being dumped somewhere in a wooded canyon. The terrain in the area surrounding her home included several small canyons, but they were fairly well traveled and not a particularly likely place to dump a body. Nevertheless, that was the indelible impression that was left on her mind.

Judy tried to shake the vision, but when it simply wouldn't go away, she decided to go down to the local police department. Once there, she drove around the block a few times, wondering what she could say that wouldn't make her look foolish. At last she went inside and asked to speak to a detective. Even then, the officer had to coax the information out of her. Reluctantly, she told him about her dream, the vivid nature of the images, and the fact that she just couldn't shake it. Intrigued, the detective took her back to a large map of the area that showed all of the canyons in the surrounding area. Without hesitation Judy zeroed in on an area to the north and east. It was a smaller canyon with only one two-lane secondary road running through it. Judy had no idea why she was drawn to that spot, but then she had no idea why she was going through all of this to begin with.

They returned to the detective's office, and he was suddenly very serious. The police, he told her, had found a truck in that general area that had been torched. It belonged to a nurse who had been missing for several days. Until Judy walked in the door, the police had absolutely nothing to go on. For all they knew, the woman could have run off with the love of her life, and vandals could have torched the truck.

"No," Judy told them, "she was murdered, and her body is still up there in that canyon."

The police agreed to launch a search and told her to go home, but aside from the one detective to whom she had spoken personally, Judy got the distinct feeling that they really didn't have their heart in it. Judy decided that she wouldn't leave it up to them.

She did go home, but still haunted by the persistent images, she gathered up her children and headed for the canyon she had identified on the map. Maybe she would recognize something, some piece of terrain that she had seen in the dream, and at least narrow the search area. When she reached the top of the canyon, she stopped and got out of the car. There was an eerie silence, and she was suddenly overtaken by feelings of anxiety. She was about to get back in the car when she noticed tire tracks. She knelt down and touched them with the tips of her fingers. Immediately the feelings of anxiety increased dramatically. This was where it had happened, she was certain, and her only desire now was to get out of there as quickly as possible.

Judy got back in the car and was hurrying down the mountain when her daughter called out.

"Stop! Back there," her daughter said excitedly, "I saw something white."

Judy backed up and stopped the car. She and her daughter got out and made their way toward the spot where the girl thought she had seen something. As it turned out, what she had seen were the white shoes the nurse was wearing. They had found the body.

"Hurry," Judy said, turning her daughter away from the gruesome sight, "we have to tell the police."

Judy hurried back to the car. They were heading down the canyon once more when they spotted a police officer. They hailed him down, told him what they had found, and described the location of the body. The officer told them there was nothing more that they could do and instructed them to go home. At last, it was over with—or so she thought.

The police recovered the body, and later that evening, two police officers came to Judy's door. They asked her to come down to the station with them. Judy quickly agreed, but when they got there, she was asked to take a polygraph test. Again she agreed without hesitation. A short time later, Judy was arrested and charged with the crime.

For the next three days, Judy was behind bars, loudly protesting her innocence. Then police got a tip and picked up three men in a neighboring county who confessed to the murder.

The prosecuting attorney was unrepentant. "She knew details of the crime that only the killer should have known," he said. "My hypothesis is, she picked up the information about the abduction on the local grapevine and fabricated the story."

The prosecutor's attitude tells us a great deal about the level of acceptance most officials have toward psychic phenomena. Faced with the reality that Judy did not commit the crime, and admitting that she knew things about it that only the killer would know, he still insisted that he did the right thing by throwing her in jail. The more obvious fact—that she could not possibly have picked up things from the local grapevine that *only the killer would know*—seemed to have completely eluded him.

For her part, Judy is a true accidental psychic. She says that she never had any kind of psychic experience before—nor in the two decades since. She hopes that she never has one again. She did, however, sue the county for wrongful arrest and incarceration.

It would be unfair to suggest that practicing psychics who volunteer their time and talents to help police solve crimes frequently wind up being arrested. In fact, the case we have just described is the only one we know of where the psychic was actually put in jail solely on the basis of the information given to the police. In most cases, the psychic is simply given a wide berth by those not directly involved with the investigation. It is also true that psychic detectives do not solve every case in which they're asked to participate. Indeed, the ledger may fall on the debit side when all the cases are added up. But that's hardly the point.

Consider the circumstances under which the psychic is asked to work. In almost every case, the police have come to a dead end. Some cases have lain dormant for years. (Remember Charlie in Chapter One?) Usually, the psychic is provided with only the barest details with which to work. And given the nature of psychic awareness, more often than not, the psychic isn't even sure what the impressions mean. Given all this, it's a wonder that psychics have any success at all.

Most psychics are fully aware of the drawbacks but continue to offer their services anyway, no matter how remote their chance of success. Dorothy Allison is one such psychic detective. She has been featured on television shows such as A&E's "Unexplained" and "Sightings" and NBC's "Dateline." She will go just about anywhere her help is requested and adamantly refuses to accept any money for her services. According to "Sightings," she has a remarkable record of achievement.

In one of her more bizarre cases, Dorothy was called by a detective and asked to come to Canada. A young girl had been missing for some time, and by the time she was called in, the police had run out of options. There were no leads and no clues. In a telephone conversation with the detective, Dorothy said that she was experiencing some kind of "psychic interference." But she agreed to come up and do what she could anyway.

Strangely, the psychic could get nothing on the girl the detective was concerned about. But she insisted that there was someone else—another girl— and something terrible had happened to her. Driving past a lake near the town where the girl had disappeared, Dorothy began to experience the same kind of psychic interference that she had during the phone call. A girl's body was in that lake, she told police, and her leg would be the first thing to be found.

A few days later, fishermen made a grim discovery. They pulled up a cement block with a girl's leg protruding from it. An immediate search was undertaken. In all, eight cement blocks were retrieved, each containing a body part of a young girl.

The detective felt certain that they had found his missing victim, but the coroner's report identified the girl in the cement blocks as another missing teenager whose disappearance had only been reported a few days earlier. The physical characteristics of the two missing girls were strikingly similar: Both were about the same height and weight, both had naturally brown hair dyed blond, and both wore braces.

Back home in the United States, a year passed before Dorothy Allison would be contacted by the detective again. He still hadn't been able to locate the original missing girl, and the psychic still could not offer him any help. But another victim *would* be found, she told him, and within a week. Dorothy gave the detective an amazingly detailed description, even though he assured her that no such person had been reported missing.

The girl would be found covered with brush, she told him. She told the detective that he would hear trickling water nearby and see a white fence. Within a week, a young girl with long dark hair was indeed reported missing. She was found a few days later, her body hurriedly buried under some brush. A nearby culvert provided the sound of trickling water, and across the road was a white rail fence.

Unfortunately, Dorothy Allison could not give the detective a description of the murderer. One more murder would occur before a young woman would come forward and confess that it was she and her husband who had committed all the murders, thus bringing to a close one of the most bizarre crime sprees in Canadian history. Although Dorothy Allison had not been able to help solve the case, the accuracy of her descriptions of the victims, *well before* their bodies were discovered, left a lasting impression on the detective.

If Peter Hurkos is the world's best-known psychic detective, it's fair to say that Dorothy Allison holds that distinction in America. Her most recent case was made public by "Sightings" in January 1998. Allison was called in to help solve the case of a grandmother who was raped and murdered in a small town in Alabama. The sheriff had never worked with a psychic before, but was impressed with his first meeting. Having only the victim's birthdate and the date of the murder to work with, she correctly identified where the crime had taken place and how the murder was committed. But there is something decidedly different in this instance. Working with a retired New York police sketch artist, Dorothy Allison has given the police, and through "Sightings" the world, a picture of what the murderer looks like. It will be interesting to see if Dorothy Allison proves to be right once again.

Like psychic healers, some psychic detectives apparently can receive their images over great distances. Gerard Croiset Jr., the son of a world famous Dutch psychic, demonstrated this ability by assisting in the case of two missing girls thousands of miles away in South Carolina. The two girls had gone for a walk along the beach near their home and were never seen again. One girl's mother, desperate to find her daughter, heard about Croiset and wrote him a letter pleading for his help.

Within a matter of days, the mother received Croiset's response. In it he drew a sketch of the beach, which he had never seen, including such details as a bus stop and a parked bulldozer, along with a page and a half of comments. "The girls," he said, will be there [on the beach] together." The police found the girls where Croiset said they would be, and they were together. They had been murdered and buried, side by side, in shallow graves in the sand.

It would be a mistake to think that local police departments are the only levels of government to use psychics. In the next chapter, our friend Gayle takes us on one last psychic journey, into the secret realm of covert operations and experimentation.

Chapter Ten

Government Psychics

Gayle had gone to visit her chiropractor, a man who routinely practiced kinesiology, dabbled with crystals, and in general kept himself abreast of the latest developments in the world of the paranormal. He was also a man she felt she could confide in and did so from time to time. In her wildest imaginings, she could not have thought of this gentle man as anything but a concerned healer, eager to do whatever was necessary for the benefit of his patients. She was therefore surprised when, on this particular visit, he said, "We think you have the skills we can use."

"What on earth are you talking about," she replied, "and who is 'we'?"

"You remember you told me how you sent an astral message to that girl that was kidnapped a couple of years ago? Those kinds of skills."

Gayle didn't remember having told him about her experience with the police and the kidnapping, but she very well might have. In fact, it was not likely that she would have mentioned it to anyone else, including her husband.

"Okay," she said evenly, "but that's not something I do every day. In fact, I'm not sure I did it then. It might have been just a coincidence."

"Yes, of course," the chiropractor said impatiently, "but we don't think so. We think you are probably capable of full astral projection any time you wish."

"Now there's that 'we' business again." She paused and looked him dead in the eye. "Just exactly *who* are we talking about here?"

"I could tell you," he said, "but then I'd have to kill you." It was an old joke, but he laughed anyway, then abruptly grew very serious. "Actually, it's not quite that bad, but almost. Once you're in the program you're in. Period."

"Okay, that's it." Gayle started to reach for her coat. "This is too weird, even for me."

"No, wait, let me explain."

The chiropractor gently touched her arm and indicated a chair. "Please," he added.

Gayle sat back down, folded her hands in her lap, and waited for whatever would come next.

"We've known each other a long time," the doctor said, "and I wouldn't bring this up except for the fact that you possess some of the most impressive psychic talent I have ever come across."

"I didn't know you were an expert in such matters," she replied, genuinely surprised.

"Actually, I don't like to make a big deal of it, but I have some, uh, talents, shall we say, and those talents have put me in touch with a very interesting project." He paused, took a deep breath, and added, "It's a government project."

"I hope you're talking about *our* government," she replied.

"Yes, of course."

The doctor didn't know it, but he had found Gayle's hot button. She was an old-fashioned girl; to her, love of country ranked right up there with love of God and love of family. There were few things she would not do if she believed it was for the good of the country.

"The 'we' you're talking about, then, is the government?"

"Well, just a small part of it, but it's an important part."

From that point on, Gayle was all ears. The "project," as it was outlined to her, had to do with remote viewing and astral projection. Her only personal contact would be with the chiropractor, but she would receive all assignments over the telephone by someone she would know only as "the general."

Gayle left her chiropractor's office that day in a state of confusion. She wasn't sure she fully understood what was expected of her, and she wasn't entirely sure she had even accepted a place in the "group." The doctor had asked what she wanted for her service. She could have "anything" she desired: a new car, the mortgage paid, whatever. Gayle assured him she wanted nothing. In the first place, if it really did have something to do with "national security," it was her duty to do everything she could. In the second place, she wasn't about to buy a pig in a poke, and she knew that if she accepted anything from "them," anything at all, she was obligated from that point on.

As she drove home, another thought was rattling around in her mind. The doctor had sworn her to secrecy. She was not to discuss any of her assignments or what she was doing with anyone. He had hinted that any breach could prove to be dangerous. But dangerous to whom? Was she putting her family in harm's way? Love of country did rank very high with her, but it was definitely below family.

Several days went by, and Gayle began to think that her refusal to accept any kind of remuneration must have discouraged them. She had all but put the conversation out of her mind when the phone rang.

"Hello," said a voice at the other end. The voice on the phone was unfamiliar and had a high-pitched quality that sounded mildly electronic. "I'm the general. Is this Gayle?"

There was a moment of silence while Gayle readjusted her thinking and tried to swallow the lump that had unexpectedly appeared in her throat. "Yes," she said at last, "this is Gayle."

"I hope you'll forgive me for using your first name without a proper introduction, but the doctor has told me so much about you, I feel like we're already friends."

"Oh that's fine, everybody calls me Gayle." There was another pause, "Uh, what can I do for you?"

"Good, right to the point, I like that." The general took a moment to gather his thoughts, then said, "We have a doctor—a Ph.D., actually—who is dying of cancer. He has a lot of information that he's willing to give us, and we'd like you to keep him alive until we can get it."

"You're kidding."

"No, we're quite serious."

"Is this some kind of a test?" General or no general, Gayle thought the whole thing sounded ridiculous, and she got a little feisty. "Because if it is, I think maybe we should start out with something a little more reasonable."

The general was nothing if not patient. "I thought you understood,

Gayle, everything we do is a test. Our entire project is one big test to see if psychics have any value in a military or national security setting. Equally important, we want to know if we have to be concerned about pyschic abilities being used against us." He paused to let that sink in, then continued. "We realize what we're asking you to do is difficult. If there were an easy way to do it, we wouldn't need *you*, now would we?"

"Sorry," Gayle said, now quite subdued, "it's just that I've never attempted anything even remotely like what you're suggesting."

"Good choice of words, Gayle, because that's exactly how we want you to do it, by remote."

"I see. Well, who is this doctor, and more importantly, where is he?"

There was a long silence.

"General?"

"I'm afraid we can't tell you that," the general said, "sorry."

Gayle could feel the frustration rising once again. "Now let me get this straight," she said icily, "you want me to find this Dr. somebody who has cancer and find some way to keep him alive until you can get information from him?"

"Precisely."

"What information?"

Gayle knew what the answer would be before the question was out of her mouth. She said the words along with the general, "Sorry, we can't tell you that."

"Okay," Gayle replied, "I'll do what I can. Is there someplace I can call you?"

"No, I'll call you. But if you come up with anything in the next few days, just pass it along to your chiropractor."

Gayle hung up the phone more perplexed than ever. Was this something she really wanted to get involved with? It wasn't as if being a psychic was her vocation. It was more of a hobby and, on occasion, something she was "required" to do, but to this point, at least, it seemed she had options. If she went ahead, her options may disappear. She spent the rest of the day going over and over in her mind all of the ramifications, pro and con. A longtime student of transcendental meditation, she decided to meditate and see if she could come up with an answer. What she did come up with surprised even her.

Gayle had no idea how long she had been in the alpha state when the image appeared. It was a man, somewhat beyond middle age, thin with graying hair, lying on a bed in a bedroom that obviously hadn't seen a woman's touch for many years. The image was as clear as a photograph. "Oh," she thought, "that's the doctor." She held the image and tried to identify objects in the room, for verification purposes. The doctor, whoever he was, lived in a messy environment.

As she watched, he sat up on the edge of the bed. A huge dark spot over his left breast became the focus of her attention. That was the cancer, she was sure of it, but it shouldn't be visible; yet she was seeing, or perhaps visualizing it in all its grotesque horror. The question now was what to do about it.

Lacking any medical knowledge of cancer or how it works, her only choice was to focus all of her attention on the dark spot on his breast. Simply put, Gayle began to "project" her energy onto that spot. She held it until the image disappeared. Since the mind works at such blinding speed, she had no way of knowing whether she had held the image for five minutes or five seconds, but coming out of her meditation, she felt certain she had discovered the "target." Whether or not she had provided him with any help was another question entirely.

Gayle called the chiropractor and described the event and the person she had seen.

"Yes," the chiropractor assured her, "that was the doctor."

His wife had died a few years earlier, and he was not a very tidy person, except in his mind. Prior to his retirement, he had been a physicist working for a major supplier of national defense technologies. Since his retirement, he had developed some new theories and ideas (such as a silent jet engine capable of hypersonic speeds), and it was that technology the government was after.

This was the beginning of a seven-year odyssey for Gayle that resulted in a number of stunning successes and some heartbreaking failures. The doctor did survive his bout with cancer and showed up on her doorstep nearly two years later. Invited to visit his home, Gayle was able to confirm virtually every detail of her first image of the man and his surroundings. (She felt certain that some of the same socks were still in the same place on the floor!) The name of the "project" was never mentioned to her, nor did she ever get to meet the "general." Several years later, however, her contact, the chiropractor, died, and the phone calls ceased.

Gayle and her family moved to another part of the country, and slowly the memories began to fade. Then one day she heard about the Stargate project. This project, she was told, was government funded and dealt with national security. It was designed to discover whether or not "remote viewing" by gifted psychics had any basis in reality.

It is likely, however, that Gayle's involvement had more to do with an army psychic spy unit that operated as a classified entity for more than a decade. According to Major Edward Dames, retired, who now heads up an RV (remote viewing) academy called PSI-Tech in Beverly Hills, California, the program had three distinct parts, each of which was separately funded by the Department of the Army. They were:

1. The operational unit, which was highly classified.
2. The medical evaluation program (Gayle's first assignment).
3. A remote viewing research and development program, which was not classified.

The army operational unit had been continuously employed since 1978 in support of actual missions, first for the Department of Defense and later for the entire intelligence community. The primary focus was on cases where all other attempts at penetration had failed or where other methods were not available.

The origins of Stargate began in 1978 with the code name Grill Flame. In the beginning, the idea of examining remote viewing took many different angles, one of the principal objectives being to see if psychics could, by pure power of the mind, have any effect on target computers. It quickly expanded to attempting to see what was going on in other locations around the world, and that in turn escalated to testing to see if a remote viewer could actually influence another person in another location. One of the tests devised was as trivial as getting target individuals to look behind them by influencing their thoughts with the notion that they were being followed.

Stargate would be funded for seventeen years, with over 4,000 missions being carried out. The cost to the government was $20 million. But what, if anything, did the government get for its money? Those who followed the project closely believe that Stargate proved beyond a shadow of a doubt that psychic talents are real. Skeptics quickly point out that the group was not 100 percent accurate all the time. That's true, but at least three different groups came up with an accuracy rating of between 55 and 70 percent (a whole flock of white crows). Keeping in mind that Stargate was a project that dealt with national security and was subject to the stiffest possible scientific controls before each session, those results are truly startling. At least one member of the group, Joseph McMoneagle, received one of the army's highest peacetime awards, the Legion of Merit, for providing more than 150 essential elements of information (EEI) to the military while a member of Stargate. Information was also submitted to the Joint Chiefs of Staff, DIA, the National Security Agency, the Central Intelligence Agency, the Drug Enforcement Administration, and the Secret Service. It was, the award said, "crucial and vital intelligence unavailable from any other source."

There seems to be little doubt in the minds of those who participated in the project or those in government familiar with the results that the project was a complete success. McMoneagle, the remote viewer regarded as the most "gifted" and the one member of the project who was there from the beginning to the end, even demonstrated his ability before a national TV audience. In the 1995 ABC Special "Put to the Test," McMoneagle was challenged to locate a target hidden by ABC. In spite of their best efforts to conceal it, McMoneagle was right on target.

The Stargate program was overseen by three different panels, and each had to give their approval before each project was funded. The results were then reviewed against strict, scientific protocols and forwarded to another board. Reviews took place once again prior to the next mission to determine whether or not the new mission was likely to obtain information that could be used for our nation's defense or security.

The very fact that this program survived seventeen years under the strictest secrecy (probably the only secret the government has kept in the past hundred years), and displayed such a remarkable success rate using only psychic means speaks volumes about the very real accomplishments of the participants. Keep in mind that our government was trying its best to keep all 4,000 of the assigned missions a secret because the Soviets and several South American countries were (and many believe still are) using remote viewing techniques themselves. The effects, it was discovered, could be profound. One remote viewer within the Stargate project was given a position in the program because he was successful in "frying" a government computer. The repair bill ran close to $1 million.

Stargate was eventually shut down. A report labeled the "AIR Report" was submitted to Congress recommending the program's declassification because, according to the report, Stargate had no value in serving the nation's security and defense. Several boxes of documents, supposedly containing all the reports issued by Stargate, were said to be the basis of the recommendation.

Some observers contend that the "several boxes" referred to in the report amounted to only about 1 percent of the documentation compiled by Stargate. The other 99 percent, they say, is safely locked up in a government vault someplace. It has also been suggested that a group of psychics, working without official sanction but with full government knowledge, continue to work their magic.

Following her seven-year involvement with whatever program it happened to be (she still doesn't know), Gayle did come to one rather startling conclusion: "There is no such thing as national security. A good psychic can get in anyplace anytime. It's a piece of cake."

Of course, no chapter on government involvement with the paranormal would be complete without some reference to the CIA. I recently visited the office of a former member of the CIA. On a wall covered with awards and photographs of himself with presidents and generals, the centerpiece was a large, poster-size plaque that read: AMERICA IS AT PEACE, BECAUSE THE CIA IS

AT WAR. In the lower right-hand corner was a personal note from former CIA director George Bush.

That the CIA operates as if it were always poised for war is indisputable and perhaps helps us understand why they are always being accused of various forms of malfeasance. That is certainly the case with "The Constantine Report No. 1," an exposé of the "remote viewing studies at Stanford Research Institute or illicit CIA mind control experimentation." (Alex Constantine is the author of *Psychic Dictatorship in the U.S.A.*, which purports to be "an exploration of electromagnetic mind control, cults formed by the CIA, collaboration with old guard Nazis, media disinformation and other outrageous acts of federal malfeasance."[1]) According to the report, there is "concrete evidence" that electronic mind control was in fact the object of the study at the Stanford Research Institute. The venerable *Washington Post* reported in 1977 that when the navy awarded a contract to the institute, "the scientific assistant to the Secretary of the Navy, Dr. Sam Koslov, received a routine briefing on various projects, including SRI's. As the briefer flashed his chart onto the screen, Koslov stormily interrupted, 'What the hell is that about?'" There, on the projected chart describing SRI's work, was the label "ELF and Mind Control."[2]

ELF is shorthand for "extremely long frequency" electromagnetic waves and has specific reference to the very slow frequencies in the brain (up to about 100 cycles per second), but it was the "Mind Control" label that had Koslov upset. He ordered the SRI research stopped and canceled another $35,000 in navy funds slated for more remote viewing studies. The navy, however (again, according to Constantine), quietly continued to lay out another $100,000 for a two-year project directed by a bionics specialist.

The report asserts that mind control was used in domestic covert operations, and during the Vietnam War, SRI was "a hive of covert political subterfuge." It does appear that EM (electromagnetic) mind control machines were supported by Dr. Karl Pribram, director of the Neuropsychology Research Laboratory at SRI. "I certainly could educate a child by putting an electrode in the lateral hypothalmus and then selecting the situations at which I stimulate it," he said. "In this way I can grossly change his behavior." *Psychology Today* has touted Pribram as "the Magellan of brain science."[3]

It would seem that EM mind control and Stargate would be far apart, but apparently, biotechnology and cyber-psi were focal points in the Stargate research as well. It was, Constantine says, the CIA that chose the American Institutes of Research (AIR) in Washington, D.C. to evaluate the validity of remote viewing. AIR apparently could be counted on to keep the secrets. And of course, it was their report that resulted in the shutdown of Stargate.

The CIA being what it is, it is unlikely that the allegations of the Constantine report will be answered anytime soon. What does seem apparent in all of this is that the government of the United States, at several levels of operation, has taken (and continues to take) psychic aptitudes and devices very seriously. Perhaps we should, too.

Stargate was by no means the only project funded by the government that proposed to do the undoable. Nor was it the first. In 1943, at the very height of World War II, the United States Navy is believed to have conducted one of the most bizarre experiments on record, but for over a decade it remained a closely guarded secret.

Our story actually begins in January of 1956. A man by the name of Morris Ketchum Jessup, a former mathematics and astronomy instructor at Drake University in Iowa and at the University of Michigan, had wandered far afield. After developing research that led to the discovery of several double stars that were subsequently cataloged by the Royal Astronomical Society, Jessup began studying Mayan and Incan ruins. He concluded that the original buildings could only have been constructed with the help of extraterrestrial technology. He abandoned his research and returned to the United States, where he began an intense effort to pressure Congress into funding experiments into Einstein's unified field theory. Jessup believed that this could provide the answer to how UFOs traveled around the universe.

On January 13, 1956, Jessup received the first of two letters from a man who signed himself Carlos Miguel Allende and also Carl M. Allen. In these rambling letters, Allen (or Allende) warned Jessup to forget his interest in the unified field theory, stating that the U.S. Navy had already tried it on a destroyer-type ship in 1943 with disastrous results.

The letters meander through a fantastic story and in some places become almost incoherent, but they blew the lid off what has become known as the Philadelphia Experiment. According to Allende:

> The result was complete invisibility of a ship . . . and all of its crew. The Field was effective in an oblate spheroidal shape, extending one hundred yards (more or less, due to lunar position and latitude) out from each beam of the ship. Any person within that sphere became vague in form but he too observed those persons aboard that ship as though they too were of the same state, yet were walking upon nothing. Any person without the sphere could see nothing save the clearly defined shape of the ship's hull in the water.
>
> There are very few of the original experimental D-E's crew left by now sir. Most went insane, one just walked through his quarters wall in sight of his wife and child and two other crew members (was never seen again). Two went into "the flame," i.e. they froze and caught fire while carrying common small boat compasses. . . . THEY BURNED FOR 18 DAYS. The experiment was a complete success, the men were complete failures.
>
> Check Philadelphia papers for a tiny one paragraph (upper half of sheet inside the paper, near the rear third of paper, 1944–46 in spring, fall or winter, not summer) of an item describing the sailors' actions after their initial voyage. They Raided a Local to the Navy Yard, "Gin Mill" or "Beer Joint," and caused such Shock & Paralysis of the waitresses that little comprehensible could be gotten from them. . . . I ask you to do this bit of research simply that you may choke on your own tongue when you remember what you have appealed to be made law.[4]

Jessup had written a book called *The Case for the UFO,* which had been published in 1955. He was the "flavor of the month," so to speak, and a topic of conversation throughout Washington, D.C. A copy of the book finally made its way to the Office of Naval Research, and that copy contains comments written above and below the text and in the margins. Careful examination seemed to indicate that the comments had been the work of at least three men, and Jessup was sure that one of them, based on the handwriting, was Allende. The volume wound up in the hands of two ONR officers, Commander George W. Hoover and Captain Sidney Sherby. Both men claimed that their interest was purely personal and that there was no tie to the Office of Naval Research. That may be, but the navy would soon take a very lively interest in the growing debate over the 1943 experiment.

Jessup received another letter from Allende. Within just a few days of the first letter, Jessup opened his mail and read:

> I wish to mention that somehow also, the experimental ship disappeared from its Philadelphia dock and only a very few minutes later appeared at its other dock in the Norfolk, Newport News, Portsmouth area. This was distinctly and clearly identified as being that place but the ship then, again, disappeared and went back to its Philadelphia dock in only a very few minutes or less. This was also noted in the newspapers but I forget what paper I read it in or when it happened. Probably late in the experiments. May have been in 1956 after experiments were discontinued. I cannot say for sure.[5]

Inexplicably, Jessup turned the letters over to the two naval officers, who for some strange reason had Jessup's book, and the annotations, retyped for greater clarity and then republished in a limited edition. Why, no one knows. Whether or not Jessup made any inquiries is unknown. His direct involvement ended on the evening of April 20, 1959, when he was found dead in his station wagon in Dade County Park in Florida. A hose from the tailpipe of the car was inserted into one of the car windows. Jessup, it appeared, had committed suicide.

But had he? Friends who knew him well insisted he was not the kind of man who would kill himself, nor could any real reason for such an act be found. UFO study was still in its infancy then, and some speculated that he had come too close to the truth and that the infamous Men In Black had something to do with his death. The fact is, nothing was ever uncovered to support anything but suicide.

Be that as it may, it was already too late for the navy. Investigators began to follow up on the correspondence between Jessup and Allende. Soon it was discovered that the ship in question was the USS *Eldridge* and that indeed, its history and that of its crew was as vague as the experiment itself.

Charles Berlitz and William Moore, two experienced authors and investigators, followed up on the Allende letters. Their investigation resulted in the book *The Philadelphia Experiment,* which recounts in considerable detail the results of a horrifying experiment gone wrong.

The essentials of the story are this: A force field was created around the ship (USS *Eldridge*) as it lay in a special berth in the Philadelphia Navy Yard. The purpose of the experiment was to ascertain if it was possible to make a ship invisible to radar—a perfectly worthy wartime goal, since German U-boats were destroying nearly half the ships going across the Atlantic. According to one report, prior to the actual experiment there was a "dry run," during which domestic animals were placed throughout the ship while the force field was applied. Following up, the scientists discovered that many of the animals were badly burned, and many more had somehow disappeared from their cages. In spite of this admittedly "negative" result, the navy decided to forge ahead.

During the actual experiment, survivors reported that the crew could see one another normally but witnesses not on board could see only the vague outline of both ship and men through the force field. They shimmered through a greenish haze before resuming their normal shape and density. But it was the aftereffects that Allende warned Jessup about that were truly horrifying. Some of the men went mad, others periodically became semitransparent, some simply died of heart attacks; but the most gruesome result was said to have been that some men were actually embedded alive in the steel structure of the ship.

The "gin mill" episode alluded to in Allende's letter turned out to be the tale of three sailors, in ragged and dirty uniforms, who suddenly appeared out of the back room in a nearby bar. The only problem was, there was no back room, and much to the consternation of the waitress, they disappeared again the same way they had come in, through the wall.

The navy, of course, denies that the experiment ever took place. The story is so persistent, however, that as late as December 1997, investigators were still telling their story on television's The Learning Channel, in a two hour special entitled "New Visions of the Future, Prophecies III." Andrew Strom (also known as Drue), an international lecturer and author, says that the men of the *Eldridge* suffered horrors that no one has ever suffered. "Death," he says, "would have been preferable." Al Bielek, author of *The Philadelphia Experiment and Other UFO Conspiracies,* points out that in fact the experiment was a success in many ways. The ship did very quickly become radar invisible, but at the last minute, something went terribly wrong and the ship became not just radar invisible but invisible period—for nearly four hours.

What happened during that four hours no one knows for certain. Allende claimed that the ship was somehow transported 275 miles away to another harbor and back again. Others agree with the change of harbor, but add that the ship, while berthed at Newport News, was also forty years into the future.

Both Albert Einstein and Nikola Tesla had given up their experiments on the unified field theory many years earlier—some say because they became convinced that the technology would never be used for the *benefit* of humankind. But both Strom and Bielek believe that the government did, in fact, test a time machine that day. They also believe that the government is still using it.

I had the opportunity of sitting in on one of Al Bielek's presentations at a UFO convention in 1993. His story is almost too extreme to be credibile. Yet, it is fascinating in all of its complexity. Even more intriguing is the fact that since that time, I have encountered a number of seemingly unrelated incidents and investigations that appear to support some of his more fantastic claims.

In a nutshell, Bielek claims that he and his brother were part of the ill-fated Philadelphia experiment and that, had they been permitted to live in their own "time line," he would now be an eighty-year-old Harvard-educated physicist and his brother (slightly younger) would be a physicist also, but with a Ph.D. from the University of Edinburgh, in Scotland. Instead, having joined the U.S. Navy, both were assigned to the Institute for Advanced Study at Princeton, New Jersey, and specifically to the ongoing Project Invisibility. According to Bielek, a completely successful test in 1940 at the Brooklyn Navy Yard led to a reclassification of the project and a new name, Project Rainbow, with offices in the Philadelphia Navy Yard.

Both Bielek and his brother, Duncan, worked on the project through 1942. In March of that year, Nikola Tesla dropped out, and the research was put in the very capable hands of John von Neumann. So far so good. But then came the *Eldridge* and the application of the invisibility research with which both Bielek and his brother had been involved.

Both men were on the ship when the experiment began, but recognizing that something was very, very wrong, they chose to jump off when it was somewhere in hyperspace. (More about that in a moment.) When they landed, they were at a secret research base on Montauk, Long Island, and the year was 1984. (This makes sense once you realize that the exact same experiment was being conducted at Montauk forty-one years after the tragedy at Philadelphia—or at least that's what Bielek claims.)

His brother decided to stay in the future. Bielek chose to return to 1943 and destroy the equipment aboard the *Eldridge,* which he did. The government, he said, would have killed him except that his molecular structure was now connected to both the 1943 and the 1984 "time rift," and they believed that if they killed him, it could cause a ripple effect that would reopen these holes. Instead, they (the government) used technology supplied by aliens to "regress" him to a one-year-old and send him back in time to 1927, where he became a replacement son for the Bielek family, who had just lost their baby boy.

The time tunnel experiments at Montauk into which Bielek and his brother had been projected continued well into the 1980s. Then, somehow Bielek's memories of his past experiences returned, and purely by accident, he was reunited with his brother, Duncan. Together once again, they were able to participate in what they claim was a fully functioning series of time tunnel journeys. Strangely, even though the technology was secure enough to take a person from one time period to another and back again so quickly that it would appear that no time had passed, they still couldn't penetrate the future from 2011 to 2013, a curious anomaly, particularly in light of some predictions we'll discuss in Chapter Twelve. When they did finally get past 2013, what they saw was a barren landscape with no visible life.

That the Montauk laboratory existed is not in dispute. It is, in fact, still there today. The project itself was shut down in the mid-1980s—destroyed, actually, if Bielek is to be believed. Tunnels and ducts were filled with concrete, and the whole complex was turned over to the state of New York to be used as part of the existing state park. Oddly, it was never used as part of the park. None of the buildings were torn down, and it was never opened as a park facility. Fences were removed so that people could go in and hike and camp during the day; but at night, park rangers made sure that everyone was out.

What they did at Montauk, apparently, was create time tunnels using a psychic as the "chair," or interface, between the device and the computer. The whole thing was sabotaged by project insiders because of some of the uses (not specified) for which the time machine was being employed. Von Neumann wanted the site preserved because of the time travel (or remote viewing) capabilities, but he was overridden by Bielek, Duncan, and others.

There were apparently other research projects being carried out at Montauk as well, but no one seems to know what they were. Classified records still exist at Lincoln Labs at MIT in Cambridge, Massachusetts, but so far, no one has been able to get access to them. One of the most interesting aspects of the entire story, however, is that it now appears that Montauk might be resurrected. In 1992, Bielek visited the site and noticed that there were new coaxial cable runs in place, and new power transformers were being put in the substations. Non-PCB cooling agents were seen on the site, the kind that would be necessary to meet modern environmental regulations, and the radar tower, formerly open to anyone who wanted to walk in, had been equipped with a new double-lock steel door.

Perhaps the last chapter in the history of Montauk is still somewhere in the future. But what is there in the modern state of affairs that might trigger such a decision? What do we know now that Einstein and Tesla didn't know?

Einstein, you'll remember, was a champion of the unified field theory—the notion that all physical laws could be unified into one simple framework (a formula, if you will, no more than an inch long). The concept consumed the last thirty years of his life, but the theory eluded him. Nor was he the only one; such great twentieth-century thinkers as Werner Heisenberg and Wolfgang Pauli struggled with the problem and ultimately gave up. Niels Bohr, founder of the modern atomic theory, once listened to Pauli explain the unified field theory, then stood up and said: "We are all agreed that your theory is absolutely crazy. What divides us is whether your theory is crazy enough."

Today, after decades of frustration, many of the world's physicists think they have finally found a theory that is "crazy enough" to be the unified field theory. It is called the *superstring theory*. We are not physicists, of course, and for any of this to make sense to the average person, some definitions are needed. (Even that might not be enough.) For the following definitions we are indebted to Michio Kaku, an internationally recognized authority in theoretical physics and the man generally conceded to be the originator of the superstring theory:

- *Hyperspace.* This is the theory of higher dimensions. It states that dimensions exist that are beyond length, width, height, and time. At present, many of the world's leading physicists believe that we may live in a ten-dimensional universe. Because this theory is the theory of everything, it may eventually answer questions that have puzzled scientists for thousands of years, such as, What happened before Creation? Can you go backward in time? Can you visit the stars?
- *Wormholes.* A wormhole is a tunnel in space. As a practical example, take a blank sheet of paper and place two dots some distance apart. Conventional wisdom says that a straight line is the shortest distance between these two points. Now bend the sheet of paper in such a way that the two points touch. The shortest distance between the two dots is the wormhole created by bending space. This, of course, presents the possibility of moving fantastic distances in space.

- *Time Travel Paradox.* If I go back in time and alter the past—for example, kill my parents—then how was I able to be here to be able to go back in time? The paradox seems immutable. Isaac Newton believed that time was like an arrow. Once fired, it could never return. Einstein thought that time was more like a river, speeding up and slowing down as it moved into proximity of galaxies and stars. The new theory suggests that the river may have whirlpools or forks. If you are caught in a whirlpool of time, you fulfill the past, thus eliminating the paradox. If, however, you alter the past (e.g., kill your parents before you are born), then time forks into two parallel universes, thus averting the paradox.

Einstein's general theory of relativity allows for the possibility of both time travel and wormholes. But there are problems. What if the wormholes and whirlpools are not stable? Quantum corrections (i.e., radiation effects) could conceivably destabilize the hole just as it is being entered. It is therefore essential that there is a theory of everything (a superstring theory) in which to calculate quantum corrections.

There is another problem. According to Kaku, it would require enormous amounts of energy to open up holes in space and time. The Planck energy, for example, is 100 billion billion times the energy typically found in a hydrogen bomb. Could the researchers at Montauk have found a way to create such energy?

Part of Al Bielek's experience, you'll recall, was the intervention of technology supplied by aliens, at least some of whom were from a Pleiadian world. Barbara Marciniak, in her book *Bringers of the Dawn,* claims to have channeled a Pleiadian definition of time that might be useful:

Time is greatly misunderstood in third-dimensional reality; you believe that time is measured in minutes or degrees. Time is much vaster than you realize. In actuality, time codes and plays with information, allowing you to move into realities simultaneously by stretching, distorting, curving and twisting time around. You can get on an elliptical curve of time and experience many realities by simply going around the elliptical curve and discovering that, as time is not "solid," neither is reality.[6]

Could it be, as some have suggested, that not only time but everything is illusional? Kaku doesn't seem to think so. "Mainstream physics," he says, "has far outstripped the imagination of any science fiction writer; physicists are now entering the tenth dimension. The superstring theory predicts that the universe is ten-dimensional. In the tenth dimension we have the unification of all known physical theories."

During the past half century, two basic theories have dominated, indeed governed, the world in which we live. The quantum theory and the theory of general relativity explain the sum total of all physical knowledge at the fundamental level—without exception. The laws of physics and chemistry can, in principle, be derived from these two fundamental theories, making them the most successful of all time. Unfortunately, these concepts are diametrically opposed to each other. The quantum theory is the theory of *microcosm,* a description of the subatomic world. The theory of relativity is a theory of the *macrocosmic* world, the world of galaxies, superclusters, black holes, and creation itself. This sad state of affairs, according to Kaku, can be compared to Mother Nature having two hands, neither of which communicates with the other.

The superstring theory, many physicists believe, has solved this problem. It has also raised a storm of controversy, with Nobel Prize winners taking positions squarely on opposing sides. The superstring theory postulates that all matter and energy can be reduced to tiny strings of energy in a ten-dimensional universe. Imagine a violin string. All the notes of the scale can be played equally, none being more fundamental than the other. What is fundamental is the string. By studying the vibrations or harmonics that can exist on the violin string, it is possible to calculate the infinite number of possible frequencies that exist.

But easily the most controversial aspect of the superstring theory is the prediction that the universe originally began in ten dimensions. Supporters of the theory find in this concept the introduction of a breathtaking mathematics into the world of physics. Detractors see the ten-dimensional hyperspace as bordering on science fiction. This is not too surprising, since humans are incapable of visualizing any spatial dimension beyond three. That does not mean other dimensions do not exist, of course. Computers routinely manipulate equations in N-dimensional space. It is a matter of biology, not physics. We simply do not have brains that can visualize movement in four directions, any more than a fish can conceive of movement in more than two dimensions. From a mathematical point of view, however, adding more dimensions to a theory always allows the unification of more laws of physics.

The superstring theory has been called the most sensational discovery in theoretical physics in several decades, but not too surprisingly, its critics have focused on its weakest point: It is almost impossible to test. The reason is rather simple. The theory of everything is necessarily a theory of Creation; that is, it must explain everything from the Big Bang down to household dust. To test the theory on earth would mean re-creating Creation, which is impossible with present-day technology.

But testing time tunnels with the technology available in 1943 must also have seemed ludicrous to the physicists of that era, and yet the evidence suggests that is precisely what was done, and apparently with some success. Could construction of the Super Collider (approved by the Reagan administration but still held up by Congress) near Austin, Texas, provide some idea of the moment of Creation? And is it possible that the facilities at Montauk are being revived once again to study the practical implications of this startling new theory?

Kaku and other physicists are now beginning to ask questions that psychics have addressed for hundreds of years: Do higher dimensions exist? Are there unseen worlds just beyond our reach, beyond the normal laws of physics? Can ghosts or people live in these higher dimensions? Perhaps the most pertinent question would be, Will the physicists and the psychics finally begin talking to one another?

Next, tragedy, triumph, laughter, and tears is the stock in trade of the city affectionately known as Tinsel Town, but not even the most imaginative scriptwriter could dream up plots equal to the real-life experiences of some of Hollywood's most famous citizens.

CHAPTER ELEVEN

TRUTH IS STRANGER THAN FICTION

MY CAREER AS AN AUTHOR AND PRODUCER spans several decades and dozens of movies, television shows, and books. I have met presidents, helped elect governors, and generally spent my life in close association with talented, intelligent, and sometimes powerful people. Many of them I am privileged to call friends. Few things in my life, however, have had the lasting effect that working with people like Uri Geller and Peter Hurkos has had. These associations have led me, over the years, to seek knowledge in areas and about subjects I would otherwise have overlooked.

I joined Erich Von Daniken in his search for ancient astronauts; traveled to the very heart of the Bermuda Triangle with Charles Berlitz as he sought to unravel that age-old mystery; and worked with Raymond Moody trying to solve the greatest mystery of all, life after death. I have met and talked with hundreds of experts and eyewitnesses about UFOs, explored the pyramids of Egypt, and studied photos of the Loch Ness monster and the Shroud of Turin, hoping to find clues to these enigmas. All of this came about because I was willing to open my mind to the possibilities that at least some of these things are real.

There was a pivotal event in my life—one I don't like to talk about much—that convinced me that there is more going on in this world than any of us dare to dream. Early in my career as a producer, and due largely to the success of some of my earlier ventures, I found myself with the means to live just about anyplace I chose. I had always loved the mountains, and so I decided to build a home behind an old mining town turned ski resort called Park City, in Utah. The spot my family picked for our home was well away from the ski runs and nestled in a small valley south of the old town of Park City. Tailings from several abandoned mines dotted the slopes, but there were no commercial roads into the area, and in the winter, the only way in or out was by snowmobile or a vehicle that travels on deep snow called a snow cat. In spite of its isolation, it was still just minutes from Park City and barely an hour from Salt Lake City. It seemed we had the best of both worlds.

As you might expect, I, my wife, and my two sons soon became proficient at handling snowmobiles. Our front yard in winter was miles of untrammeled powder, and a number of hills and small canyons stretched off in every direction, unknown to just about anyone except the local deer hunters. It was not unusual for the boys to take off in the morning on their snowmobiles and spend the entire day breaking a trail into some previously unexplored canyon. But one day, my oldest son, Don, didn't return. At first we weren't too worried. He was eighteen years old, an experienced outdoorsman, and he knew the terrain well.

"He'll be all right," I told my wife, "he's just off doing something."

When he didn't return, we all loaded up and went out to look for him. At the time, I was a volunteer police officer for Wasatch County, and when we didn't find any sign of Don on our own, we asked for a full-scale search. The County Search and Rescue team, Park City ski patrol, and hundreds of volunteers scoured the area for weeks. Brokenhearted, we finally gave up. I cannot remember a colder winter or more devastating time in my life. Hunters found my son two years later in the spring, deep in an isolated box canyon. We were never able to determine exactly what happened, but it was a terrible loss for our family.

A short time later, my wife divorced me, and I sold the home and moved. I threw myself into my work, producing several motion pictures in the space of just a couple of years, most of them very successful. The industry being what it is, I attracted the attention of a studio in Los Angeles that I knew to be primarily interested in horror films. Frankly, I was surprised to hear from them. My reputation was built on movies that were a far cry from the kinds of things usually put out by this studio.

As it turned out, they had been intrigued by one of my films, *The Amazing World of Psychic Phenomena,* and wanted to know if I would be interested in doing the same kind of picture for them, but one that dealt strictly with the occult and devil worship—"the dark side of the same coin," as they put it. My first reaction was to turn it down, but as we talked, my resistance began to dissipate. I had nothing going right at that moment, and the one thing I wanted to avoid at all costs was *not* having something to do. Finally, we got around to the matter of money. A check for $50,000, they said, would be in my hands by the end of the week. That was just to get started. I still had misgivings, but I finally agreed.

The check arrived, and I began delving into the subject at hand: black magic, Ouija boards, devil worship, and the like. I found it uncomfortable at first, but as I got more familiar with the trappings, I began to lose my apprehension. I actually began to enjoy my research into the occult. I now feel that I had put myself in peril by unknowingly opening up a "channel" into the dark side.

Then one night, midway into the project, something brought me out of a sound sleep. One instant I was asleep and the next I was wide awake and staring at someone standing over me staring into my face as I lay in my bed. I recognized him immediately. It was my son. No words passed between us, but there was a look of disappointment, even sadness, on his face. To this day, I cannot explain how I knew, but the message was clear. He was telling me not to go on with this picture.

I have no idea how long his "visit" lasted, but after he left, sleep was impossible. There was no question in my mind as to what I would do. It was more a matter of how to do it. Producers who walk out in the middle of projects tend to be marked in the industry. And besides, I had already spent some of the money. But by the time I got out of the shower, all hesitation had vanished. I called the studio and told them that I was dropping the project and that a check for the full $50,000 would be on the way to them that afternoon.

It was an expensive lesson, but in that brief moment I shared with my son, I knew that if I continued, something terrible would happen to me. I have never regretted the decision to walk away from that picture. Somehow I know that my son was sent to rescue me from something horrible. That alone is enough to overshadow any doubts or regrets.

I have since discovered that a great many of us who work in the motion picture industry have had more than our share of psychic encounters. And the industry itself has never been shy about dealing with subjects that defy explanation. A case could easily be made that the supernatural has been a staple of the movie business, literally since its inception. You can find Frankenstein in film catalogs dating as far back as 1908, but it was probably Erich Pommer's 1919 production of *The Cabinet of Dr. Caligari* that really started the ball (or the cameras) rolling with respect to the supernatural. From that first effort to last week's *An American Werewolf in Paris,* Hollywood has always relied on the odd, the outlandish, and the unbelievable to bring audiences into the theater.

Less known but almost as consistent has been the correlation between the images on the flickering screen and the strange and often frightening private lives of the stars, writers, directors, and producers who make it all happen. In the 1920s, it was the unquestioned king of Hollywood, Rudolph Valentino, and his wife, Natasha Rambova, who made mediums and spirit teachers the *thing to do* in the film colony. When Valentino died in 1926, Natasha channeled messages from her dead husband and pretty much established the precedent of trying to commune with dead movie stars. On just about any given day in Hollywood, you can find mediums and channels claiming to make contact with the spirits of Rock Hudson, John Wayne, Sal Mineo, John Lennon, Elvis Presley, and Princess Grace of Monaco. The spirit form of Marilyn Monroe is said to have appeared in several of her favorite (pardon the word) haunts, and at least one former husband claims that she materialized physically in his presence.

Mae West wrote scripts under the direction of her spirit guide, and the great comedian Peter Sellers firmly believed that he was being guided by a spiritual entity. These two lead a long list of Hollywood greats and near-greats whose lives and careers were directly affected by their belief, and often participation, in the psychic world. Lee Marvin, Susan Strasberg, John Travolta, Linda Evans, Elke Sommer, Clint Walker, Lindsay Wagner, and of course Shirley MacLaine are among that imposing group.

MacLaine, of course, is known as the celebrity spokesperson for the increasingly popular notion of reincarnation, but she certainly doesn't stand alone. Robin Williams believes that he has had several past lives, at least one of them as a Shakespearean actor. And such great stars as Willie Nelson, Ernest Borgnine, Sylvester Stallone, Loretta Lynn, David Carradine, Glenn Ford, and John Travolta all believe that this life is just another in a long line of continuous incarnations. It is not too surprising, then, that Hollywood has hosted more than its share of strange occurrences.

Unfortunately, witchcraft, Satanism, and other black arts have also been part of the scene. W. Somerset Maugham, early in his career, wrote a book called, *The Magician.* It was based on the life of Aleister Crowley, a remarkable and demonic magician who lived in Hollywood in the 1920s and became the leader of a cult of devil worshipers that some say is still going strong. This son of a wealthy Englishman, who billed himself as the "wickedest man in the world," had a career that brought ruin not only to himself but to those around him. Yet, Rex Ingram, one of the great directors of the silent era, made Maugham's book into a movie. Ingram could never explain his fascination for Crowley, but the residue of that evil legacy lingers on today. Some contend that Crowley planted the seeds in Hollywood that eventually grew into real life monsters like Charles Manson and Richard Ramirez, the night stalker.[1]

It is interesting to note that the range of Hollywood experiences covers just about every aspect of the paranormal: ESP, remote viewing, precognition, dreams, crystal balls, tarot cards, clairvoyance, and of course astrology. Literally and figuratively, the stars of Hollywood have seen it all.

It would be a mistake to assume, however, that there is anything in the occupation itself that *causes* these things to happen. More likely, talented and sensitive people simply bring their gifts to town with them. Basil Rathbone, for example, most often remembered for his role as the supersleuth, Sherlock Holmes (he starred in fourteen Sherlock Holmes films), often told of a prophetic dream his mother had when he was just a small boy that saved the lives of his entire family.

The Rathbones were preparing to leave South Africa, where Basil had been born just four years earlier. They were returning to their ancestral home in England, and even though it would be a long sea voyage, everyone was looking forward to the trip. Just prior to their departure date, Basil's mother, Barbara, had a terrifying dream. She saw their ship sinking in the Bay of Biscayne off the coast of France. Her description of the event was so vivid and so profound that Basil's father changed their plans and set a new departure date. Events transpired just as his mother had seen. The ship they would have been on sank in the Bay of Biscayne. There were very few survivors.

Rathbone himself seemed to have inherited his mother's ability to dream of future events. Born in 1892, he was just old enough to go into the army during World War I. His brother John was also in the army, and one night, Basil was engulfed in a nightmare in which he saw his brother killed. Try as he might, he could not hide the anxiety he felt over what he felt certain was a prophetic dream. Several weeks later, while in the trenches, he was overcome by an ominous foreboding. He would later learn that it was on that very day that his brother was killed in action.

Death seems to be one of the most powerful ESP-producing events. Why, we can only guess, but psychic awareness becomes more acute when the final curtain is the text of the message.

Ida Lupino was the descendant of a British theatrical family going all the way back to the seventeenth century. She starred in a number of important films in the late 1930s and 1940s, but is probably best remembered for her role in the 1941 classic, *High Sierra*. Her father, the famous British comedian Stanley Lupino, had remained in London, even though the Nazis were busily trying to destroy the city on an almost daily basis. Londoners, he believed, had precious little to laugh about, and he refused to leave his beloved city.

On a Hollywood soundstage in 1942, at the height of the Nazi blitzkrieg, Ida Lupino was in a rehearsal. Suddenly she interrupted herself in mid-speech and shouted, "My father has just been killed in London." A number of people on the set knew who her father was, and they did their best to reassure her that everything was surely all right in England. Ida, however, was inconsolable. Two weeks later, she received a letter confirming not only that her father was dead, but that his death, London time, occurred at precisely the same time that Ida Lupino had become aware of it in Hollywood.

Apparently, neither distance nor time is any barrier to the transmission of psychic messages. All that is necessary is for transmitter and receiver to be in tune. Anyone who has tried to find a favorite radio station while traveling in a car shouldn't find that concept too difficult. Most of us seem to struggle with the idea, however, and anyone with the courage to try and teach us how to use our *own* transceiver will likely face more ridicule than reason. Just ask Shirley MacLaine.

Shirley MacLaine traces the beginning of her climb to stardom to about age three. She remembers herself in a four-leaf clover hat, standing in front of an audience, clutching an apple and singing "An apple for the Teacher." Her life as a performer gave her, she believes, the opportunity to "perfect the craft of communication." She now uses that craft to try to "make simple sense of complicated concepts of spirituality"[2] for audiences all over the world. Her books and seminars, while always well attended, usually draw a number of hecklers as well.

Not long ago, shortly after the completion of one of her extensive lecture tours, MacLaine decided to apply certain spiritual techniques to her acting. Many of us remember the delightful and engrossing character of Madame Sousatzka, played to perfection by Shirley MacLaine in the movie of the same name. As a producer and director of motion pictures, I remember being very impressed with the depth of character portrayed by MacLaine. As a member of the audience, I was enchanted by the story as it unfolded. I wasn't aware of it at the time, but MacLaine had done something very unusual in preparation for that role. We'll let her tell you about it in her own words:

> Madame Sousatzka was a part and a half: a domineering teacher of classical piano, commanding, manipulative, outrageous, funny, vulnerable, and, in the end uplifting. Whatever my character Aurora Greenway might have been in *Terms of Endearment,* Madame Sousatzka made her look like a quiet day at the beach. As I hadn't worked since *Terms* (aside from playing myself in *Out on a Limb*), I was excited at the prospect of trying a new way of working.

I proceeded to sculpt, with Schlesinger's help [Director John Schlesinger], what Sousatzka looked like, what she wore, how her hair was styled, what jewelry clanked on her wrists, how she walked, talked, ate, breathed, laughed and cried. Then I molded and refined her in my mind. She became a complete reality; a real, living, breathing character, fashioned from our creativity. After I finished my composition of thought, I let her go. I threw her up to the universe and said, "Now you play yourself through me."

I had seen so many channels and mediums over the past few years, I decided I would apply the same thing to show business. I simply put my conscious ego aside, got out of my own way, and channeled a character that we had created and I absolutely adored. We actors are continually looking for techniques to inhabit the characters we are asked to play. This time I allowed the character to inhabit me. Instead of trying to become Sousatzka . . . I just let her play herself through me.[3]

Apparently, the channeling worked, though not always to the comfort of MacLaine. Sousatzka was a compulsive eater, and MacLaine gained fifteen pounds while working on the picture. Sousatzka had a bad back, and every time MacLaine went into a scene, her back hurt. Sousatzka had been a great concert pianist, and much to MacLaine's surprise, she discovered she could learn the music with just a few hearings because Sousatzka "knew how to direct my fingers to the right keys on the piano!"[4]

Shirley MacLaine's experience of channeling spiritual energy in her seminars had been translated into the practical world of acting. Based on the result, I'd say that there are a number of actors and actresses who could profit from the technique. A lot less ridicule and just a little more reason would be an enormous help.

Many Hollywood types, in fact, avoid discussing their personal intuitive experiences for precisely that reason: They want to avoid looking foolish in the eyes of their colleagues. In that regard, Shirley MacLaine has exhibited enormous courage. But there have been others willing to share their insights.

When the movie *The Conqueror* was scheduled to be filmed in St. George, Utah, a small town on the Utah-Nevada border, no one was aware of the enormous health hazard created by that area's being directly downwind from the Nevada nuclear test site. The sad fact is that John Wayne, Susan Hayward, Agnes Moorehead, Pedro Armendariz, Thomas Gomez, and Dick Powell (in his first stint as a director) all died from cancer that many believe was the result of the months spent on location in what was later described as a nuclear fallout zone.

Only one of the picture's major stars escaped: John Hoyt, who, interestingly enough, played the role of the shaman, a wise man who knew the ways of the spirit. All of his scenes, with the exception of a few exterior long shots, were already "in the can," having been filmed on the studio soundstage in Hollywood. When the time came to depart for the location shooting, Hoyt declined.

"My inner voice simply told me not to go," he said, adding, "I felt that something very unpleasant would happen to me if I did."

A double filled in for Hoyt's location scenes, which amounted to nothing more than riding a camel across the desert at a considerable distance from the camera. Hoyt escaped the fallout and lived to enjoy a career as a grandfather in the television show "Gimme a Break."

It's sometimes a toss-up as to whether you ignore advice from your inner voice or ignore advice from someone else. The sad fact is that most of us tend to ignore both. The famous evangelist Billy Graham, pastor to presidents and well known among the Hollywood elite, was also apparently capable of precognition. In her autobiography *Debbie, My Life*, Debbie Reynolds tells the following story.

A man she knew from the Bel-Air Presbyterian Church who also worked for 20th Century-Fox Studios called her one day and told her that Billy Graham had called him and said that he had been given a vision of the death of Marilyn Monroe. Graham, it seems, was convinced that it was not yet Marilyn's time to go, and he wanted Debbie to warn Marilyn that she was in terrible danger.

As Debbie relates the story, she didn't know Marilyn, but her friend said that the evangelist was insistent that someone tell Marilyn about his vision. Finally, Debbie remembered Sidney Guilaroff, a hairdresser who she knew had done Marilyn's hair. Debbie called him, and he agreed to give Marilyn the message, disagreeable as it was. To his credit, Guilaroff tried on two separate occasions to give Marilyn the message, but his attempts to speak to the actress alone were frustrated. The following Sunday, Debbie learned that Marilyn Monroe was dead, a victim of what many believe to be an accidental suicide.

Not all messages are that direct. Sometimes a certain amount of interpretation or just plain old fashion faith is required. Elke Sommer, the famous German beauty who starred in such hits as *The Prize* (1963), *A Shot in the Dark* (1964), and *The Art of Love* (1965), announced to the press in 1972 that she was going to take a long overdue trip back to her home near Nuremberg to visit her mother. The announcement didn't cause any great stir in Hollywood, but it was big news in Nuremberg. Unfortunately, so was news of a serial killer that the German newspapers had dubbed the "midday killer."

Frau Rosa Bratter, a German psychic, was leafing through the morning paper when her eyes fell on the latest story concerning the murderer. His most recent victim had been an innocent man who had accidentally bumped into him on the street. Rosa disliked such stories and quickly turned the page and saw a picture of a smiling Elke Sommer. She knew the family. Elke's father had been a Lutheran minister in a small town just twenty miles away. Her real name was Elke Schletz, and the story was filled with glowing reports of her success in America and how her mother was looking forward to her visit.

Suddenly the psychic's fingers began to shake. A dark foreboding seemed to fill the room, and she felt compelled to turn back to the story of the midday killer. As she once again began to focus on the news of the murderer, the picture of Elke materialized and became superimposed over the story of the killer. With a psychic's inner sense, she knew that if Elke didn't alter her plans to visit her mother, something dreadful would happen to her.

Frau Bratter wrote a brief note to Elke in Hollywood. She identified herself as a psychic and told her she was certain that Elke would be in mortal danger if she didn't change her plans. When Elke received the letter, she was faced with several choices. The trip had already been announced to the press and the travel arrangements made. In addition, she didn't want to hurt her mother's feelings. Furthermore, she had never even heard of Rosa Bratter. Why should she pay any attention to a letter that might have come from some hysterical fan?

Fortunately, Elke decided to postpone her trip. It was a decision she will always be grateful she made. On the day that she would have arrived in Germany, the midday killer struck again. His victim was a man who attempted to stop him from stealing a woman's purse. But this time he didn't get away. Once they had him in custody, the officers went to his apartment and discovered a leather-bound diary in which the killer had kept a detailed record of his crimes. On the last page, they found an entry in large block letters: ELKE SOMMER—KIDNAP HER.

The killer later confessed that he had indeed planned on kidnapping the star when she came to visit her mother. He claimed that he had intended to demand a huge ransom from the studio for her release. But investigators believe that he had something far more sinister in mind. Among his possessions, they discovered a veritable arsenal of rifles, knives, hand grenades, and handguns. One of them, a pistol, was clearly marked for a very special victim. Etched into the metal were the words "FOR ELKE."

Upon hearing of these grim events, the grateful star wrote to Rosa Bratter to express her heartfelt thanks. She would later explain why she had so willingly changed her plans on the say-so of someone she had never met. "I've always believed," she said, "that beyond our everyday world, there lies the paranormal realm, and my experience with Rosa Bratter has only strengthened those convictions."[5]

A few years ago, we were doing a television series called, *Miracles and Other Wonders.* Included in one of the shows was a short segment concerning an incident that happened to Mickey Rooney. At the time this event took place, Rooney's career had bottomed out. He hadn't worked in a long time, and no one seemed interested in an aging child star, no matter how prodigious his talent. And there was something else: Mickey's personal life had been less than exemplary for a long time.

Rooney and some friends had gone to dinner at one of their favorite restaurants in the Pocono Mountains of Pennsylvania. There was nothing special about the evening—that is, it wasn't anyone's birthday or any kind of special occasion. But during the meal, a young man with long, flowing golden hair approached Mickey directly.

"At first I thought he was a busboy," Rooney remembered, "but there was something different about him."

It wasn't just the hair, of course. In those days, young men with long hair of just about any color were a dime a dozen. This young man seemed to have a "glow" about him, and he spoke only to Mickey Rooney.

The conversation was totally one-sided and lasted only a moment or two. He came over to the table and simply told Rooney that Jesus loved him. He smiled, a bright warm smile, as if to emphasize the message, then he turned and left. For perhaps the first time in his life, Mickey Rooney was speechless. Finally, he turned to his friends and asked if they had seen that remarkably good-looking busboy. None of them had.

Before they left the restaurant, Mickey asked the maître d' about the new busboy with the long blond hair. The man said he knew of no employee that fit that description. Puzzled, Rooney asked other customers who were seated nearby if they had seen the young man. No one had. He left the restaurant that night a very puzzled but a very changed man.

"I desperately needed some meaning in my life," Rooney said, "and the 'angel' with the golden hair provided it. My life is much better now. I know God loves me, as He loves us all."[6]

Shortly after this encounter in the Poconos, Rooney was selected to do *Sugar Babies* on Broadway with Ann Miller. The show was a smash hit and rejuvenated what had been a badly slipping career. Rooney is quick to give the credit to a brief encounter with a golden-haired "angel" who spoke to him only once and said just three words: "Jesus loves you."

The concept of guardian angels or spirit guides seems to be almost universal. Stories of metaphysical beings that suddenly materialize to help or protect humans are told by people in every walk of life and every income level. But there are other entities that go by various names—ghosts, poltergeists, and restless spirits, just to name a few. These entities are frightening because no one knows quite what to make of them, and anything we don't understand tends to frighten us. Some of these entities are mischievous, but most appear to be rather benign.

The ghostly image of Humphrey Bogart, for example, is reported to have been seen several times and always near a replica of the Maltese falcon, a statue made famous in the motion picture of the same name. Bogart initiated the role of Sam Spade, private eye, in the movie that had as its central thesis a statue of a falcon believed to be fashioned of pure gold. It is one of Bogart's most memorable roles, and it stands beside *Treasure of the Sierra Madre,* and *Casablanca* as one of his definitive performances.

No one seems to know why Bogart's ghost should appear around these replicas. However, certain purchasers of the Maltese falcon have told friends and investigators that they have seen "Bogie" standing near the statue dressed in his trademark trench coat and fedora hat. Some psychics have suggested that the falcon may act as a kind of magnet, drawing Bogart's image from the "other" side. Whatever the reason, nothing as sinister as the plot of the movie is ever implied. He seems to be satisfied with simply hanging around.

Mitzi Gaynor's "pet" ghost, on the other hand, actually helps out with the housecleaning. Both Mitzi and her husband, Jack Bean, have long held an interest in the paranormal, which might be due to the "live-in" ghost that has been terrorizing the household while tarrying about the house. One maid quit after she witnessed sheets and pillowcases being tossed around the room.

Mitzi, however, takes a philosophical view. She calls the ghost Mrs. Walker, after the previous owner who had died while still in possession of the house. According to Gaynor, Mrs. Walker takes a lively interest in what is done to the place. Shortly after moving in, Mitzi had a number of chandeliers hung in various rooms. Mrs. Walker apparently didn't approve of two of them: They both came crashing down almost as soon as they were installed. The electricians were called in to find out what had happened, but they were unable to discover any reason why the chandeliers should have fallen. Meanwhile, this tidy ghost goes about cleaning the chandeliers she does approve of. Occasionally, during the night, the faint sound of tinkling crystal can be heard. Mrs. Walker is doing the one chore the maids never do—removing the dust from the chandeliers.

Probably no ghost in history has been reported seen more often and in more places than Elvis Presley. Few know, however, that Elvis himself once saw something that had a profound impact on his life. In 1965, Elvis was driving the bus bringing his tour group into Los Angeles. Suddenly he stopped, awestruck by something he saw on the horizon.

"I saw the Christ and the Antichrist," he sobbed, clinging to an astonished Larry Geller. "For the first time in my life God and Christ are a living reality. Now I know I'll never have to doubt again. God loves me."

One of Elvis's longtime friends told reporters: "When he was alive he had so much love in him. He helped everyone in need that he possibly could. If he could figure out a way to come back he'd do it."

A nineteen-year-old girl and her family think he may have found a way. The girl, lying in a coma brought on by an inoperable brain tumor, said it was Elvis that "sang her back to life." Two years later, the same girl was struck by a truck and sent into yet another coma. According to her mother, Elvis came through once more. She began playing Elvis's records near her daughter's bedside, and twenty-eight days later, much to the surprise of the doctors, the girl awoke once again.

But Elvis isn't the only Hollywood celebrity credited with being an after-death healer. Princess Grace of Monaco has an enviable record in this regard. A little French girl had her sight restored after she saw Princess Grace in a dream; an eleven-year-old girl was blessed with the sudden cure of her blindness as she placed flowers on Grace's tomb; and actor David Niven is said to have told his butler that the spirit of Princess Grace was comforting him and helping him through his own final days of pain and anguish.[7]

Finally (though we have just scratched the surface of Hollywood's affair with the supernatural), an article in the *New York Times* quoting Mercedes McCambridge vindicated for me my decision to drop the occult movie project I had so reluctantly begun. Mercedes was never seen on screen, but she was the voice of Lucifer in the movie *The Exorcist*.

"Speaking those vile, blaspheming words," she said, "was an agony for me. For sixteen years I sat in front of a pulpit hearing about the horror of evil incarnate, and now I had to play evil incarnate. I had to think evil. If there was any horror in the exorcism," she said, "it was me." After filming was complete, Mercedes was ill and could barely speak. She said she thought she was being punished for doing the picture.

Not everyone, of course, is subject to the same set of influences. But I know that if I had been required to "think evil," it would have put an end to my career. The course I have chosen to follow, with the help of my son, has been every bit as mystical, much more enlightening, and ultimately a good deal more satisfying. Many questions still remain to be answered, of course, but the reality seems to be that somehow, every now and then, a particular person develops psychic talents so powerful and so amazing that the rest of us find it hard to believe. Yet, there must be something to it.

Trying to discover what that something is has been one of the goals of this book. Can our minds open into some other dimension? Are we all capable of psychic feats? You have met a number of people who believe we are. And if our minds can tap into this other dimension, does that suggest that there is a Supreme Being? Maybe there is a greater purpose to our lives than we have yet imagined.

In the next chapter, we will examine that idea from the standpoint of some who have been there—and come back. Are such things as ghosts, apparitions, and poltergeists a reality or simply a figment of someone's imagination? Do people actually die and come back with incredible visions of the future? To find out, all you have to do is turn the page.

Chapter Twelve

Ghosts, Apparitions, and the Afterlife

P ROBABLY A DOZEN TIMES SINCE THEIR DEATHS I've heard my mother or father, in an ordinary, conversational tone of voice, call my name."

That comment is not too surprising except for the fact that the speaker is none other than the famous astronomer and debunker of all things metaphysical, Carl Sagan.

"They had called my name often during my life with them," Sagan went on to say. "I still miss them so much that it doesn't seem strange to me that my brain occasionally will retrieve a kind of lucid recollection of their voices."

Sagan was true to his "scientific" roots to the very end. Not even his own personal experiences could alter a mind set so firmly grounded in things physical.

Is that the answer, then? Our brains simply retrieve a "kind of lucid recollection"?

According to Raymond Moody, author of *Life After Life* and *Reunions, Visionary Encounters with Departed Loved Ones,* "the study of apparitional sightings is largely a study of stories, tales told by people who see ghosts and volunteer their accounts to researchers." Moody, like most psychologists, found that approach to studying the paranormal phenomena quite frustrating, since anecdotal information is not the stuff that science is made of. With the release of *Reunions,* he offered researchers and the public an opportunity to put ghostly and apparitional experiences "to the test," so to speak. The process used to accomplish this is called *mirror gazing.* The idea is certainly not a new one, although serious researchers into matters metaphysical will more likely remember it as crystal gazing. A book by that name was in fact written by Northcote Thomas, and was the inspiration for Moody's study.

We bring this up because throughout our book, we have tried to provide you with some means of testing your own psychic or paranormal skills. While we cannot reproduce Moody's entire work, we thought that you should be aware that in the introduction to *Reunions,* he makes the following promise: "By using the techniques described here, a considerable number of you will actually be able to experience visionary reunions with loved ones who are lost to death."[1] If ghosts, poltergeists, and apparitions are things that interest you, you will undoubtedly want to give Moody's method some attention.

This might be a good time to establish some general definitions, since we will be dealing with several different "types" of paranormal visitations in this chapter:

- *Ghosts* are almost always complete strangers to the person coming in contact with them.
- *Apparitions* are almost always an identifiable likeness of someone well known to the person. Usually, as in my own case, they only appear once.
- *Poltergeists* are ghosts with a mischievous nature that make their presence known through some physical means. Some suggest that poltergeists are actually a form of psychokinesis—mind over matter that is actually a projection from the victim.

These definitions are by no means exhaustive, and many spiritual visitations will exhibit characteristics of all three. The ghost of Hamlet's father is an excellent literary example. Because he was well known to everyone who saw him, he more properly fits the definition of an apparition, and indeed, Hamlet addresses him as such. On the other hand, his multiple appearances give him more the characteristics of a ghost. And the famous "Marian apparitions" (visions of the Virgin Mary) are always seen by many people and return dozens, even hundreds of times, as we shall see in a later chapter. In short, there is no clear-cut definition of specific entities, but it is useful to have some means of separating them for the purposes of discussion.

Ghosts and apparitions are invariably visible in some form to the person being contacted. Poltergeists, on the other hand, are never seen, but they might drop a chandelier (as per Mitzi Gaynor's experience) or, as in the following case, even write you a note. According to an eposide of the A&E television program *The Unexplained*, aired in 1997, Bob and Beth Batzel have suffered from not just one, but a whole army of poltergeists throughout their married life.

Beth was divorced and caring for her young daughter when she met Bob Batzel. The two fell in love and got married. Bob, shortly thereafter, adopted Beth's daughter. It seemed to Beth to be an idyllic family arrangement when they moved into their first home in New Brunswick, New Jersey.

This part of America is rich in history. New Jersey was one of the original thirteen colonies and figured significantly in the Revolutionary War. Washington Valley Road still winds across the countryside, following almost exactly the route taken by Washington's army as it traveled from one battle to the next. Homes that boast a 300-year history are not uncommon. Some of them still have the original wood floors, held in place by wooden dowels. The home purchased by Beth and Bob Batzel in historic New Brunswick was an older home, but it took a very disagreeable set of circumstances to lead them to discover just how old it was.

Beth told investigators that they had barely settled in before strange occurrences began to take place on a daily basis. Lamps would swing back and forth with no one near who could have touched them; doors would open and close of their own accord; and various objects would suddenly disappear and reappear in the wrong place. Soon they began to detect the smell of rotting flowers in various rooms in the house—as if the odor was coming from the very walls. The temperature would soar to sweltering levels for no apparent reason, and before long, knives, forks, and baby bottles darted around the house.

"I felt very scared," Beth said. "We didn't know what to expect; we never knew what was coming next."

What came next might be some small object hurled at them by some unseen force or a door slamming in the middle of the night. Whatever it happened to be, it was always out of place and a frightening surprise.

Needless to say, the stress level in the Batzel home was extremely high, though they tried to maintain some semblance of an ordinary life. Then one day, Beth had some friends over for afternoon tea. Suddenly, out of nowhere, the rubber stopper from the bathtub shot between them, as if hurled with great force. And just as suddenly, a pleasant afternoon chat turned into a desperate attempt to explain what had been going on in their home—with very unsatisfactory results. When something can't be explained, Beth would learn, everyone thinks it's your fault.

A few nights later, Beth and Bob stood frozen with fear as they watched a lighted cigarette drift slowly down to the kitchen floor. "We didn't know what to do," Beth explained. "We didn't know if someone was holding it, if it would hit the floor and start a fire. We didn't know what to do."

Beth had never believed in ghosts, but the events taking place in her home forced her to confront the possibility that her family was experiencing a genuine "haunting." The word soon spread, and a group interested in paranormal activity asked if they could conduct a seance in the home. Bob and Beth both quickly agreed.

The group assembled around the dining room table, and Beth, still skeptical, set up tape recording equipment. If anything substantial were to take place, she wanted it on tape. The seance began, and the psychic conducting it called out to the spirit. As if waiting for the opportunity, the spirit began to speak through her. The tape recording demonstrates two clearly distinct and different voices, that of the psychic and that of the spirit.

"Can you tell us your name?"

"It's my land—you get out," came the angry reply.

"If we could investigate and see if it is your land," the psychic said, "maybe we could get out. But you have to help us. Could you tell us your name?"

"My name is George Baxter," the spirit replied in the same belligerent tone. "This land belonged to me. I bought it in 1872. Now you look that up, mister."

The next day, Beth went to the New Brunswick library to research the history of the house. A George Baxter had indeed purchased the land in 1872. Beth was surprised but still skeptical. After all, the psychic could have done the same research in the library and found out who had owned the house. Of course, that didn't explain the floating cigarette or the flying bathtub stopper or any of the other strange occurrences. But even if it was the ghost of George Baxter, she thought, maybe they could work out an accommodation.

That idea went out the window a few weeks later when the family awoke to find threatening messages in lipstick scrawled across walls and mirrors. "Go" and "Dead" were the two words they saw everywhere and around them hastily scrawled graveyard crosses. Then, according to Bob, the same deadly message, as well as others, was scribbled on notes and left throughout the house.

The angry ghost had now become brazen, and Bob and Beth began to fear for their daughter. They had no way to protect her from the belligerent spirit. Reluctantly, they packed up and left, thinking they would leave the nasty poltergeist behind.

The Batzels moved to an apartment in Clifton, New Jersey, miles across the state from New Brunswick, but they had barely moved in when some unseen force pushed all three of them down the stairs. This time they didn't wait to argue with the spirit. They moved again, even farther away, to a town called Flemington. They had just completed unpacking when, to Beth's horror, she found a large butcher knife impaled in the kitchen door frame. She knew that they had not yet eluded the vicious spirit.

But was George Baxter following them around? Or was there some other explanation? Could it be that Beth herself was somehow attracting the malevolent entities? No one seemed to know, least of all Beth and Bob Batzel.

From 1971 to 1985, the Batzels moved eleven times, always seeking some place where they could live a normal life with their family, which had now grown by one. They had been blessed with another daughter, and it was not just the children's physical well-being they were concerned about, but their mental and emotional states as well. But their lives were anything but normal. Friends shunned them. People avoided the Batzels as if they were somehow responsible for everything that was happening. In desperation, they made one more move.

Bob and Beth decided to build their own home from the ground up. Surely, no greedy poltergeist could claim that they were invading "his" home. They bought property near a small lake in Pennsylvania and built the home of their dreams. They moved in with every expectation that the terror of the past dozen years was now behind them. They were wrong.

Within a week of putting the finishing touches on the interior of their new home they discovered the most gruesome message of all. Sometime after midnight Bob and Beth were awakened by the sound of their older daughter's terrified screams. They rushed to her room to find the pet cat hanging by the neck in the doorframe. Its eyes had been gouged out. This poltergeist, it seems, had broken the rules. It had found a way to do harm to living things.

Unwilling to be chased out of the home they had built, they decided to stick it out. Another week went by, and then one night the glass in all the picture frames throughout the house exploded, sending shards of glass flying across almost every room in the house.

Lloyd Auerbach, a respected paranormal psychologist, would find these last two events quite out of character for a poltergeist. His thesis at the convocation I attended was that there were no "monsters." Rather, a poltergeist was simply a question of mind over matter, or psychokinesis, an unwitting projection of the victim that in reality was nothing more than a series of small irritations or changes, not things being smashed. Auerbach apparently had never spoken with the Batzels.

Leon Lederman, a Nobel Prize-winning physicist, takes an even dimmer view. "People are either dishonest or disillusioned," he says, and adds emphatically, "Science has no room for ghosts."

Karl Schlotterbeck, a psychologist, takes a completely different position. When he was called to the Batzels' home, he became a believer very quickly. "There was a different feeling in different rooms," he said. "In one room it was difficult to breathe, and recordings made in that room were fainter than in others." Schlotterbeck was so convinced of the reality of the Batzels' experience that he co-authored a book with Beth. They call it *Lion of Satan, Lion of God.* There is no scientific verification, of course, but Schlotterbeck believes that these spirits are attracted to Beth because of some undefined quality in her they find inviting. He suggests that Beth might be an "undeveloped" psychic. Whatever the answer, the Batzels are still asking the same questions: "Why me?" and "Why here?"

Steven Spielberg, the famous Hollywood producer and director of such outstanding motion pictures as *Close Encounters of the Third Kind, ET,* and the much less heralded *Poltergeist,* suggests that "probably every fourth person you talk to has had an experience with a poltergeist or ghost—or knows someone who has."

Our experience suggests that just might be true, but what about Spielberg himself?

"It is a very, very personal thing that I won't discuss," he says. "I've always wanted to see a UFO, and I never have. But ghosts—that's another story."

One, we hope, he may eventually tell on film.

Nick Nicerino, director of the Institute of Psychic and Hypnotic Sciences in Pinole, California, has been pursuing "whatever ghosts are" as a parapsychologist, a psychic researcher, and a paranormal consultant since 1944. He is also one of the country's most respected photographers of paranormal events. Nicerino's photographic files cover hundreds of events. Most of his photographs (*not* taken for publication) are taken at night on black and white ASA 400 film. Indoors the lighting is likely to be a single candle. Outdoors he uses only available light, which between 9:00 P.M. and 5:00 A.M. isn't likely to be very much.[2]

According to Nicerino, there are four fairly clearly defined causes for ghostly appearances: First is the ghost of someone who has been murdered and whose death has been improperly recognized: "Maybe it was officially recorded that the death was a suicide or an accident and the deceased wants to set the record straight and have it known that he was murdered." A close variation of that type of haunting, Nicerino says, is the ghost of someone who has been improperly buried.

Second, there is the confused spirit of one who had been forcibly kept from society—men and women who were kept chained in cellars or attics.

Third is the haunting precipitated by someone bringing home an antique or a Native American relic. "In one particularly dramatic case involving an ancient Chinese vase," Nicerino says, "the owner became so desperate that we all went along to throw it in the ocean. We all saw it sink into the waters, so imagine our consternation when we returned to the house and found it waiting for us."

Fourth, there is the spirit that travels with people from a haunted area. Nicerino gives this frightening example: "There was a bar that had a ghost that would follow customers into their cars, then manifest while they were driving, grabbing at the steering wheel, pushing at the brakes. A lot of accidents were caused by this entity."[3]

Which brings us back to an earlier question: Can ghosts harm living things?

Nicerino doesn't think so. He suggests, instead, that ghosts have the ability to put things into a person's mind that make them think that something is happening when in reality it isn't. Ghosts, after all, don't have bodies, and as Lloyd Auerbach pointed out, "People carry guns and knives, ghosts don't."

There are, of course, more benign stories of hauntings, some of them even quite entertaining—like the story of the bartender at the Banta Inn, in Banta, California. His name was Tony, and quite unexpectedly he dropped dead from a heart attack one day while pouring a drink for a customer.

Tony had been behind that bar for a number of years and was well known to all the regulars. He had a few little idiosyncrasies that were likewise well known. For example, Tony liked to have the jukebox playing while he was at work. It was almost as if silence was an insult. He also had everything placed in specific spots so he could easily get his hands on them. Things like the bar towel, the nuts, and the premix for certain drinks, such as a Bloody Mary, all had their spot either on the bar or behind it. Then there was the matter of the cash drawer. Tony liked all the coins arranged in a certain way, neatly stacked from the larger to the smaller denominations. Those things didn't make a whole lot of difference to the customers, but they apparently made a big difference to Tony.

Shortly after Tony's untimely demise, the new bartender began to notice strange things happening. Not as tidy as Tony, he would nevertheless find his bar towel neatly folded and next to the ice bin. Drink glasses left next to the sink would somehow find their way into the soapy water, and on several occasions, he would open the cash drawer to find the coins all neatly arranged, largest to smallest. On more than one occasion, the juke box would suddenly begin to blare with no one near it and once when it wasn't even plugged in! But it wasn't until one of the regulars said he saw Tony in his accustomed place behind the bar that they began to put it all together. Tony, taken by a turn of fate before he was ready to go, was apparently hanging around to make sure things stayed nice and neat at *his* bar.

People returning from the dead in ghostly form to correct a problem or right a wrong of some kind is certainly not a new idea. The cult of the dead among the ancient Greeks was widespread. Deceased persons would frequently return to the land of the living to complete some task overlooked in their lifetime or sometimes simply because the funerary rites had been botched. Usually, these spirits spread terror throughout the household, but in the case of Eukrate's house, the spirit returned with tenderness, even a poetic sadness.

Eukrate had lost his beloved wife, and together with the body, all of her belongings had been consigned to the funeral pyre. Seven days later, as Eukrate was reading Plato's *Phaedra* to try and escape his grief for a few moments, his wife entered and sat beside him. One of her golden sandals, she told him, had escaped the fire. It had, in fact, fallen behind the chest. As she spoke, so the story goes, the Melitian dog barked, and she vanished. The sandal was found and appropriately burned, and the dead woman never returned again.[4]

Nothing, it seems, is too trivial to command the attention of departed spirits. On the other hand, there are concepts of transcendent importance that can result in certain types of hauntings.

The state of Texas, for all its size, is almost bereft of natural scenic attractions. Someone once said that a trip across Texas is a trip that covers miles and miles of nothing but miles and miles. Steve Lee, a truck driver from Dallas, often found himself carrying loads from Texas to Colorado, and the stark contrast between the plains of his home state and the beautiful and rugged Colorado Rockies had a profound impact on him. Steve decided that he wanted to raise his family in more scenic surroundings, and so the first chance he got, he moved his wife and two boys into a log home in the spectacular Black Forest, not far from Colorado Springs.

Steve was unaware of it at the time, but according to a Hopi Indian legend, there are hidden places in the mountains of Colorado where the spirits of the dead make their way from this world to the next. For the spirits of the dead, these are sacred portals for the passage we must all make in and out of this world. To the living, they are simply mysterious gateways.

Even if Steve had been aware of the legend, it wouldn't have made any difference to him. Steve was, after all, a practical man, not much given to stories of the supernatural. Besides, their new home gave his boys the freedom and spirit of adventure he had hoped it would. It would take more than a few itinerant ghosts to dampen his enthusiasm for his new home. In fact, he was busy, at every opportunity, taking pictures of the home, its surroundings, and his boys to send back to his friends in Dallas.

The first roll of film, however, was a big disappointment. Streaks of light seemed to invade every print. At first Steve chalked it up to a bad roll of film, but the second and third rolls produced exactly the same result. And there was something else. The light streaks seemed to have some consistency. An orange beam of light appeared on every photograph of his younger son, while a greenish glow seemed to be hovering around the older boy. On some prints, the vague outline of faces would appear—faces that shouldn't have been there.

Steve had his camera checked; there was nothing wrong with it. Steve became fascinated with the pictures. The more he took, the more consistent the results became. Then one day, he took a picture of the mirror over his dresser. The faces staring back at him from the mirror terrified him (shades of Raymond Moody). They were not the faces of people he recognized, but their features were distinct, and their eyes seemed to glow like points of light. What's more, the faces were not always the same. Different people would appear, then the image would dissipate, only to be replaced by another. Steve also became aware that different parts of the house seemed to be more active than others.

Steve refused to believe that he had ghosts, but he couldn't escape the notion that something was definitely going on. He installed surveillance cameras to see if the lights and images might be human-made. When his tapes showed nothing, he decided to call in an expert. Bill Gibbens, an electronics specialist and sometime psychic investigator, was called in to see if there was anything electric or magnetic about this particular area that might be causing the phenomenon.

Gibbens set up a video camera of his own, but he set it up outside. He also brought a spectrometer with him to test for electromagnetic or radio wave anomalies in or near the house. The first videos supplied some startling pictures. Waves of light, moving through the darkness, seemed to be in a motion pattern that made them seem as if "they had a mind of their own." And while the spectrometer failed to show any real anomalies, an ordinary compass did. At one corner of the house, it would swirl uncontrollably.

When Dennis Hauk, author of *Haunted Places,* was asked to look at the videotape and photographs, he said that the number of strange images surprised even him. It was as if hundreds of spirits had gone through this particular spot, and he could find no earthly explanation for the anomalies.

Steve Lee still isn't ready to admit that his house is haunted, but he and the other investigators who have seen the evidence wonder if maybe a part of his house is built on one of the spiritual passageways spoken of in the Hopi legends. Is it possible that the Lee house is filled with spirits traveling in and out of this world through one of these legendary portals?

Be that as it may, one portal of the spirit would seem to be the body itself. That spirits do travel in and out of the body has been widely attested to by those who have gone through a near-death experience. In the international best seller *Embraced by the Light,* Betty Eddy chronicles in detail her own experiences. Dozens of other people could be cited as well, all of them saying more or less the same thing: The spirit leaves the body and for some period of time is permitted to watch the efforts being made to revive the earthly body. The spirit is then drawn into a tunnel of light and whisked to some other sphere, where often loved ones or even Christ himself is waiting to welcome it. The spirit is then, for various personal reasons, "required" to return to the earthly plain.

The three stories we are about to relate are all pretty much like that, but something new has been added. In each case, a limited gift of prophecy was given to the woman in question, with the expectation that she would pass her visions along upon her return. Each of the women described here was the subject of an interview recently on The Learning Channel as part of a special production called, "New Visions of the Future, Prophecies III."

The year was 1992, and Cassandra Musgrave was waterskiing with two friends. It was her turn on the skis, and everything was going beautifully until she caught a tip and fell. Through some strange quirk of fate, her arm got tangled in the tow rope, and she suddenly found herself being dragged through the water headfirst and unable to get air. Her friends, forgetting the first rule of water safety, were chatting away in the boat, oblivious to her predicament.

Cassandra, meanwhile, was drowning. As that realization came over her, she was suddenly and inexplicably outside of her body. She watched with surprising detachment as the boat continued to drag her body through the water. Then, on what she described as an "inner level," she found herself being pulled through a dark tunnel. She continued on until she came to a "wide open space" with stars all around, like an open view of the universe. At that point, Cassandra says, she was given a glimpse of the future, specifically, twenty years into the future—the year 2012. During this period of time, she says, things will be greatly accelerated here on earth, and that acceleration will be manifest through great earth changes: earthquakes, floods, tidal waves, and great winds.

"I also saw that there will be certain areas that will be particularly affected," Cassandra told the reporter, "the East coast, which was a surprise regarding earthquakes, and I remember very clearly, Japan slipping into the ocean. I was shown that there would be something akin to three days of darkness. I don't feel it was thermonuclear war, it was more a feeling, like a series of natural disasters, with smoke from volcanoes that simply block the sun. We're all going to be on a roller coaster ride, but it's not forever. If we have darkness for three days, we will always have the light."

Then, suddenly, Cassandra was back in her body, and the moment she reentered her body, the boat stopped. Frantically, her friends pulled her back in the boat and untangled her arm from the tow rope. To their amazement, Cassandra seemed none the worse for her experience. What her friends couldn't know was that her experience had taken her into the spirit world and given her a glimpse of a disturbing future.

Elaine Durham was rushed to the emergency room after suffering a stroke in her sleep. By the time they got to the hospital, Elaine was no longer on the gurney looking up, but rather floating alongside at about eye level. She was aware of the body on the gurney, but says that she felt no particular relationship to it.

The next thing she remembers, she was running across a field of grass. There were several people waiting there for her, among them her grandmother, who had died when Elaine was nine years old, and her husband's Aunt Virginia, who had just recently passed on.

Suddenly she was "slammed" back into her body. The medical team was working frantically to save her, but when Elaine's heart stopped again, they gave up and moved her aside to be prepared for the morgue.

Once again, Elaine's spirit left her body, but this time it entered a, "spiritual realm of light." She was pulled into a place filled with "billions and billions of diamondlike sparkles . . . and I was one of them."

It was at this point, Elaine says, that she was shown visions of the future. Interestingly, these visions are not unlike those seen by Cassandra. "I have seen the destruction that earthquakes create," she says, and adds, "The Pacific rim is really going to take a beating . . . and there's no way around it. I have knowledge of icebergs melting and raising the water table. The water didn't come in and cover all the land, it left areas where there were large islands."

As to the fate of the United States specifically, Elaine says: "America was not destroyed but we reached that pinnacle where we could have tipped and gone the other way."

Elaine's experience ended when she "woke up" in the morgue, completely unaware of how she came back. There was just the feeling of being back in a cold, clay body with tears streaming down her face.

Jessica Cade was practicing backflips from a "low board" (a 1-meter diving board) at a local swimming pool when she misjudged her distance and cracked her skull on the bottom of the diving board. Drifting slowly toward the bottom of the pool, she felt herself black out. The next thing she knew, she was hovering about 15 feet above her body. Jessica remembers wondering, "What's happening here?" Then, she says, she "left this world."

Jessica told the interviewers that she saw a light tunnel, and light beings from the tunnel were lifting her higher and higher. There was, she said, the most profound feeling of peace and love she had ever experienced. It was at this point that she was given a brief glimpse of prophetic vision. Jessica was shown some-one in her family, an uncle, who would commit suicide, and she was also told that there would be more prophetic visions at some point in the future.

Suddenly, Jessica was back at the pool, landing back in her body with a "thud." She was lying on the concrete at poolside with a lifeguard desperately administering CPR. Far from being grateful, Jessica was angry at being pulled back from the light tunnel and the feelings that accompanied the whole experience.

A short time later, her uncle did, in fact, commit suicide, but Jessica pretty much forgot about the promised visions of the future until a few years later, when she drowned once again. This time, Jessica was tubing down a quiet river when she somehow was thrown from her tube into the murky water. She felt herself being drawn down into the green, gloomy depths, and somehow she knew what would happen next. The life-extinguishing water brought her face to face with the glowing light beings. This time they opened her eyes to the future.

"The light beings surrounded and filled me with light," she said. "I saw them unrolling a scroll before me. It looked almost like an Arabic or Greek text."

Like Cassandra and Elaine, Jessica was also shown earthquakes all along the "ring of fire" (Pacific Rim). "I saw pictures of horror, of one world gov-ernment; the return of concentration camps. I saw diseases and implosions of germ warfare. These visions of essential horror were not lasting. There would come another time of peace, another time of joy and love." And she was told, "You and others would be safe."

Suddenly, Jessica shot to the surface and took a huge gulp of air. Amaz-ingly she was able to make it to the river bank on her own, none the worse for having drowned—again.[5]

For those of us who have received some evidence of life beyond the grave, whether as a result of ghosts, apparitions, poltergeists, or a near-death experience, the extension of the life cycle into some other sphere or realm is a fore-gone conclusion. It is not terribly surprising, however, that the world of science "has no room for ghosts," since it is a world that is, by its own design, self-limiting. Fortunately, there have always been those who, like Columbus, have known that simply because we cannot see beyond the horizon, it doesn't mean that there is nothing there.

It seems a strange paradox that, on the evidence, human beings desperately want to know what the future holds, but seem to be deathly afraid of the people and processes that make the future available to them.

In the next and final section, we will face that paradox squarely. For nearly 6,000 years, prophets have been warning of the evils of our generation. Do we really want to know what the future holds? Do we have the courage to face it?

You are about to see what some of the great prophets have had to say about what just might be the rest of our lives. The year 2000 is upon us, the most fabled year in the history of the world. Is that world, as we have known it, on the threshold of irrevocable change—even destruction?

PROPHECIES AND PREDICTIONS

*Time present and time past
Are both perhaps present in time future,
And time future contained in time past
If all time is equally present.*
T. S. ELLIOT, *"Burnt Norton"*

ALL OF US WOULD LIKE TO KNOW what tomorrow will bring, or even the next hour, for that matter. It is one of the foibles of human nature to want to know the outcome from the outset, and as we have seen, for some that appears to be a very real possibility.

From the beginning of recorded history, there have been men and women who claimed to have a special knowledge of things to come. Some of them have proved to be astonishingly successful at the task. Their methods for divining the future vary widely and over the centuries have assumed certain nationalistic characteristics.

The *I Ching* (pronounced "ee jing") for example, is generally regarded as peculiarly Chinese, although it is believed that the Samurai warriors of Japan consulted the *I Ching* in planning military strategy. Today, virtually all followers of Confucius rely on its hexagrams. Also known as "the Book of

Change," it states that we must not fight against the whirlpool when we are cast into it but instead move with it in order to survive.

Palmistry might have originated anywhere, but it was the gypsies of Spain and central Europe who made it part of their culture. On the other hand, tarot cards can be found virtually anywhere on the planet.

From sand paintings to crystal balls, from the movement of the stars to the bumps on your head, from the pages of the *I Ching* to the pages of the Bible, the process of trying to predict what will happen tomorrow, next year, or perhaps even 4,000 years from now has always been the grand passion of the human species. But does our investigation thus far prove that it can actually be done? More specifically, can you and I do it?

There seems to be a significant body of evidence that suggests that some of the techniques used by various prophets and seers have been very successful. In the next few chapters, we will introduce you to people and prophecies who, if they are correct in their predictions, will have a powerful impact on the rest of your life and the lives of your children.

Perhaps it is time to open our minds to every possibility. After all, the future is where we are all going to live.

CHAPTER THIRTEEN

PROPHETS, PSYCHICS, AND SEERS

IN THE SEVENTEENTH CENTURY, A MAN by the name of William Lilly predicted that London would be destroyed by fire. Fifteen years later, in 1666, his prediction came true and in such precise detail that a government inquiry was held to determine whether or not Mr. Lilly had some hand in creating the disaster he had so eerily forecast.

A hundred years earlier, a French physician made the same prophecy, and he named the very year. Nostradamus, with uncanny foresight, wrote: "The blood of the just will be demanded of London, burnt by fire in three times twenty plus six."

William Lilly consulted the stars. Nostradamus, it is said, used an elaborate mixture of a wand, a tripod, and a kettle of water. Yet, both of them arrived at the same conclusion, albeit a hundred years apart.

The world's largest ocean liner, the new *Titan*, on its maiden voyage in 1898, struck a huge iceberg and sank with enormous loss of life. But wait, wasn't it the *Titanic*, and didn't it sink in 1912?

True! But *The Wreck of the Titan,* a novel by an obscure British writer named Morgan Robertson, predicted, in horrifying detail, the fate of the *Titanic,* fourteen years before it happened, very nearly to the exact day. In Robertson's story, the *Titan,* a huge ship believed by its builders to be unsinkable because of its unique structural design, struck an iceberg on a cold evening in April; the *Titanic* began her maiden voyage on April 10, 1912. The *Titan,* in what the author called a story that wrote itself, struck an iceberg and sank to the bottom; fourteen years later, the *Titanic* relived the same horror. In Robertson's little-known tragedy, most of the 2,500 passengers were lost, as were most of the *Titanic* passengers, because there were lifeboats on board for only about half the passengers. Who or what moved Robertson's pen across the paper?

Even closer to home and nearer in time: In the fall of 1952, Mrs. Jeane Dixon, by all accounts a deeply religious woman, entered St. Matthew's Cathedral in Washington, D.C., for her morning devotions. According to her own account, as she knelt to pray, the White House suddenly appeared before her in dazzling brightness surrounded by a kind of indistinct haze. As she watched, numbers pushed through the haze above the roof and formed the sequence 1-9-6-0. She had no more than taken this in when an ominous dark cloud appeared, covering the numbers and dripping onto the White House lawn. Then she saw a young man, tall, blue-eyed, a shock of thick brown hair, quietly standing in front of the main door. She was struggling to understand this vision when a voice came out of nowhere and told her that this young man, a Democrat, would be seated as president in 1960 and would be assassinated in office.

Eleven years later, that prophecy was fulfilled when President John F. Kennedy, a Democrat elected to the presidency in 1960, was gunned down on a main thoroughfare near Dealy Plaza in Dallas, Texas. Jeane Dixon made several attempts to persuade President Kennedy not to make the trip to Dallas. Something in her psychic awareness told her that this would be the time when her awful vision would become reality. The president, however, weighed down with the pressure of politics and probably skeptical of anything so "unscientific" as visions and prophecy, ignored her warning, much to his, the nation's, and perhaps the world's detriment.

We will never know if John Kennedy felt even the smallest trepidation over the warning. If he did, he kept it strictly to himself. Interestingly, the funeral mass for Kennedy was delivered in the same church in which Dixon had beheld the vision and received the warning of his death.

This, of course, is not the only instance where a prophetic warning was ignored with dire consequences. In the case of the *Titanic,* a number of dire predictions were recorded. Some of them were heeded, and those lucky (and perceptive) individuals lived to tell the world of the journey they didn't take.

Most of the stories, however, were similar to that of W. T. Stead, a British journalist.

Stead had consulted two seers, both of whom told him to avoid taking any journey by water. One even told him he would sail to America within two years of their session. He told Stead he "saw" more than a thousand people struggling in the water with no hope of survival, Stead himself included. Nor was this a subject with which Stead was unfamiliar. Some years earlier, he had written a magazine article in which he described the tragedy of a ship hitting an iceberg. In his story, there was only one survivor. Incredibly, Stead also told friends that he had had a dream in which he saw himself standing on the deck of the *Titanic* without a life vest as the last lifeboat vanished in the dark. Yet, in spite of all the warnings and omens, W. T. Stead booked passage on the maiden voyage of the *Titanic* and was among those lost in the icy waters of the Atlantic.

These are just a few examples of the power of prophecy, and they are all fairly recent in origin. In fact, there does not appear to be a time in the history of humankind when there were not prophets, soothsayers, or oracles in whom was vested the responsibility of foretelling the future. The most widely known, of course, are the prophets of the Old Testament. The historic landscape seems to be littered with disasters that befell those who ignored their prophets. Yet, today we appear to be even less inclined to listen to those who claim to have prophetic insight, as witnessed by fates of both W. T. Stead and John F. Kennedy. That being the case, a little jog through our prophetic past might prove instructive. It might even be essential.

We are now on the brink of the turn of the century and the very millennium that has been the subject of prophecy and divination for at least 4,000 years. It therefore seems appropriate to look back at those prophets who centuries (even millennia) ago looked forward to what they believed would be "the last days."

The last days! The phrase is one that most of us have heard since childhood, and it still has an ominous ring. Wars, rumors of wars, famine, pestilence, and disease are all harbingers of the scenes that some believe are literally upon us. But where did these grisly scenes originate? Did a lonely exile on the tiny island of Patmos really see the end of the world? Have other prophets, ancient and modern, seen anything remotely like the scenes described in the Book of Revelation? If so, what have they had to say about the present and the future—if there is to be one? Hopefully, in all of this we will discover something about the nature of prophets and prophecy and their relationship to an often skeptical and sometimes hostile world.

The island of Patmos is a tiny (13-square-miles) pile of rocks in the southeast Aegean Sea. John, the brother of James and a cousin of Christ, was the last of the original apostles still living. He had been banished to this inhospitable spot by the Romans, who were hoping to stamp out the last vestiges of this upstart new religion called Christianity. According to the text, John is out walking when he hears a voice commanding him to write down what the speaker tells him. John turns to face the voice and discovers a personage that claims to be Christ himself,[1] but in some highly celestialized form.

He first gives John messages specifically for the seven churches, but from Chapter 4 onward, the book takes on a completely apocalyptic character, which most scholars concede was John's vision of "the last days."

Written in a form of Greek that was unknown in his own day, and speaking in images and metaphors quite unlike anything else in the Bible (with the possible exception of Daniel), the prophecies of doom and destruction pour forth and define a judgment day that few Christians, Jews, or Gentiles of that period could recognize. The words do, however, resonate in a very meaningful way for many who study the book today. For example, John speaks of mechanized "horses" and describes an army of 200 million men,[2] something that would have been unthinkable in the last ten years of the first century A.D.

But John was not the only prophet to write about these things. Hundreds of years earlier, Ezekiel talked of an army that—"shalt come up against my people of Israel, as a cloud to cover the land" and adds, "It shall be in the latter days."[3] Zechariah also describes "that day" when "a great tumult from the Lord shall be among them: and they shall lay hold everyone on the hand of his neighbor."[4] Ezekiel is even more explicit: "And the wicked shall slay the wicked and fear shall come upon every man."[5]

According to many biblical scholars, this will be the time of a great cleansing of the earth. While it is Babylon that is named specifically, it seems clear that the name is symbolic of some city, perhaps many cities, far greater than the Babylon located in modern-day Iraq. It should be pointed out, however, that Saddam Hussein is working feverishly to restore the city of Babylon to its original splendor. Perhaps some Iraqi leader less fixed on waging war may do it. One thing seems certain. Babylon was never destroyed as the Book of Revelation says it must be. It has simply withered away and over the centuries turned into little more than a dusty village. But Revelation tells us: "Alas for the great city, the mighty city of Babylon! In a single hour your doom was struck."[6] Such an event is yet to come.

There is more, much more, to this cleansing. There will be an earthquake "like none before it in human history, so violent it was. The great city was split in three; the cities of the world fell in ruin."[7] But before that takes place, there will be plagues and infestations, and the sea will turn to blood, likewise rivers and streams. And the great winepress of God's wrath, "was trodden outside the city, and for two hundred miles around blood flowed from the press to the height of the horses' bridle."[8]

As you can see, John is not stingy with the details. He names the star, Wormwood, that will shoot from the sky like a flaming torch and poison a third of the waters. Hail and fire mingled together will burn a third of the earth, and a great blazing mountain will be hurled into the sea, killing a third of every creature in it and sinking a third of the ships thereon.[9] (At least two recent movies deal with a huge comet or asteroid plunging into the earth and destroying life as we know it. The writers haven't necessarily been reading the Bible, they are taking their cue from modern astronomy.)

In the sixth chapter, peace is taken from the earth, people slaughter one another, famine rages, and pestilence rules the land. All in all, it is not a very pretty picture, and according to the biblical time frame, as best the scholars can pinpoint it, the year A.D. 2000 is the benchmark.

There is, of course, much more to the Book of Revelation, but there is very little of a more positive outlook. Unfortunately, we will not be able to verify the accuracy of these prophecies until they actually happen, and according to the book itself, no one knows when that will be. How, then, can we measure the validity of these prophecies?

There are some biblical prophets we can look to to see what kind of record the Bible actually has. Isaiah, for example, prophesied the birth of Christ fully 700 years before the actual event. Several Old Testament prophets warned various kings of Judah and Israel that their kingdoms would be overthrown and the people scattered, and certainly that seems to have taken place. But these are prophecies whose fulfillment is self-contained within the pages of the book. Are there biblical prophecies that have been fulfilled in what we could call "modern" times? If indeed these are the last days, then surely there is something to help us identify that fact.

According to Paul Boyer, professor of theology at the University of Wisconsin in Madison, "One of the most striking and precise examples of biblical prophecy essential to the ushering in of the last days occurred in 1947. In that year the gathering of Israel promised by Ezekiel became a reality."

Twenty-five hundred years ago, while still a captive himself, the prophet Ezekiel wrote:

> Oh my people, I will open up your graves and bring you into the land of Israel . . . I will take the children of Israel from . . . whither they have gone and will gather them on every side and bring them into their own land. . . . I will make them one nation in the land upon the mountains of Israel and one King shall be King to them all."[10]

"It is not a stretch of the imagination," Boyer says, "to see the liberation of the German prison camps as 'opening the graves' of the Jewish people who were still there. The rest of Ezekiel's prophecy has been fulfilled without the slightest change." The establishment of a Jewish homeland in Palestine, bringing them "into the land of Israel," certainly seems to meet the criteria. It also set the stage for a continuation of the struggle between Israel and her

Arab neighbors, a struggle that has gone on since the dawn of history. But that, too, fits in with the ancient prophecies.

Daniel wrote that there would be a period of trouble such as never was "since there was a nation." Surrounded by hostile neighbors of enormous wealth and power, tiny Israel weathers one political storm after another. It would be difficult to identify a time in the history of the Middle East when the nation of Israel was in a more troublesome spot.

In the New Testament, the apostle Luke warned that nation would rise against nation and kingdom against kingdom, and great earthquakes would occur in diverse places, and there would be famine and pestilence and fearful signs and great sights. These prophecies were all given as signs that the last days would be upon the world. It's difficult to look around and not see evidence that all of these things are happening.

All of this suggests that what the biblical prophets told us either came true or is in the process of coming true. But is there any corroborating evidence? Have there been other prophets, psychics, or seers who have predicted the end of the world as part of the modern epoch? The answer, not too surprisingly, is yes—some of them ancient, some of them in our lifetime.

Hundreds of years ago, ancestors of today's Hopi Indians carved symbols in the living rock on Black Mesa, in Arizona. The elders were told (and they passed the word from generation to generation) that these were symbols of a great devastation that would come into the world. Centuries later, these symbols, the Nazi swastika and the Japanese sun, combined, just as the carvings suggested, and burst upon the world as the battle flags of massive armies bent on conquering the world. To the Hopi, the terrible devastation of World War II was the fulfillment of the ancient warnings and a sign that what they call the Great Purification (a concept not dissimilar to "cleansing") has begun.

According to Thomas Banyaca, a Hopi elder, author, and lecturer, each generation of Hopi leaders has been warned to watch for a series of three world-shaking events, each accompanied by a particular symbol. The symbols are the swastika, the sun, and the color red. These symbols are also carved in the sacred gourd rattles used in Hopi rituals. These symbols, according to Banyaca, represent the purifiers who will shake the world with violence and destruction. When Germany, with its swastika, merged with Japan, the land of the rising sun, the Hopi were convinced that all of their prophecies were coming true.

If that's true, then the world is in for a very rough time. According to the ancient Hopi writings, there will be earthquakes and floods, causing enormous devastation. There will be changes in the seasons, famine in all of its forms, and confusion and corruption among the leaders of the world. Amazingly, their description of coming events sounds eerily similar to those we read about in both the Bible and the morning paper.

It is a geological fact of life that the incidence of earthquakes has been increasing in number and severity ever since the beginning of this century. Flooding, too, has become so commonplace as to be expected on an almost seasonal basis, and each flood seems to exceed the last in terms of destruction and devastation. As for political confusion and corruption, well it doesn't take a psychic to watch the news.

But the worst is yet to come. "Wars," Banyaca says, "will come like powerful winds. Armies will spread across the land like red ants. According to the prophecies, we must not go out of houses to watch. When these things happen, then will come the final purification." Banyaca is deadly serious when he adds, "We see the signs and omens all around us and our prophecy foretells the outcome."

What will that outcome be? The color red is the third symbol in their prophecy and is identified as the symbol of a people who will be recognized by their red cloaks or hats. Some believe that this symbol, like the swastika and the sun, also represents a great army. Frank Waters, another Hopi elder who has watched the signs for many years, adds an even more startling insight. "These people of the red hat and cloak," he tells us, "will have a huge population. If the Hopi knowledge is rejected the color red will come from the east in the form of an aerial invasion by men who will darken the sky like a locust swarm."

The Hopi knowledge, according to Waters, is contained in secret teachings that the Hopi have now released for the benefit of humanity—"how to protect the earth mother, how to be one with all creatures and how to show gratitude for the gifts of the great spirit. But humanity must accept these teachings in order to help offset the final, great purification."

Given the political complexion of the world today, it is impossible not to look toward China as that great population symbolized by the color red and capable of fielding an army that could fill the sky like a swarm of locusts. But surely there's no connection between the Hopi Indians and China.

Or is there?

It is truly amazing how sometimes the warning voices of seemingly unrelated prophets echo across the centuries from different parts of the world and come together in ways that the seer could not have imagined. According to an eighth century Buddhist prophecy, a time will come when iron birds will fly and horses will run on wheels. When that time comes, the prophecy continues, great sadness will come to the "land of the Red man."

If a Buddhist prophet of the eighth century could in fact see our day, he would surely believe that iron birds can fly. And of course, our horses do run on wheels. (Don't we still classify almost anything that moves according to its "horsepower"?) How could anyone 1,200 years ago imagine such things? And what flight of fancy could conceive of the "land of the Red man" fully 600 years before its discovery?

We are left with several interesting things to contemplate. The warning, remember, also refers to a "great sadness." Is it yet to come? Could it be the great purification the Hopi speak of? Will it be our generation who watches as the army of "red hats" pours from the skies?

Perhaps the question we should be asking is, Has the world accepted the ancient knowledge that the Hopi have tried to share? The answer is discouraging.

Over twenty years ago, the Hopi, along with several other Native American nations, tried to take a petition to the United Nations calling for greater protection of the earth, an end to strip mining, and an end to war. Their petition was never read to the assembly.

According to John Lansa, a Hopi leader, his people have always seen themselves as the guardians of a way of life that values honesty, purity, simplicity, and perseverance. It is a self-image that has been sorely tested the past hundred years, and it is being tested even more today at a place the Hopi call Tukunavi. To the rest of the world, it's known as Black Mesa, the site of a major electrical power plant. "This is the spiritual center of the continent," Lansa says in *Prophets, Psychics, and Seers,* an unreleased television special:

> We were told to keep this land undefiled. The Great Spirit entrusted this land to the Hopi to be tended with prayer and fasting in order that the balance of nature can be preserved for the whole world. It was intended to be a Holy place where all the good people would be protected. But the world's greed for electrical power interferes with Mother Earth and saps her energy. Man is tearing at the very heart of Mother Earth and if this continues nothing can prevent her death throes and the coming of the final purification.

The notion that Black Mesa is the heart of Mother Earth may seem like a primitive metaphor, but Elizabeth Rausher, of the Stanford Research Institute, reports that magnetometric research in that area has detected intense geomagnetic anomalies. Black Mesa does, in fact, support the highest concentration of lightning phenomena on the North American continent. Sadly for the Hopi (and for the rest of us if their prophecies are to be believed) it is also the current site of the largest energy-generating power grid in the entire world—a power grid that, the Hopi say, destroys the natural energy flowing through Black Mesa. According to Lansa,

> There are shrines out there in the spiritual center. They are markers for spiritual routes which extend to the edge of the continent in all four directions. Our ceremonies keep the natural forces together, our prayers go to all parts of the earth. This is the sacred place; it must not have anything wrong in it.

The Hopi prophecies drawn on the rocks in Black Mesa say that there will be paths in the sky, and cobwebs in the air, and a gourd of ashes will be dropped from the sky that will boil the oceans and burn the land, causing nothing to grow for many years. The prophecy also says that humans will travel to the moon and the stars, and then they will know that the time of the great purification is very near.

Humankind's great leap to the moon and continual probing of the nearby planets are already established facts. The Hopi see jet contrails as paths in the sky, and a cobweb of power lines that extends outward from Black Mesa in every direction fulfills that part of the prophecy. Given these realities, they are easily persuaded that the "gourd of ashes" cannot be far behind.

China recently boasted that between her standing army, reserves, and militia, she has an army of 200 million—exactly the size of the army the apostle John tells us will come to do battle in the last days. The Hopi legend suggests that it will be an army that significantly displays the color red that will be the instrument of the great purification. Could the Hopi prophecy, the Buddhist prophecy, and the Book of Revelation all be looking toward the same set of events?

According to Lansa, the Great Spirit said, "I was the first, I will be the last." The Bible records almost the same thought: "I am Alpha and Omega, the beginning and the end, the first and the last." Could the ancient prophets on opposite sides of the world all be tapping into the same source? Or is it something else?

One of the constants of prophecy, regardless of the source, is the basic assumption that time is linear. That is, yesterday happened, today we are engaged in the only activity over which we have any control at all, and tomorrow will eventually come with who knows what. "Time," the old news-reels used to tell us, "marches on." Omar Khayyám's *Rubáiyát* says it this way:

The moving finger writes; and having writ
Moves on: nor all your Piety nor Wit
Shall lure it back to cancel half a line,
Nor all your tears wash out a word of it.

But there are those who question this notion. These theorists suggest that the past, present, and future are all the same: John the Apostle, the ancient

Hopi shamans, Nostradamus, and all those who have peered into the future have simply seen what already *is*.

John William Dunne, a British aeronautical engineer during World War I, wrote a book called *An Experiment with Time*. According to Dunne, this was "the first scientific argument for human immortality." Strange prophetic dreams led him to the conclusion that he was "compelled to perceive . . . large blocks of . . . experience displaced from their proper position in Time."[16] In short, the theory suggests that time is its own entity, separate and apart from all other planes of experience. We do not "pass through," but rather "exist within" time. According to this notion, the past, present, and future are inseparable. We leave one and approach the other much as an airplane takes off from one airport and goes to another. The destination is already there, and we approach it knowing full well there is nothing we can do to change or alter the landscape. The further assumption is that we could go back as well as forward in this realm.

That concept would seem to explain two very different yet similar events that took place in different parts of the world nearly a half century apart. Both involved aircraft. In 1934, Air Marshal Sir Victor Goddard was lost over Scotland in his Hawker Hart biplane. Caught in a heavy storm, he needed a familiar landmark to get his bearings. Dropping down closer to the ground, he began searching for an old abandoned air field he knew of called Drem. If he could find it, he would know exactly where he was. A short time later, he did indeed spot it, but Drem, far from being abandoned, was a bustling military airfield, well lit, even in the storm, with mechanics and other personnel busily servicing a number of bright yellow military aircraft. Surprisingly, no one on the ground paid the slightest attention to his Hawker, even though it was flying low enough to skim the rooftops.

The air marshal was puzzled, but now knowing where he was, lifted back up into the clouds and went on to his original destination. But Goddard had been correct. In 1934, Drem *was* abandoned and run down. Incredibly, however, four years later, in 1938, authorities reopened Drem as an RAF flying school, and sometime between 1934 and 1938, the color of British training planes was changed from silver to yellow. The air marshal, it seems, had taken a little side road four years into the future.

Some forty years later, two amateur pilots, a man and a woman, flying over the Caribbean, also lost their way. Running low on fuel, they headed in the direction of Grand Turk Island, hoping they were not so far off course that they wouldn't be able to see its comparatively large and distinctive shape against the backdrop of the ocean. A short time later, they did in fact spot the island and dropped down, expecting to be able to land and refuel on the airstrip they knew was there. But as they flew over the island, it appeared to them to be totally pristine. They could see no buildings or roads and certainly nothing that looked like an airport.

On the ground, the people heard and saw the plane and tried in vain to contact it by radio. They could hear the two occupants of the plane discussing what they were seeing below, but nothing that the airport manager or tower transmitted got through to the plane's radio. The people on the ground knew from the conversation that the plane was in trouble, but why neither the pilot nor his passenger could hear them they couldn't imagine. What's more, the runway had been carved out of the forest and was easily discernible from the air. Still frantically trying to make radio contact, the people on the ground watched helplessly as the couple turned their craft away and flew into oblivion. This airplane, it seems, had taken a side trip into the past.

Neither event has ever been satisfactorily explained.

This particular theory of time presupposes an unalterable destiny for everyone, something that appears to contradict the notion of free will and an ability to alter present conditions to change future circumstances, which many feel is the whole purpose of prophecy. The opposing view of time, of course, is simply that time, like gravity, exists. It cannot be altered and the events of any given point in time cannot be known until one actually arrives at that point. Prophecy in this context takes the position that people can affect their future if warnings and premonitions that are received (sometimes by ourselves and sometimes by others) are heeded and acted upon. In other words, these strange, psychic gifts have a purpose and value.

Then there are those who seem to be on both sides. Jeane Dixon, quite possibly America's most famous psychic, held the view that those prophecies received through visions were unalterable, and "no power on earth" could change the outcome. On the other hand, she allowed that intuition, premonition, psychic warnings, and precognitive dreams, if heeded and the circumstances changed, could indeed alter the predicted situation.

The ancients, of course, were not troubled by any of this. Time was measured by the rising and setting of the sun and the rumblings of the stomach. But for those, ancient or modern, who see beyond the veil of time, it is a matter of very serious concern. Whether or not it should be of serious concern to the rest of us is one of the things we hope to discover.

Next we consider the last days as seen by the two famous healers we met earlier. Even though they lived 400 years apart, is it possible that they both opened the book of time and turned to the same page?

CHAPTER FOURTEEN

THE TELESCOPE OF TIME

THE YEAR IS 1936. A MIDDLE-AGED MAN, nondescript in appearance and lacking any significant formal education, is preparing himself to go into a trance. In the living room of his home, a small couch for this purpose has been arranged. Several men are seated around the couch and will be permitted to ask questions. Just to the left of his head, a young woman with a stenographer's pad and pencil waits expectantly. She will take down every word. No one in the room is surprised by these arrangements. Edgar Cayce, known far and wide as the sleeping prophet, has been doing this sort of thing for years.

In the early days (some say he began receiving his visions at the age of six), his prophecies were almost always of a healing nature. Someone was ill. The patient would send a letter or sometimes a friend to intervene with Cayce and request a cure. According to his own records, Cayce "treated" some 30,000 patients prior to his death in 1945. Many times the patient wasn't even there. Not infrequently, the person desiring the cure would be hundreds of miles away. Distance proved no barrier to Cayce's remarkable healing ability. He would simply slip into a trance, and with nothing more than a photograph or name to work with, prescribe a cure. If his directions were carefully followed, the person requesting his help invariably got better.

The session today, however, is not to discuss healing. The men present have been engaged in a long and sometimes bitter discussion regarding the "end time," or what biblical scholars refer to as "the last days." As always, the issue is time. When would this period begin? Finding no hint anywhere between Genesis and Revelation, they have determined to put the question to

Mr. Cayce. Having agreed to the session, Edgar Cayce is now preparing to respond to their request.

Cayce loosens his tie and waistcoat and stretches out on the couch, his hands folded comfortably across his chest. The glasses he almost always wear have been placed on a small table next to the couch. The woman standing behind him watches his every move. She will signal to the others when the questioning is to begin.

"I am ready, gentlemen," Cayce informs them. "If you will be so kind as to wait for my wife's signal before asking your questions, I will appreciate it. Please be as quiet as possible, and if you ask your questions one at a time, it will be most helpful."

All eyes are on Mrs. Cayce as she waits for the now-familiar deep and even breathing that signals that the sleeping prophet is in a trance. She looks up at one of the men and nods.

"Mr. Cayce," the first man intones softly, "you have told us that the great changes in the earth, foretold in the Bible, will soon begin to occur. Can you tell us when these changes will begin to be apparent?"

There is a moment of silence. Then in measured tones, Edgar Cayce gives his answer: "When there is the first breaking up of some conditions in the South Pacific and those as apparent in the sinking or rising of that, that is almost opposite same, or in the Mediterranean and the Etna area, then we may know it has begun."

In 1936, the science of plate tectonics was hardly known, and it is quite probable that Cayce's reference to a "breaking up" in the South Pacific and a corresponding sinking or rising in the Mediterranean meant very little to the person asking the question. To a modern geologist, however, that answer would have enormous significance.

We now know that there is a point in the South Pacific where the western boundary of the Pacific plate breaks up to form the southwestern curve of what is popularly known at the "ring of fire" because of the great number of volcanoes that continue to erupt all along this perimeter. According to geologists, an area between the Fiji and Tonga island groupings has always been one of the most seismically active locations on earth. But in 1967 and 1968, something truly extraordinary took place. Massive seismic activity was registered here, so cataclysmic that entire islands appeared and disappeared. Meanwhile, on the other side of the globe, as far back as 1959, a Reuters dispatch from Athens reported that water levels in several Greek harbors had dropped far enough to expose the seabed. And in 1975, Mount Etna itself erupted.

Edgar E. Cayce, the son of the "sleeping prophet," is a retired civil engineer and a lifelong scientist. He tells us: "My father was not a trained geologist. All he knew about earthquakes was that the ground shook. I believe," Mr. Cayce continues, "he was the conduit for an important warning the world needed to hear."

The answer given by the senior Edgar Cayce was carefully recorded, as were all his trance sessions. His words were clear and unmistakable. The changes foretold in the Bible could be said to *begin* with a breaking up in the South Pacific and a raising or lowering at an opposite point in the Mediterranean, even specifying Mount Etna. If, as his son tells us, Cayce knew nothing of geology or plate tectonics, then how could he know, some thirty-five years ahead of time, that all of this would take place? Is it possible that the earth is even now undergoing the great changes spoken of in the Bible? Did the prediction by Edgar Cayce actually pinpoint when it began? According to his son, "Based on what geologists now know, my own judgment is the great earth changes of which my father and the Bible speaks probably began around 1960."

A word here before we proceed.

We realize that it is always risky in a work dealing with the paranormal to mix the prophets of the Bible with the secular psychics and prophets. The risk, of course, is that you can very easily offend everyone. On the one hand, those who read and love the Bible are likely to feel that the book and prophets mentioned are being trivialized. On the other hand, those who reject the Bible's sacred origins will contend that such references have no place in a work that pretends to be objective.

There is, however, a third view: The prophecies recorded in the Bible cannot be ignored simply because the prophets claimed that their inspiration came from God. In fact, there is sufficient archaeological evidence to strongly suggest that these prophets wrote when they said they wrote and the fulfillment of their predictions occurred at the approximate times recorded in the Bible. It would therefore be both unwise and unfair to suggest that prophecies uttered and recorded in, say, 700 B.C. and fulfilled to the letter seven centuries later should not be considered simply because God is claimed as the source of inspiration. This view also rejects the notion that comparisons with modern psychics trivialize the biblical prophets. Indeed, the exact opposite may be true. It should not be forgotten that many prophets not associated with the Bible (including Edgar Cayce) have claimed the same source for their inspiration.

Hoping, therefore, to offend no one, but eager to present the widest possible view of prophets, psychics, and seers, let us go on.

Taken in the context of the question asked Edgar Cayce in 1936, and assuming that subsequent geological events have proven him correct and could those events in fact be the beginning of the "end time"? Using 1960 as a benchmark, as we look down the telescope of time, has anything happened in the past thirty-eight years to suggest that things are progressing according to the biblical schedule of events? For example, Ezekiel, Daniel, and John all speak of "earthquakes in divers places." There have always been earthquakes, of course, but is there evidence that these events are increasing in number?

According to Hal Lindsey, minister, lecturer, and author of the best-selling book *The Late Great Planet Earth,* the increase has been both specific and dramatic:

> In each decade from 1890 to 1960, we averaged 2 to 3 major earthquakes per decade. In the decade of the 60s alone there were 15 major earthquakes. In the decade of the 70s, 54 major earthquakes were recorded around the world and in the decade of the 80s, 86 earthquakes wrecked havoc upon citizens of the world. From 2 to 3 every ten years to 86 is an enormous difference.

We are, of course, on the slippery slope of assumption if we base all of our conclusions on the utterances of just one psychic. There have been other seers that have looked at our time, some of them through a much longer lens. For example, there are those who are convinced that the "last days" will begin with the end of the papacy—that is, a literal end to the office of the pope. One of these "prophets" was a pious Catholic priest named Malachi O'Morgain. Father Malachi lived nearly a thousand years ago in Ireland and led a small congregation in the village of Bangor.

Sometime during his stewardship, no one knows quite when, Malachi O'Morgain wrote what has become known as the "papal prophecy." In this astonishing work, he named every pope, in succession, from 1134 to what he describes as the "last pope." That last pope, according to the prophecy, will be the one elevated to the papacy when the College of Cardinals gather on the death of the present pope.

But the world might never have known about this remarkable prophecy if Father Malachi hadn't decided to make a pilgrimage to Rome in 1155. It is a story worth repeating because it demonstrates that not all prophets or seers seek or desire notoriety.

On the day Father Malachi was set to depart on his pilgrimage, a cold wind blew in from the Irish sea and brought with it pelting drops of freezing rain that turned the ungainly ruts in the road into a long, continuous puddle of ice. Father Malachi opened one of the shutters in the small stone chapel that served as his home and office as well as a house of worship and looked out at the bleak landscape. For a moment he thought of postponing his trip until later in the spring, but he quickly put it out of his mind. He couldn't explain the sudden sense of urgency that compelled him to undertake such a long and arduous journey, but there was no denying that the urgency was there.

Father Malachi closed the shutter and turned back to the travel bag on the table that stood against the wall. He took one more hand-spun wool shirt from the chest at the foot of the bed and put it in the bag.

"Do you need some help, Father?" His traveling companions were obviously anxious to get started. It would be bad enough traveling in this weather in the daytime. They did not want to get stranded someplace between villages after dark.

"No, no thank you," Father Malachi replied through the closed door. "I'll only be a moment more."

The priest took one last look around the small and sparsely furnished room, tied the bag, and started to leave. He was about to lift the latch on the door when something made him stop. Turning back into the room, he placed the bag on the table and turned to the one bookshelf in the room. Carefully he began to remove some books.

"The mules are loaded father. We need your bag."

"Yes, yes, I'll just be a moment."

Father Malachi removed several sheets of parchment from their hiding place behind the books. He glanced at them briefly, then lifted his eyes to heaven as if in prayer. A moment later, he rolled the sheets of parchment tightly and bound them with a strip of cloth. Gently placing them under an article of clothing in the top of his bag, he hurried out the door.

Several days later, Father Malachi and his traveling companions were seated around the large table in the dining hall of the priory of Clairvaux. Father Bernhard, the abbot of Clairvaux, was an old friend of Father Malachi and had looked forward to his coming.

"It is a long journey from Bangor to Rome, Malachi. How are you bearing up?"

"Mostly on the backs of my good companions I fear, Father. We have looked forward to Clairvaux and your hospitality."

Malachi might have wanted to say more, but he was interrupted by a violent siege of coughing. Obviously, the journey had been very difficult for him.

"Are you all right, old friend?" Father Bernhard asked, genuinely concerned for the priest's welfare.

"I think a good night's sleep in one of your warm rooms, Bernhard, and I will be fine."

Father Malachi smiled weakly and started to rise, but the strength in his legs suddenly failed him and he collapsed to the floor. Grasping the chair next to him, he tried to rise but was seized by another spasm of coughing and slipped back onto the floor.

"Father Malachi, let me help you," Bernhard cried as he rushed to his side. In a moment, Malachi's traveling companions were also bending over him, and between them they got the weary priest to his feet.

"This way," Father Bernhard told them. "We will take him to my chamber."

The following morning, Father Malachi awoke to the first streaks of light streaming through the stained glass window in Father Bernhard's bedchamber. For a moment, he didn't realize where he was, but slowly the events of the previous evening came back to him. Suddenly he sat upright. His bag. Where was his bag? Anxiously he glanced around the room until his eyes fell upon it. The bag had been placed on the floor near the door to the chamber. Slowly he started to get up and retrieve it, but even this small effort resulted in another spasm of coughing. Gasping for air, he fell back against the pillows.

In a large chair near the fireplace, Father Bernhard was awakened by the coughing. He had spent the night sitting up with his old friend, bathing his fevered brow with cool water. Only when Malachi slept would Bernhard steal a few moments of sleep in the chair. He was at Malachi's side in a heartbeat.

"Don't waste your strength, old friend. I am here and you must rest."

Malachi pointed at his bag sitting on the floor, but there was not strength enough in his body to form words.

"What is it, Malachi?" Bernhard asked. He turned to look where his friend was pointing. "Your bag? Is it your bag you want?"

Malachi nodded, and Bernhard quickly retrieved it and placed it on the bed near his friend. With Father Bernhard's help, they managed to get it open, and Father Malachi reached in and carefully removed the roll of parchment sheets. Beckoning to Bernhard to come closer, Malachi handed him the sheets and whispered, "You must keep these pages close to your heart. What is on them I know to be true. It came to me here in Clairvaux the last time I visited. Guard them well I pray you." Exhausted from the effort, Father Malachi collapsed back against the pillows.

Malachi O'Morgain never made it to Rome. According to the church historians, he died in the arms of Bernhard, Bishop of Clairvaux.

We can only guess at what went through the mind of the good bishop as he read the names on the list. And it is not known whether Father Malachi asked Father Bernhard to withhold the prophecy or not. What is known is that it went unpublished until 1595, when it was discovered in the Vatican archives and included in a larger work. It is interesting to note also that both Malachi and Bernhard were elevated to sainthood by the Catholic Church.

Since its publication, the papal prophecy (which ends, remember, with the end of just one more papal administration following the present one) has been compared to the predictions of Nostradamus, whose forecasts and warnings have had much to say about various popes. But to look into these prophecies, we will have to fast-forward another 400 years.

In one of his most famous papal visions, Nostradamus, at the time a physician and fortune-teller to the queen of France, was walking along a muddy road when he saw several monks approaching. He stepped aside to let them pass, but as one of the youngest of the group, a newly ordained cleric by the name of Peretti, drew abreast of him, Nostradamus dropped to one knee and bowed his head low.

"What is this?" exclaimed one of the monks. "Does Nostradamus mock us? Why do you bow before brother Peretti?"

"I must yield and bend a knee before his holiness," Nostradamus replied, touching the hem of the young monk's robe.

"You must be mistaken, sir," a slightly embarrassed Peretti replied. "The Lord has only recently delivered me from a pig sty."

Nostradamus, according to the historians, stood up slowly, his eyes never leaving those of Peretti. "Nevertheless," he said solemnly, "one must give honor where it is due."

The monks laughed, and one of them slapped the young monk on the back. "Well what do you think of that, brother Peretti? The queen's own fortune-teller says a swineherd will be pope."

Nostradamus, it is said, ignored the mocking and continued on his way. It is not recorded what became of the other monks, but forty-five years later, nineteen years after the death of Nostradamus, the lowly swineherd, Felice Peretti, became Pope Sixtus V.

So we have an Irish bishop, now a saint, who lived in the twelfth century and a French physician and astrologer who lived in the sixteenth century, both leaving written documents predicting that from this point in time, there will be only two popes. Some have suggested that Nostradamus must have read the papal prophecy and published his own version to correspond to it. The difficulty with that explanation is that Nostradamus published his own papal predictions in 1555, a good forty years before the publication of the papal prophecy. Furthermore, it is unlikely that Nostradamus could have had access to such an obscure and little-regarded document. Besides, there is no record of Nostradamus ever having visited the Vatican.

But what exactly did these two very religious Catholics have to say about the future papacy?

Well, both of them describe John Paul I as "the Moon," and John Paul II as "the works of the Sun." But it is their agreement on the events surrounding the last pope that is particularly striking, even down to the name. Malachi is expansive in his description and very clear: "Peter, the Roman will lead his sheep to pasture in the midst of numerous tribulations. The City of Seven Hills will be destroyed. The twilight settles, indeed, the depth of night before the promised dawn." Nostradamus, characteristically couches his predictions in more obscure terms, referring to the last pope as "the Rock" of the church, which, according to Catholic teaching, is "Peter." Both prophets agree, however, that there will be great tribulations and that a man named Peter will be elected and serve as the last pope. Nostradamus, in one of his more forthright quatrains, puts it this way:

Oh vast Rome,
your ruin is approaching.
Not that of your walls
but of your lifeblood substance.

We should perhaps note here that Nostradamus places these events in or around the year 2024, giving us twenty-six years instead of just two to either prepare for the course of world events, or try to change them.

But having brought Nostradamus back into the conversation, let's take a closer look into what this amazing man had to say about the future of humankind. He is (apart from the prophets of the Old Testament) the most famous of all those who have taken it upon themselves to look into the future. His *Centuries* has been published in at least eighty languages. His range of prophecy extends from one side of the globe to the other and from his own day to the end of the world. Except for the Bible, the Nostradamus books of mystic predictions are the oldest and most sought after books still in print. There are, in fact, those who suggest that his predictions concerning our day might well be the most useful of all time if we can just learn to decipher them correctly.

What is there in the history of this man, apart from the startling accuracy of his predictions, that so captivates the entire world? Why are experts trying so desperately to uncover the meaning of the quatrains that look through the telescope of time and focus directly on us? It is fair to say that Nostradamus was much more than a fortune-teller to the court and a favorite of the queen. Long before his psychic abilities became known, he had been renowned as a physician of great skill and bravery.

Nostradamus was born Michel de Nostredame on December 23, 1503 (by the old Gregorian calendar) in the province of St. Rémy, in France. He was born into what had been a prominent Jewish family, but in September 1501, King Louis XII issued an edict that required everyone to either convert to Catholicism or leave Provence. The family converted.

Nostradamus, by all accounts, never made any secret of his Christian piety, fully embracing the Catholic Church throughout his life. But by the same token, he never rejected his Jewish heritage, which, traced through his mother, made him a member of the lost tribe of Issachar, the tribe that could read the moon and stars and interpret the heavens. Whether or not that is true, he was fascinated by the study of astrology from a very early age.

By the time he was twenty-one, Michel de Nostredame (he was not yet using the latinized form of his name) had been given a license to practice as a physician. Because the rigors of attaining such a lofty goal were much more pronounced then than they are today, the achievement speaks volumes about both his intelligence and his stamina. His courage would soon be tested during one of history's most devastating episodes, the ravages of the great plague of 1546.

Nostradamus refused the magic coat of seven colors that was believed to protect physicians from the diseases they treated. Instead, he proceeded to go among the people hardest hit by the disease with what, for the day, were some very unorthodox methods. Nostradamus would throw back the dingy curtains and let in fresh air and sunlight. He insisted that any standing water be thrown out and only fresh water brought to the patient. His "antics" angered many in his profession, but his success at curing patients was undeniable. Prescriptions for his own unique cures were published in 1552. By the time his book of cures was published, he had been authorized to wear the black, four-cornered cap of the D.Phil. (today's Ph.D.) for twenty years. He would wear it proudly all of his life.

Nostradamus was given his doctor's title and doctor's cap, October 23, 1529, and was offered a teaching position at Montpellier, which he occupied for about a year, but some strange wanderlust urged him to move on. He traveled the countryside, practicing for a while in Bordeaux, La Rochelle, and Toulouse. Then one day he received an invitation from the renowned international philosopher Julius Caesar Scaliger to stay at his home in Agen. There, embraced by all the physical and intellectual comforts, Nostradamus seemed to settle down. He met and married a beautiful and highborn young lady who gave him two lovely children, a son and a daughter. Life, it seemed, was complete.

Unfortunately, the plague eventually found its way to Agen, and all of the skill that had proven so successful elsewhere failed him when his own family contracted the dread disease. His young wife and two children died. The loss sent Nostradamus wandering the countryside once again, and eventually he arrived in Salon. Here he married again, a rather well-off widow, who gave him six children, the oldest of which he named Caesar. And here begins the public awareness of Nostradamus's prophetic gifts.

For many years, the young physician had entertained the gentry with small demonstrations of his psychic ability. One of the more famous stories is particularly revealing, since it puts Nostradamus in a seemingly impossible situation. It is the tale of two pigs.

Nostradamus, so the story goes, was invited to the home of a particular nobleman who, having heard of his peculiar abilities, was determined to expose him as a fake. Upon Nostradamus's arrival, the nobleman pointed out two piglets, a black one and a white one.

"Can you tell us what fate will befall these two little fellows?" he asked mockingly.

Without hesitation, Nostradamus replied, "The white one will be eaten by a wolf, we will eat the black one."

The nobleman then instructed his cook to prepare the white one for their dinner that evening and told him to make sure there was no mistake. Dutifully, the cook killed and began to prepare the white piglet, but a wolf cub belonging to one of the servants made off with the main course. The cook, in a panic, quickly killed and prepared the black one instead.

Later that evening during the course of the dinner, the nobleman, secure in the knowledge that his cook would not dare go against his wishes, pointed out to Nostradamus that the company was eating the white pig, and that Nostradamus was therefore no prophet. Nostradamus politely but firmly insisted that they were dining on the black pig.

"Is that so," said the nobleman. Turning to one of the servants, he ordered him to bring in the cook.

Upon entering, the terrified cook admitted that, indeed, the black pig was the main course that evening and further confirmed the rest of Nostradamus's prediction—that a wolf had, in fact, made off with the white one. Silence hung heavy in the air as the nobleman, somewhat chagrined, glanced over at Nostradamus, who lifted his knife and with a smile said, "My compliments to the chef."

For some reason, the birth of Nostradamus's first son from his second marriage was the occasion for putting frivolous things behind him. Most historians believe that Nostradamus had been having his apocalyptic visions for some time, but had chosen to keep them secret. In a remarkable letter to his infant son, Nostradamus tells him, and us, why he felt it important to do that:

Although I have often foretold long before what has afterward come to pass, and in particular regions, acknowledging all to have been done by divine virtue and inspiration, I was willing to hold my peace by reason of the injury—not only of the present time but also of the future—because to put them in writing, the Kingdoms, Sects and Regions shall be so diametrically opposed, that if

I should relate what shall happen hereafter, those of the present Reign, Sect, Religion and Faith, would find it so disagreeing with their fancies, that they would condemn that which future ages shall find and know to be true. Consider also the saying of our Savior, *"Such alone as are inspired by the divine power can predict particular events in a spirit of prophecy."*

Nostradamus, as we pointed out earlier, was no fool. He knew what the reactions of the people around him would be. His reason for deliberate confusion bears repeating. Looking toward a time when his son would be old enough and wise enough to ask, he added in his letter:

For this reason, I have withheld my tongue from the vulgar and my pen from paper. But afterwards, I was willing for the common good to enlarge myself in dark and abstruse sentences, declaring the future events, chiefly the most urgent and those which I foresaw, (whatever human mutation happened), would not offend the hearers, all under dark figures, more than prophetical.

Nostradamus gives us several important insights in this letter, which was obviously intended for his son's edification and perhaps even protection at some later date. He tells us that he has been having prophetic visions for a long time but has kept them a secret for fear of reprisals, which would seem to indicate that he knew things about the current regimes that they wouldn't like. He tells us that even if his contemporaries disagree with his prophecies, "future ages shall find and know [them] to be true." And he also gives us what he believes to be the source of his amazing gift: "Such alone as are inspired by the divine power" can prophesy.

Finally, he tells his son that he decided to publish his prophecies for "the common good," but even here, there is a feeling of trepidation. Nostradamus felt it essential that he obscure the meaning of his verses in "dark and abstruse sentences." In that he certainly succeeded. Scholars have argued over the meaning of his quatrains for centuries, and even today, many of the quatrains—perhaps as many as a thousand—remain a complete mystery. Some, however, like those cited earlier, are quite clear. And some become clear only after the event takes place. For example, the following quatrain had been a complete enigma to experts for 450 years, until the ill-fated flight of the space shuttle *Challenger:*

> Nine will be set apart from the human flock, separated from
> judgment and counsel. Their fate to be determined on departure.
> The unripe fruit will be the source of great scandal
> Great blame. To the other, great praise.

The notion that someone in the sixteenth century could foresee the explosion of a spaceship staggers the mind. Yet there are those who believe that Nostradamus was just playing a cosmic practical joke on his contemporaries. If that's true, then his predictions about submarines, aircraft, mechanized warfare, and the rise and fall of governments—including names of people and places—were all just lucky guesses. We find that harder to believe than the predictions.

That being the case, what did Nostradamus have to say about our day beyond his prediction of the end of the papacy? Adding to a long list of things that most of us would like to ignore, Nostradamus saw the twentieth century ending with a worldwide plague, the worst in history, even threatening the ability of the world to reproduce. He saw the earth itself in a mad turmoil of natural disasters. He prophesied that the anti-Christ would arise out of the confusion and violence in the Middle East and delude the world into a massive confrontation that could bring on global war.

All of that will sound vaguely familiar to those acquainted with the Book of Revelation. But Nostradamus, as he did from time to time, also got very specific. In three separate references in the letter, he appears to have forecast the destruction of New York City:

1. "Earthshaking fire [which] will cause tremors around the New City."
2. "The sky will burn at 45 degrees, fire approaches the Great New City."
3. "King will want to enter the New City."

Earthquake? Invasion? Perhaps a combination of both. Nostradamus appears to be convinced that the entire nation will ultimately be involved in a cataclysmic third world war.

All of which, interestingly enough, brings us back to Edgar Cayce. In 1936, the same year he predicted the beginning of the "end time," Cayce had an apocalyptic vision of the destruction that would come upon the world sometime between the year 2000 and the year 2100. In this vision, Cayce said he had been reborn in the year 2100. He still retained the knowledge of his life, but he was apparently on some sort of scientific mission. Flying across the land in an odd-shaped craft at fantastic speeds, he and the other scientists with him landed among the ruins of what had been a great city, then in the process of being rebuilt. When he asked the name of the place, he was told it *had been* New York City.

But that was not the end of the vision. He also saw massive changes in the United States and the world. Nebraska had become the West Coast after massive earthquakes toppled the western half of the nation into the Pacific Ocean. Los Angeles and San Francisco no longer existed. Alabama was partly under water. Much of Japan was likewise submerged. And great upheavals had altered, almost beyond recognition, all of northern Europe. Meanwhile, new lands had appeared in both the Atlantic and Pacific Oceans.[1]

Thus, in 1936, Edgar Cayce joined a long list of prophets, psychics and seers going back hundreds, even thousands, of years who have foreseen almost universal destruction of the world somewhere around the year 2000.

But it is not only individuals who are involved with prophecy and predictions. Entire kingdoms and cultures have been known to invest the future of their people on the word of their prophets and seers. Astonishingly, more often than not, the prophets were correct.

Chapter Fifteen

The Fate of Nations

In the ancient world, the Druids where known as the "race of oracles." All the great cities of Persia, Greece, and the Roman Empire had their Druid seers, who were considered far superior in foretelling the future than even the fabled magi of Persia. Julius Caesar, as did most Roman generals, kept the same personal Druid seer with him throughout the Gallic wars. And it was another Druid seer, Vestricius Spurrina, that tried to warn the imperial Roman of his fateful day.

Caesar was perfectly willing to listen to the seers and even plan battles according to their visions, but when it came to his own personal safety, he apparently just laughed it off.

"Well, old Vestricius," Caesar chided him, "what do you say of your dire warnings now? As you can see, the ides of March have come and I am none the worse."

"Aye, Caesar," the old Druid replied, "the ides of March has come but it has not yet gone."

Later that very day, as every student knows, Caesar was struck down by those closest to him, including his beloved Brutus. His dying words, "Et tu, Brute" ("You too, Brutus"), have become synonymous with treachery.

Unquestionably, however, the most famous of all Druid seers was the man called Merlin. For many years relegated to the land of myth and legends, Merlin was regarded as no more than a figment of some fertile imagination. There was no Camelot; ergo, there was no Merlin.

But Merlin, it turns out, was very real. A Welsh Druid priest, he was known far and wide for his remarkable prophecies, many of them as far-ranging as those of Nostradamus nearly a thousand years later. Seven long centuries before there was a conquering Islamic people known as the Saracens, and long before a unified kingdom had emerged out of the impenetrable English mists, Merlin wrote this incredible prophecy:

> The Lionheart will 'gainst the Saracen rise
> and purchase from him many a glorious prize.
> But whilst abroad these great acts shall be done,
> all things at home shall to disorder run.
> Cooped up and caged the Lion then shall be
> But after sufferance ransomed and set free.
> Last, by a poisonous shaft shall the Lion die.

Seven hundred years later, Richard the Lionheart fought against the Saracens. While he was gone, his brother John usurped the throne, and the Barons forced him to sign the Magna Carta. There was so much disorder in England that only a Robin Hood could save it. Unfortunately, Robin Hood *was* just a legend.

Actually, Richard was not a very good executive. He spent little more than nine months of his entire reign at home as a working king. He was, in fact, taken captive on his way home from the Crusades and ransomed out of Austria. During the siege of Limoges Castle, which his forces took, he was struck by a poisoned arrow and died three days later. Merlin's prophecy had been fulfilled to the very letter. For hundreds of years, the fate of England was there for all who dared look. Yet, Merlin disappeared into the mists of myth, and no one, it seems, paid any attention to what he had to say, least of all Richard the Lionheart.

The English have always had their fair share of prophets and seers, and not all of them have been men. One of the most beloved of all English seers was Mother Shipton, a remarkable woman who is still revered to this day.

Mother Shipton was born in Yorkshire about 1488. Her mother's name was Agatha Southill. Her father is unknown; he was a mystery figure that legends say was more than mortal. Some even suggest that he was not of this world, a notion that might fit nicely into some of today's UFO theories. In any case, he disappeared soon after his daughter was born. Agatha named the child Ursala, left the infant to the parish, and joined a convent, where she soon died.

Ursala was not a terribly attractive little girl, but she was unusually bright. Unfortunately, as with many orphans, the very fact that she was different was enough to elicit spiteful and taunting cruelties from the other children. Something of a celebrity among the villagers because of the strange circumstances surrounding her parentage, Ursala also got more than her share of attention from the folks in the town. It was not long before they discovered that she was "different" in many ways. She had, it was whispered, inherited some of her father's supposed powers.

Ursala was twenty-four years old when she was courted by an ordinary country lad named Tobias Shipton. They were married and began what would turn out to be a short but extraordinary life together. Tobias was apparently a good provider, but he didn't live very long. Upon his death, instead of the usual "Widow Shipton," for some reason everyone referred to her as "Mother Shipton," an appellation that has remained to this day.

Mother Shipton soon became a favorite of the community. She had an uncanny ability to predict things that would shortly come to pass: the weather, the best time for planting, or sudden freaks of nature. She never failed to correctly predict the sex of an unborn child and what, if any, problems would occur during the birthing. She was still a young woman when her fame reached such heights that even the nobility and the gentry were beating a path to her door. Nothing was too important or too trivial to ask her to divine. Among other things, she had the sibylline gift for seeing alternate futures. Many marriage contracts were either made or avoided because of her vision of what the couple's future would be.

As might be expected, the local clergy, always suspicious of such gifts, found her activities suspect and resented the attention she was getting. But Mother Shipton proved equal to the occasion. She could be brash in both her opinions and her predictions. For example, Cardinal Bishop Wolsey, rich, vain, and ostentatious, was the most powerful man in the realm, save only the king. It was never wise to offend him, and he was easily offended. Upon hearing that the cardinal was intent on moving his residence to York, Mother Shipton offered the following:

> The mitered peacock shall now begin to plume himself and his train will make a great show in the world. He will want to make his residence in ancient York with pomp and parades. See York, he shall but he shall not enter it.

The good cardinal was so annoyed when he heard her prophecy that he dispatched three of his knights to threaten her with the stake if she repeated it. The knights, however, proved to be more interested in hearing Mother Shipton clarify the prophecy than in menacing her about it, though one of them did tell her that Wolsey would surely burn her as a witch if she continued in this vein.

"He knows well I am not a witch," Mother Shipton replied. Taking a handkerchief from her bosom, she tossed it into the fireplace. "So far as burning goes," she said, nodding toward the handkerchief, "if this burns so shall I." The knights stared in wonder as a few moments later Mother Shipton removed the handkerchief from the flames without so much as a scorch mark.

Sometime later, Cardinal Wolsey and his entourage arrived in the village of Carwood, from where they could see the fabled spires of York. Unfortunately, the good bishop was arrested there for treason and died on the way to his own execution in London. Just as Mother Shipton predicted, he never entered York.

As her fame spread throughout England, she widened her prophetic range and began to prophesy about great political and international events. Her many historical prophecies began with Henry VIII's invasion of France in an alliance with the German emperor, Maximilian I. She wrote:

> English Harry and his German ally will win the field from the French though their resistance be gallant. The dull horse of the north will bring

confusion and shame on the enemy, though not through its intention. Confusion and not courage wins the field and the day.

History, of course, confirms that Henry VIII did invade France with the aid of the German emperor Maximilian. What is not so well known is that the fighting was basically a standoff until Henry's mount was struck accidentally and bolted headlong toward the French lines. The cavalry, thinking that the king was leading a charge, galloped after him. The French forces broke and were defeated. Indeed, just as Mother Shipton prophesied, it was confusion, not courage, that saved the day.

In Mother Shipton's day, the "divine right" of kings was beyond question. The king was the anointed of God, his kingship sacred. Even to touch the king in anger was not just treason—it was sacrilege. Yet, Mother Shipton predicted the rise of the commoner Oliver Cromwell, who would seize the English government and behead its divinely appointed king more than 150 years into the future. Her predictions for the British Empire, in fact, remain startling reading even today. She saw the British flag in India, Africa, and the unknown wilderness of the recently discovered land of America. But perhaps the most intriguing of her visions was of the coming industrial age and the birth of mass transportation. Not only did she describe automobiles and railroad trains; she predicted their routes, where the roads and tracks would (and ultimately did) run. She even pinpointed the cities that would spring up along these routes with uncanny accuracy.

In an age when she could easily have been accused of witchcraft and suffered the penalties for that crime, she was instead admired and respected. She left behind a remarkable number of predictions that were still being fulfilled 200 years after her death. Not incidentally, she also predicted the date and place of her own death precisely. And we should perhaps take note of the fact that she warned future generations that the end of the world would come 400 and some years after her death. That should make it right around the year 2000 if she is right—again.

The Gaelic people of the remote Hebrides Islands have always taken the gift of prophecy pretty much for granted. Second sight, as it is sometimes called, is only remarkable when it is missing. Everyone, they believe, has a touch of it. Even today, there's scarcely a family that doesn't boast of an enchanted relative or two—all of which makes the gift possessed by Kenneth Odhar even more wondrous. His abilities were so superior that he was referred to simply as "the seer" by the islanders.

As with Mother Shipton, there are any number of legends surrounding his birth and the source of his prophetic powers. In all likelihood, however, he was born to poor parents and orphaned very young. There is ample evidence that he worked as a common farm laborer and shepherd until a grown man.

But somewhere in the course of his growing up, Odhar discovered the strength of his gift. A loner by nature and close to no one, he avoided the company of people whenever he could. He seemed to prefer the Highland glens of the misty isles, where even today the last vestiges of the ancient Druids can be found. It is not too surprising, then, that in the seventeenth century, many people believed that Kenneth Odhar was a reincarnation of the great Merlin.

Odhar was still a young man when he learned that prophecy could pay handsomely. He was unquestionably the best, and he charged accordingly. That he never worked another day in his life after the age of twenty is strong evidence that he made his gift pay very well indeed. Everyone, it seemed, had need of his service at one time or another. To the sheepman he might say: "Put no flocks on the west slopes of Galamoor before June. Ice storms in May will kill the lambs." Invariably, whatever he told them proved to be true. To the fisherman his advice might be: "Sail due west for three days and north for two. You'll find the haddock swimming there five days and no more." Fishermen from a dozen parishes refused to put out to sea without a scrying from Odhar.

Few marriages were made without consulting the seer: "If you give the girl in marriage to Donneal, she will be back upon you, a bairn in arms, big with another and the dowry gone and spent." Such a scrying would, of course, doom poor Donneal to searching for a bride elsewhere.

It is also a fact that Odhar was consulted about sickness and death more often than the local doctor. One famous prophecy read: "Care more for your father and less for what he'll leave. A grave you hurry him toward may be waiting for you as well." It is widely believed that the old man was afforded much greater attention and far greater care after Odhar uttered those words to a wavering son.

By the age of twenty-five, Odhar, the Brahan seer, as he was now called, had come to the attention of the nobility on the mainland. This was both good and bad for Odhar. His very nature pitted him against an aristocracy that he actively disliked. On the other hand, he did very much like their money, and he charged them according to their lofty station. In this strange love-hate relationship, he bordered on being scornful, even contemptuous of his "betters." But in the beginning, at least, his fame and his incredible abilities put him beyond the reach of such petty resentments.

In the meantime, his prophecies continued to pour forth, many of them completely indecipherable to his contemporaries. Who among them, for example, could have imagined water mains and gas lines under the streets 200 years into the future when he said, "Water and what becomes fire, streams under every street of Inverness." Or which of the noblemen of the day would have nodded with understanding when, like Mother Shipton, he spoke of the coming of railroads and automobiles: "Coaches made of iron and glass make great noise, smoke and smells in the streets and move by invisible means." It is likely that Odhar himself little understood the visions he received.

Unlike Mother Shipton, however, who made many friends with her prophecies, Kenneth Odhar made none. The surly and often insolent Brahan seer was respected, even feared, in some quarters, but it all combined to bring him to an untimely end. It also left us with his most enduring and haunting prophecy.

The Earl of Seaforth had been in France far longer than his wife deemed necessary. She feared for his safety and summoned Odhar to tell her what had befallen her husband. Odhar would tell her only that the earl was safe, but that wasn't good enough for the grand dame. She insisted on knowing more. Odhar stubbornly refused, telling her that there were some things better left unknown. This was too much. The haughty lady cursed and threatened this insolent bumpkin. She scorned him for a liar and threatened to have him thrown into the dungeons.

It was probably the slur on his gift that finally broke the barrier between his sense of propriety and the hatred he held for the nobility. But whatever the reason, Odhar suddenly changed his mind. He would, he said, tell the lady everything—which he did, and probably with a certain vindictive delight. The earl was in no danger, he told her; he was having a love affair in Paris and was simply in no hurry to return to the Highlands.

The countess, already infuriated, flew into a rage. She had Odhar indicted as a heretic and practioner of black magic. His longtime enemies in the church quickly condemned him solely on the basis of her charges. He was to be executed by being lowered feetfirst into a vat of boiling tar.

Odhar probably couldn't believe what was happening to him. His visions had never been questioned or gone unrewarded. But by the time the arrogant seer finally realized that the countess had doomed him to a horrible death, it was too late for repentance. The Brahan seer made one last, terrible prophecy:

> Then look to the end of the house of Seaforth. The lady who is stained with infidelity and murder leaves from her high place to follow on my heels into darkness. Before many generations this line will end in shame and contempt. The last chief will become deaf and speechless, father of four sons, they will all go before him into the grave. A white-hooded lassie from the east inherits all and she shall kill her sister. The last of the Seaforths will have for neighbors, short Gairloch, Chisolm the Fat, Grant the coward and stuttering Ramsey. By these signs know the Seaforths are no more.

The Earl of Seaforth returned on the day of Odhar's execution. He was horrified by his wife's actions, telling her that Odhar had not lied, but alas, it was too late to save the Brahan seer. It was not too late for Odhar's final prophecy to begin unfolding, however. Within six months, despised and put away by her husband, the countess did indeed leave her high place. She leaped from the parapet of the castle to her death.

For the next three generations, trouble and misfortune plagued the house of Seaforth. The last Earl of Seaforth lost his hearing and his speech as the result of scarlet fever in his adolescence. He had four sons, who, just as

Odhar predicted, preceded him in death. The white-hooded lady from the east was Lady Hood, the eldest daughter. She was wearing the traditional white of widowhood when she returned from India to settle the estate. During her stay, the buggy she was driving suddenly lost a wheel and overturned, killing her only sister.

But even more astonishing, perhaps, is the almost trivial matter of the neighbors. The records indicate that the four closest associates of the last Earl of Seaforth were "little" Sir Hector McKenzie of Gairloch; Chisolm of Chisolm, who was reportedly too heavy to ride in an ordinary carriage; Grant of Grant, who had run away in battle; and the Earl of Ramsey, who is known to have had a speech impediment. The Brahan seer had foreseen it all on his dying day two centuries before.

Kenneth Odhar's most enigmatic prophecy still remains to be fulfilled. He said that a dun and hornless cow will emerge from the waters off Carr Point with such a bellow as will knock off all six chimneys from Gairloch house, and added, "Afterwards all life will be extinguished by a horrid black rain." In Odhar's time, Gairloch house had a thatched roof and no chimneys. Today it has six. And there is a nuclear submarine base in Holy Loch nearby. Most Highlanders believe that the prophecy may well prove true in the "year with the most eyes"—the year A.D. 2000. The moving finger does indeed continue to write, and the countdown to the year 2000 persists.

Whether or not the Brahan seer was the reincarnated Merlin is open to question. We do know, however, that Merlin's influence was felt far beyond his own time. Almost a thousand years before the actual event, Merlin prophesied that "a marvelous maid will come from Nemus Canutum to free France and make a healing of nations." Translated, Nemus Canutum means "oak grove." Sometime in or near the year 1412, a baby girl was born to one Jacques d'Arc. He named her Jeanne. Just behind his farm stood an oak grove.

It might be expected that the world would forget such an obscure prophecy after nearly a thousand years. But barely thirty years before Jeanne d'Arc's (Joan of Arc) birth, the famous prophetess Marie d'Avignon dreamed of arms and armor while being told by voices that they were for "a maid who should restore France."

The life of Joan of Arc, the Maid of Orléans, was, it appears, preordained. But the prophetic dreams did not end there. When Joan was eleven years old, her father dreamed that he saw her leaving home, dressed in armor and accompanied by soldiers.

Nevertheless, Joan was a quiet and obedient girl, even though she was raised with three boisterous brothers. Then, at age thirteen, she had her own prophetic experience. Alone in the fields with her family's small herd of sheep, Joan heard a loud clap of thunder come from a cloudless sky. Terrified, she fell to her knees. But then a voice, clear and unmistakable, spoke to her: "Lift up your head Joan and hear my words."

She was told that she had been chosen to do marvelous deeds that would loose the chains from France and that she would live to see the Dauphin consecrated her king. She was also told that she would wear the clothes of men and put armor upon herself.

"You will go forth," the voice said, "and become a captain in war."

It is difficult to imagine what must have gone through the mind of a thirteen-year-old girl in the early fifteenth century when told she would become, not just a soldier, but "a captain in war." Such a thing was totally unheard of. Yet, over the next four years, Joan repeatedly heard the voices that she came to identify as Michael, the archangel, Saint Catherine, and Saint Margaret, among others.

By the time Joan was seventeen, France was in tatters. The English and their allies besieged them on all sides. The Dauphin, Charles, was still uncrowned, and the great city of Orléans was about to fall. The Dauphin needed a miracle. Little did he suspect that it would come riding in on a plow horse in the form of a small girl dressed in a soldier's battle armor.

But Joan was having difficulties of her own. Almost no one believed in her voices, and the few that did still could not get past the notion that girls simply were not warriors. At long last, she convinced two of her brothers that hers was a prophetic destiny, and together they rode off to war. She was accompanied by just six men at arms.

Joan's problems were far from over, however. Three times she tried to see the Dauphin, and each time the rough officers of the royal guard laughed at the little peasant girl and sent her away. But each time she would tell them what the outcome of some battle or campaign would be, and as each of her predictions came true, the laughing stopped. Still she was not permitted to see the Dauphin. She pleaded with them, explaining that her voices told her that she only had one year and a little more to drive out the enemy and see the Dauphin crowned king of France. Probably more to get rid of her than because of any belief in what she told them, the officers sent her on to the Dauphin in Chalon.

Her appearance at Chalon, as you might expect, did not overly excite the Dauphin either. Before he would agree to give her an audience, he ordered an interrogation of the "little prophetess in armor" by the doctors of the church. Somehow she managed to persuade the priests that she was not a witch and that her voices were indeed divine. Still, there was the one inescapable barrier that somehow must be overcome. She was, well, a "she," and in those days, women were little more than chattel, not unlike a horse or cow. Regardless of what the Dauphin might think of her piety, dedication, and bravery, no one in the realm believed that "she" would be given any responsibility with regard to the army of France.

It is one of the great miracles of the entire episode that the Dauphin did listen to her story and did in fact set what was probably the world's first militant feminist above all his marshals and officers. He gave her full command of all the troops and strategy in lifting the siege of Orléans. To understand the enormity of this decision, imagine an ignorant, untrained girl, with no knowledge of military combat or logistics whatsoever, suddenly replacing General Eisenhower in 1944.

As the world now knows, the Dauphin's judgment proved correct. In one of the most stunning battles ever fought, anytime or anywhere, Joan of Arc's smaller force of second-rate, undisciplined troops vanquished the best of the English army's veteran soldiers at the battle of Orléans. At the head of her conquering army, she rode into the city of Reims and saw the Dauphin consecrated Charles VII of France, exactly as her voices told her she would.

Merlin had also predicted that the maid would cause a "healing of nations." History records that the stunning victories of the French army in the year following the battle at Orléans brought the adversaries to the conference table, where terms for ending almost a century of war were hammered out. Meanwhile, Joan was taken prisoner by the Burgundians at the Oise River and sold into English hands for 10,000 francs. Her year and a little more had come to an end, just as she had insisted all along.

But now the English had a problem. This little peasant girl turned warrior-prophetess was a great embarrassment to the English general staff. How could this mere girl have outfought the best army in Europe, perhaps in the world? There must have been some unnatural way all of this was brought about. Their answer, of course, was witchcraft.

Compromise, it seems, was also to the advantage of the French in the peace talks that were then under way. Furthermore, the French knights could understand the English resentment. After all, great men fought and won battles, not little girls. Perhaps, they agreed to their everlasting shame, the maid was bewitched. The cynical politics of accommodation were practiced once again, and Joan of Arc was given over to a church court to be tried for heresy.

The charge against the Maid of Orléans was that in claiming to have been divinely inspired by her "voices," she set herself above the church and her priests, and that was heresy, a capital crime. Several times she was given the opportunity to save herself by simply confessing that the voices were either lies or unholy spirits that possessed her. But in the end, she did neither. The saintly voices had told her the future and what her destiny would be. She had not sought them out, nor did she have any control over them. Her only response was to obey. Yet, her prophecies were the most intensely witnessed and precisely recorded of any in history, and that record demonstrates that everything she prophesied came true, even as she played out her ordained role to the very end.

For following her "voices" and fulfilling her destiny, Joan of Arc was found guilty of heresy, excommunicated from the church, and burned at the stake on May 30, 1431. She was nineteen years old.

But these are all ancient prophets and prophecies. Is there nothing closer to our own time that portends good or evil for the nations of the world? There is indeed. There is a man who walks among us, appears on our television shows, and is the recipient of international honors—a man whose entire life, from its beginning to this very day, is a testimony to the power of prophecy. Let's go back about a hundred years.

It is morning in the land of snows. The sun is already high in the sky before it creeps above the top of the giant Himalayas. Far below, at the base of the jumbled mountains and rocky crags, stands the ancient city of Lhasa, capital of Tibet and home to the thirteenth Dalai Lama, the political and spiritual leader of over 300,000 people, all of whom practice a form of Buddhism called Lamaism. On this particular morning, the Dalai Lama is deeply disturbed. Through most of the night, sleep was chased from his eyes and replaced by troubling visions of terror and destruction for his people. Perhaps the most troubling of all was that his successor, the fourteenth Dalai Lama, would be forced to flee from his country and would be the last of the Dalai Lamas.

These disturbing prophecies were recorded in the early part of the twentieth century, when Tibet was at peace with itself and the world. But the current Dalai Lama is living testimony to the accuracy of his predecessor's predictions. He was forced to flee the country under a brutal military takeover by the neighboring Chinese. Yet even in exile, he is still revered by his people, notwithstanding a decades-long effort by the Chinese to stamp out all vestiges of Tibetan religion and culture.

The Dalai Lama, as this is being written, is in the United States. He is the subject of a popular motion picture and has appeared from time to time on television and radio. Most recently, he was a guest on the Larry King show. Yet, Tibetans seek no other spiritual or political leader. Their devotion remains solidly invested in this man.

Where does such extraordinary power over people's lives originate? It is interesting to note that for over 2,500 years, when a Dalai Lama died, no election was ever held. Nor was there a firstborn son to take over the leadership of Tibet. And there has never been even the slightest hint of a political struggle to possess the enormous power that the Dalai Lama holds over his people. Instead, the nation relies totally on the shamans, or monks.

It is not known how they do it, but there is apparently a very precise method for determining where the Dalai Lama has reincarnated. (The body may change, but the Dalai Lama is always the same spirit and continues on in another body.) In this particular instance, it took four years for the Tibetan monks to find his new incarnation. In 1937, through a series of mystical signs and manifestations, the monks were led to the village of Amdo, 1,000 miles northeast of Lhasa. The signs, according to the monks whose ability to read and understand such things is never questioned, indicated that a small boy in that village might be the object of their search. But if in fact this boy was the incarnation of Buddha's wisdom, he would have to pass some very rigid tests.

Arriving at the boy's home, the monks quickly made their preparations. A small table was set up across the bed upon which the boy would be placed to undergo the test. While several monks were in attendance, only one would be in the room with the boy while the examination was administered.

The preparations were made in complete silence. The boy's parents would not be permitted to even remain in the house while the monks were there. What's more, they knew that if their son met the requirements of the monks, he would be taken from them immediately. They might not ever see him again. In either case, they would have no say in the matter whatsoever.

One of the monks took four pairs of objects into the room and carefully placed them on the table. Each pair consisted of two identical items. There were two black rosaries, two small ivory drums, two walking sticks, and two yellow rosaries. When everything was ready, the monk turned and left the room. Moments later another monk entered; with him was a small boy, barely two-and-a-half years old. The monk picked him up and placed him on the bed with great care, positioning him so that he could see the items on the table.

One item of each of the pairs of items now before the boy had been a special favorite of the thirteenth Dalai Lama. The test was a simple one: The boy would have to pick the right item, and without the slightest hesitation. Only the monks who attended the Dalai Lama could have known which of the items was correct, and one of them was now in the room with the boy.

The monk indicated the black rosaries. Immediately, the boy picked up one of the rosaries and slipped it over his head. He looked up at the monk with an assured smile. Neither of them spoke. Next the monk indicated the walking sticks. The boy reached for one of them, and there was just a flicker of concern in the monk's eyes. The boy touched the stick, then pulled back and took the other from the table, laying it across his lap. The monk, showing no emotion whatsoever, moved on to the yellow rosaries. The result was the same as with the black rosary. The boy unhesitatingly grasped one of them and slipped it around his neck. Patiently, he waited for the monk to indicate the next item.

The final selection was perhaps the most important. With one of these small drums, the Dalai Lama had daily beat out the tantric ritual. The monk was especially watchful now as he indicated the drums. With complete confidence, the boy reached out and took one of the drums from the table and immediately started the twisting motion that begins the rhythmic beating of the tantra.

The monk bowed slightly and backed out of the room. In the next room, the other monks were waiting eagerly. We can imagine that the conversation went something like this:

"Well, is he the one?"

The monk who had been in the room nodded gravely. "In each case, he selected the authentic item: the rosaries, the drum, the walking stick. Each time he chose the one used by the Dalai Lama."

"And this without hesitation?" another monk asked.

"Only with the walking stick did he hesitate slightly."

"But was not the duplicate used by the Holy One for a brief period?" a third monk asked.

"It was. And there was something else."

All of the monks turned their eyes to him expectantly. "When he selected the drum, he immediately began to beat the tantric ritual."

At that point, the monks would not have been surprised to see the boy come out of the room, the two rosaries around his neck dragging on the floor, the drum in one hand, the walking stick being pulled along behind. These items were, as far as they were concerned, the property of the fourteenth Dalai Lama.

There were some other tests, all of them predicated on the oracles provided by the monks. But before his third birthday, the boy was declared the new incarnation of Buddha's wisdom. All that remained was to take the four-teenth Dalai Lama immediately to Lhasa. In this particular instance, his mother went with him. It is not known what happened to the boy's father. But if anyone had any lingering doubts about the authenticity of the monks' findings, there was one more startling confirmation to come.

Arriving at the huge and ornate thousand-room palace in Lhasa, several monks ceremoniously escorted the small boy to his quarters. As they opened the door and ushered him into what would be his room from that time on, the boy stopped, turned to the monks, and pointed to a small porcelain box on a table next to the bed.

"My teeth are in there," he said with an air of finality.

One of the monks hurried to the box and opened it. There, just where the thirteenth Dalai Lama had left them, was a set of dentures.

So far as the Tibetan Buddhists were concerned, the fourteenth Dalai Lama had been chosen in the "usual" manner.

It was this same child who, when barely sixteen years of age, was required to face the challenge of his predecessor's prophetic warnings. Many years earlier, the thirteenth Dalai Lama had written that the Dalai and Panchen Lamas, the Father and the Son, and all the revered holders of the faith would disappear and become nameless. Monks and their monasteries would be destroyed, and "all beings will be sunk in great hardship and overpowering fear."

As a teenager, with the weight of both the political and spiritual leadership of the nation resting on his shoulders and Tibet itself standing on the brink of destruction, this same boy faced precisely that kind of disaster. It was, in fact, just a matter of a few years when, with the Chinese takeover of that tiny nation, virtually everything the thirteenth Dalai Lama had predicted came true. The present Dalai Lama was forced to flee to save not only his life but the culture of his people, something the Chinese are still bent on destroying. Perhaps the conquerors would be well advised to remember all of the prophecies concerning the Dalai Lama.

There is still the prophecy that warns that there will only be fourteen Dalai Lamas and that the last one will have to leave Tibet. But it also says that he will return as the spiritual and political leader of the country once again.

With the Chinese firmly in control of Tibet, it is difficult to imagine the circumstance that would return the fourteenth Dalai Lama to his throne, but it should be remembered that this man, that same young boy plucked from his home at age two-and-a-half, won the Nobel Peace Prize in 1989 and is still today a leader in the quest for world peace.

Will he be the last Dalai Lama? In a filmed interview taped in Denver, Colorado, in 1993, his personal secretary, Lodi Gyari, was asked that question. Mr. Gyari replied:

> The Dalai Lama is the fourteenth, but when he speaks of being the last Dalai Lama he does not mean he will cease to reincarnate. In fact he always makes it clear he will reincarnate. There are a number of prophecies that indicate he will return, then there will be happiness again in the land of snows. We Tibetans certainly believe he will return; in fact, every day Tibetans both inside and outside the country are working and making plans for that.

So far, it would seem that the Dalai Lama's entire life has been the fulfillment of one prophecy after another. But the fourteenth Dalai Lama is no longer a young man, and most experts believe that China would have to abandon its claim to Tibet before he could return and bring with him the ancient harmony and rituals. We may yet have an opportunity to see if all the Tibetan prophecies will be fulfilled—or just some of them. In any case, so far as the Tibetan people are concerned, the fate of their nation and perhaps the fate of the world hinges on the accuracy of the prophecies.

The last Dalai Lama? The last pope? The beginning of the last days? Will we be the generation that sees the "gourd of ashes" of the Hopi and the killing "black rain" of the Brahan seer? Will we be the *last* generation to ignore the prophetic warnings?

In our last chapter, we face squarely the challenge of the end of the decade, the end of the century, and the end of the sixth millenia of our recorded history. Will it also be the end of us?

CHAPTER SIXTEEN

THE END TIME

As we mentioned at the beginning of this section, the world now stands at the threshold of the sixth millennium of recorded history. We are the generation that will usher in the year 2000, the "year with the most eyes." Millions of people believe that this will be a time of special significance in the history of humankind. The apocalyptic visions of such Old Testament prophets as Ezekiel, Daniel, and John the Revelator have pointed toward this moment in history for thousands of years. Even Christ himself spoke of "the last days." But how did all of these prophets and prophecies come to settle on the year 2000?

There can be little doubt that the seeds of the end are found in the beginning. In the Book of Genesis, God requires six days, usually interpreted as 6,000 years, to complete his work. On the seventh day he rested. The earth, it is widely believed, will have a probation equal to the amount of time required for its creation. The Bible records 4,000 years of history before the coming of Christ. It has now been nearly 2,000 years since that seminal event, or a total of 6,000 years. (Many scholars believe that Christ was actually born in the year 4 B.C., which means that the magic, 2,000 years was completed in 1996. But those are quibbles in the grand scheme of things.) If this timetable is accurate, the number of plagues about to come upon the world will make the ancient Pharaoh's problems with Moses look like a walk through the park.

Unfortunately (or fortunately, depending on your point of view), in the twelfth century, the great Jewish philosopher and jurist Maimonides pronounced the heavens closed. Most Christian denominations believe that the window between human and God slammed shut at the conclusion of John the Revelator's final vision sometime before the close of the first century A.D. That means, of course, that for the past 1,000 to 2,000 years, there has been no communication between God and humanity to help clarify the events of the "end time."

Or has there?

In 1820, near Palmyra, in upstate New York, a fourteen-year-old boy named Joseph Smith shocked the Judeo-Christian world by claiming to have had a vision in which he saw God and Jesus Christ, side by side. Over the next several years, Smith, as a boy and as a man, managed to enrage the Christian community even further by declaring that the heavens were in fact open and that he was indeed a "prophet of God." Furthermore, he asserted that it was through the process of revelation that the last dispensation of the world would be ushered in.

As to the truth of that, we'll leave it to the religious scholars. But it is clear that Joseph Smith did have some remarkable prophetic insights. For example, on Christmas day, 1832, the young prophet told a gathering of friends:

> Thus saith the Lord concerning the wars that will shortly come to pass, beginning at the rebellion of South Carolina, which will eventually terminate in the death and misery of many souls. . . . For behold, the Southern States shall be divided against the Northern States and the Southern States will call on other nations, even the nation of Great Britain as it is called, and they shall also call upon other nations in order to defend themselves. . . . And it shall come to pass after many days, slaves shall rise up against their masters, who shall be marshaled and disciplined for war.[1]

There were two remarkable things about this prophecy. First, it was the only time in nearly 2,000 years that a prophetic warning was prefaced with "Thus saith the Lord." Second, the American Civil War occurred when, where, and why the young prophet said it would. It is hard to imagine a more graphic and literal fulfillment of the warning voice. But perhaps being literal isn't so remarkable. When we look carefully at the past, prophecies attributed to or authorized by God all seem quite literal in their fulfillment.

This was just one of dozens of prophecies attributed to "Old Joe Smith," as his detractors called him, that he did not live to see fulfilled. For example, he warned of the health hazards of tobacco 150 years before the first surgeon general's warning was ever printed on a pack of cigarettes. But his claim that his prophetic powers came directly from God was too much for the fundamentalists of his day. He was murdered by a mob while being held in jail at Carthage, Illinois, on June 27, 1844; he was only thirty-eight years old.

But what of this notion that the heavens are open once again and that God actually communicates with human beings? The orthodox Judeo-Christian view is that God still isn't speaking to us—and won't until the second coming. If that's true, the proscription apparently doesn't apply to children.

In 1917, near the town of Fatima, in Portugal, three children—Lucia, age eight, Francisco, age nine, and Jacinta, age six—were busy playing among the rocks surrounding a small field where their families sheep were grazing. Suddenly, out of a clear blue sky, a brilliant flash of light riveted their attention. At first they thought it must be the harbinger of a storm, and they ran to gather the sheep. But before they could get back to the gate, another flash of brilliance focused their attention on a small oak tree near the pasture wall.

As they gazed in wonder, a beautiful woman dressed in white appeared. She seemed to be standing in the air above the tree, but her feet were not touching it. A marvelous aura of light surrounded her and reached out to embrace the children as well. Her hands were pressed together in an attitude of prayer, and from them fell a string of pure white beads, ending in a white crucifix. This apparition, now known as a Marian apparition, spoke to them:

"Do not be afraid. I will not harm you."

Lucia was the first to speak. "What is it you want of us?" she asked hesitantly.

"I want you to come here to this same place on the thirteenth of every month from now until October," the apparition announced, and added, "If you are willing to give your lives to God's service I will tell you who I am and what you must do."

That event took place on May 13 and marked the beginning of a remarkable experience for those children as well as everyone in and around Fatima. The children, of course, told everyone what had happened to them, and they dutifully returned on the thirteenth of each month, just as the apparition requested. On July 13, the pasture was overflowing with people, and a very significant event took place. During the appearance of the apparition, the people nearest the children heard them gasp and watched as they grew visibly pale. Their attention was fixed on a point just above the tree for a long time. Finally, the light seemed to gather up within itself and disappear. The entire event was viewed by a vast throng of people. As the light vanished, the children slumped to the ground. Quickly their mothers rushed to them and helped them stand. Anxiously they made their way through the crowd and out of the meadow.

Later that evening, Lucia told her mother that the lady had shown them a terrible vision and that she, Lucia, was to write what they had seen in a letter. She was free to speak about the first two parts of the vision, but the last part was not to be released until 1960, some forty-three years into the future. Lucia, remember, was just eight years old. The task of describing the vision in all of its parts must have seemed overwhelming, but she stayed with it until the job was done.

The message the child received contained three prophecies. The first was that the world war, then under way, would end soon, but another and more terrible war would begin in the reign of the next pope. The second prophecy specified that Russia would spread "terrors" throughout the world, but would eventually cease to be a threat to other nations. Both of those prophecies have been fulfilled.

But what of the third prophecy? What was the secret that was to be kept for forty-three years? As a matter of fact, we still don't know. The contents of Lucia's letter, according to some observers, seemed to strike terror in the heart of the Vatican. One report, never denied, said that when Pope Pius XII read it, he fainted.

In any case, the third part of the Fatima prophecy was carefully written down by the child, just as she was instructed. It was then delivered to the pope in a sealed envelope. Some reports have it that it was read before the College of Cardinals. Others insist that only the popes have read it. Whatever the truth, the message exists and has been acknowledged on several occasions. But it has not been released, in spite of the apparition's instructions to give it to the world in 1960. (Wasn't that roughly the date Edgar Cayce arrived at for the beginning of the "last days"?)

What could a mere child of eight have written that would have such a profound impact on the papacy? Could it be a warning of the last great war? Could it be a timetable counting down to the end of the world? Could it be a confirmation of the visions of Malachi O'Morgain and Nostradamus, spelling out the end of the papacy and the destruction of Rome? The year 1960 came and went with no word from the Vatican as to the contents of the message.

By 1967, there was enough pressure brought to bear that Pope Paul VI felt it necessary to issue a statement. A Vatican spokesman told the waiting world that Pope Paul had concluded that the time was not yet at hand to disclose the contents of Lucia's letter.

Another twenty years went by, and suddenly the third message of Fatima began to take on new and dangerous proportions. The first two prophecies had been fulfilled in almost stunning detail. Now a waiting world was getting impatient. In some quarters, the third prophecy was becoming a fixation. On May 13, 1981, the sixty-fourth anniversary of the first Fatima vision, Pope John Paul II was shot by a Turkish national named Mehmet Ali Agca because, he said, the pope refused to release the third prophecy of Fatima. The attempt on the pope's life and the subsequent trial of the would-be assassin overshadowed the fact that barely eleven days earlier, an ex-Trappist monk hijacked an Irish jetliner, demanding that the Vatican publish the third portion of the Fatima message. Clearly, there are those who take the words of Lucia very seriously. Yet today, eighty years after the fact and nearly forty years past the deadline set by the apparition, there is still no response from Rome. A year after the attempted shooting, John Paul went to Fatima to worship at the shrine and was attacked once again, this time by a knife-wielding, dissident priest. In 1991, on May 13, exactly ten years from the day he was shot, Pope John Paul II once again visited the shrine in Fatima. It was, he said, to thank the Virgin Mother for saving his life.

What is the message of the third prophecy? Joseph Cardinal Ratzinger, a senior Vatican official who is reputed to have read the prophecy, will only say that the secret is not made public "to avoid confusing religious prophecy with sensationalism." Must we then conclude that the third prophecy is in fact "sensational"? Whatever the message, it has not been revealed, even to this very day. Considering the accuracy of the first two prophecies, perhaps we really *don't* want to know what's in it.

It isn't necessary to go back eighty years to discover a heavenly messenger speaking to children. Today, near a small village in blood-soaked Bosnia-Herzegovina, there is an ongoing series of messages that began on the evening of June 24, 1981. Another of the many Marian apparitions appeared near a remarkably plain cement cross situated on a hillside just outside the village of Medjugorje. And in spite of one of the bloodiest civil wars in history, thousands of people risk their lives to go there every year.

On that evening in 1981, the apparition appeared to six teenagers on Mount Podbrdo. She spoke to them and gave them instructions and said that she would return the following day. Amazingly, the apparition has continued to return at the same time every day from that day to this. Her message always begins the same way: "I am the queen of peace. I am the mother of God. I am the mother of all people on earth." Unhappily, she is also telling the visionaries that this will be her last visitation on earth.

At first one wonders why she would choose to speak to children amid the heartbreak and tumult of the Bosnian obscenity; but on closer reflection, if the purpose is to make certain that everyone listens, the time and place make sense. Surely a light, even a small light, beaming into this dark corner of the world will attract more attention than even a spotlight in some happier place.

In any case, the apparition had been appearing each evening for ten years when suddenly, in August of 1991, the tone of the warnings seemed to take on a sharper edge. And there was something else, something that seemed to give an even broader meaning to the message. On that evening, she spoke of her previous appearance at Fatima.

Over the years, the children of Medjugorje have received ten secrets, or forecasts, of things to come. They were told to reveal each event three days before it is to take place. These events will result in a great deal of suffering for the world, but the apparition also injected a ray of hope. She told the children that prayer and fasting will stop war if people have faith. Apparently, what has been foretold can be forestalled.

This is just one of the aspects of the Medjugorje apparition that makes it unique. The number of visionaries that both see and hear the apparition is also unprecedented, as is the frequency and duration of the appearances—which means, of course, that there has been ample time to verify the efficacy of the appearances.

According to Mark Mirravalle, head of the theology department at Franciscan University, in Steubenville, Ohio: "Over the past twelve years these children, now young men and women, have been hypnotized, psychoanalyzed, questioned, threatened, and traumatized like no one else in modern history. Their faith and their story is unshakable."

In addition, thousands of people, including the clergy of many faiths, have made the journey to Medjugorje and have witnessed the miracle themselves. The visions, however, are under the "supervision" of the Vatican, which takes the position that the visions are simply of a "verified nature."

The other very unique aspect of the Medjugorje apparition is the direct reference to Fatima. Of all the apparitions reported over the years, this is the only time there has been any reference to a previous appearance. The most nagging question regarding Fatima is, of course, the sealed third prophecy. If the instruction to release it in 1960 actually came from Mary herself, and if the apparition at Medjugorje is, as it claims to be, "the mother of God" and has again validated her appearance at Fatima, then why have successive popes for nearly forty years refused to obey her wishes? If the heavens are open once again, the question is fairly asked, *Is anybody listening?*

Given everything we have seen so far, we still have to come to grips with the fact that we don't really know when any of this is to take place. Cayce, you'll remember, gives us a starting point of sometime around 1960. Is it simply a coincidence that that was also the year the third prophecy of Fatima was to have been revealed?

That is not our only resource, by any means. There are other things that must happen, other "signs of the times" that will give us clues to the beginning of the end. For example, John the Revelator writes of a man who will virtually take over the world and will wield such enormous power that no one will be able to buy or sell without carrying his mark. This is the anti-Christ (or, some say, *ante*-Christ), whose name is the numerical value of 666; this is the beast who will perform great miracles and be granted authority over every tribe and people, every language and nation.[2]

Is such a person anywhere on the political horizon?

Jeane Dixon, based on what she called "the most significant and soul stirring" vision of her life, may have seen this man. According to the report, on the morning of February 5, 1962, at precisely 7:17 A.M., she arose and gazed out of the window of her Washington home. But instead of the bare-limbed, wintry streets of the city, she saw an endless desert landscape. The sun boiled down upon this scene, and when its rays parted, she saw the ancient queen of Egypt, Nefertiti, hand in hand with her Pharaoh. In her free arm, the queen held a baby in soiled and ragged clothing, a stark contrast to the royal couple who were magnificently arrayed.[3]

Dixon's initial interpretation of this vision was that there was a child born somewhere in the Middle East, at 7:00 A.M. (EST) on February 5, 1962, who will revolutionize the world. She wrote:

> Before the close of the century he will bring together all mankind in one all-embracing faith. This will be the foundation of a new Christianity, with every sect and creed united through this man, who will walk among the people to spread the wisdom of the Almighty Power."[4]

According to John, "The whole world went after the beast in wondering admiration."[5] Jeane Dixon seemed to feel that this was a man who would reshape the present world into a world without wars or suffering; but some years later, she modified her initial interpretation of the vision:

> I am convinced that on that morning the anti-Christ was born somewhere in the Middle East, possibly a descendant of the ancient Egyptian royal line

of Nefertiti. . . . There is no doubt that he will form a new religion based on what will be seen as his almighty power and it will be far removed from the teachings and the life of Christ.[6]

As of this writing, that would mean that a thirty-six-year-old man, a world leader, born somewhere in the Middle East, should be in his ascendancy. Age eliminates Saddam Hussein; the birthplace eliminates Bill Gates.

The latter name, of course, is offered tongue in cheek, but consider this: Plans for a cashless society are already well under way. All transactions for buying and selling would be handled through means of a card, not unlike a credit card, and amounts would simply be debited or credited as the transaction required. Computers large enough to process every transaction in the world already exist, and some say they are already in place. The technology to reduce the size of the card to just a tiny chip is also available. It has, in fact, been suggested that the "card" would never be lost if it were implanted in the forehead or in the back of the hand.

If that sounds implausible, be aware that such implants, carrying critical data as to ownership and location, are already being used to identify pets. It has even been suggested that implants be used instead of name tags for newborn babies. GPS satellites, so the reasoning goes, could track the child for the rest of its life, making kidnapping impossible. Of course, that means that the government, too, could also track the child for the rest of its life. But the point is that the technology is no longer a once and future thing. It is here. Only the moral argument and the biblical warning against the beast identified as 666 stand in the way.

There are those who insist that the man who controls commerce controls the world, and today the man who controls the computers controls commerce. Has anyone checked Bill Gates's birthday lately?

Certainly, at this moment in time, the man strutting on the world stage as the personification of evil is Saddam Hussein. Even the kindest reports portray him as a madman who has demonstrated an almost sadistic willingness to murder even his own people. No one questions his resolve, and no one doubts that he would, if he thought he could get away with it, unleash the most terrible plagues upon the world in the form of chemical and bacteriological weapons. These plagues could easily match the descriptions given in the Bible.

All of that notwithstanding, Saddam Hussein may be fulfilling biblical prophecy in a far more important way than even he is aware. In fact, whether or not he is the anti-Christ is almost irrelevant. Saddam Hussein is the man who has taken it upon himself to rebuild Babylon into the city portrayed in the Bible.

Babylon! The name itself has a ring of historic importance. It is a name that signifies great power and conquest, the site of one of the seven wonders of the world—the famous hanging gardens. Now it appears that Saddam Hussein is determined to restore Babylon to its former greatness. The Bible mentions Babylon over 280 times and tells us that this once great city will indeed be rebuilt. Hussein claims to be the spiritual reincarnation of Nebuchadrezzar, the man who will make the biblical prophecies come true.

According to Charles H. Dyer, professor of theology at the Dallas Theological University and author of: *The Rise of Babylon: Sign of the End Times*, the ancient city of Babylon, while a great center of power in the Middle East during its heyday, has never been anything close to the kind of world power the Bible says it will become:

> Isaiah tells us that Babylon will become the "Jewel of Kingdoms . . . the glory of Babylonian pride." For the past two decades Saddam Hussein has been trying to restore Babylon to just such a position of power in the world community. He has also declared himself to be the great successor of King Nebuchadrezzar, whose ancient kingdom included all of today's Iraq, Syria, Lebanon, Jordan, Saudi Arabia, Israel, and Kuwait. Could it be that he hopes to reclaim the entire kingdom of Nebuchadrezzar?[7]

There are many who see this goal as Hussein's prime motivation for the invasion of Kuwait in August, 1990. If Iraq controlled enough of the world's oil, Hussein would have not only enough money but also enough power to force all nations to seek accommodation from Babylon. He could then establish that city as the center of the world oil monopoly. That could well have been his motive in trying to take over Iran as well, but whatever his motives, his attempts at conquest have so far failed.

In the building of Babylon, however, Hussein has been more successful. Two decades ago, Babylon was little more than a dusty village. Today, a visitor to Babylon will see the southern palace of Nebuchadrezzar, including Procession Street, a Greek theater, many temples, the throne room of Nebuchadrezzar, and a half-scale model of the Ishtar gate. And the building continues.

In all of this, Saddam seems to have overlooked the last part of the biblical prophecy, which states very clearly that this glorious new Babylon will be so utterly destroyed that not even the bricks will be used again. There are those who suggest that the prophecy has already been fulfilled, but in fact, Babylon has never been destroyed. According to Professor Dyer:

> It just sort of faded out of the historical picture and dwindled away but the prophecies are very clear: Babylon will be a great city, truly a world power, and it will be destroyed utterly. In my opinion the rise of Babylon is definitely a sign of the last days.[8]

In his book, Dyer makes it clear that the rise of the anti-Christ and the rebuilding of Babylon are two distinct and separate events; but by all biblical accounts, both are necessary before the great and final battle. In the Bible, Daniel, Isaiah, Zechariah, and Jeremiah all speak of the destruction of Babylon. They also describe it as a great and powerful city. Could it be that we are in fact history's witnesses to the beginning of the millennium?

It seems unlikely that all of that could take place in just the couple of years left until the turn of the century. But perhaps we have more time than that. Nostradamus left us a number of clues. He saw the twentieth century ending with a worldwide plague that would be the worst in history, even threatening the ability of the race to reproduce. He saw the earth itself in massive turmoil with natural disasters of every kind occurring at the end of this century. He prophesied that an anti-Christ would rise out of the strife and violence in the Middle East and delude the world into a massive confrontation that could bring on a global war before the year 2000.

The quatrains of Nostradamus, as noted earlier, are deliberately obscure and therefore subject to a great deal of interpretation, but at least one Nostradamus expert, E. Ruir, is deeply convinced that all of the events foretold by Nostradamus will be realized before the year 2023. That turns out to be a very interesting year when coupled with the last words in the Book of Daniel. This great prophet of the Old Testament, having seen all of the strange beasts and collapsed kingdoms, was, like most of us today, concerned about the time frame, and having access to the source, he asked how long it would be before these things transpired.

"It shall be for a time, times and a half," was the reply.[9]

"I heard but I did not understand," Daniel persisted, "and so I said, 'Sir, what will the issue of these things be?' He replied, 'Go your way Daniel, for the words are kept secret and sealed till the time of the end.'"[10]

Daniel was told further that only the wise leaders shall understand, and his book concludes with the following:

From the time when the regular offering is abolished and "the abomination of desolation," is set up, there shall be an interval of one thousand two hundred and ninety days. Happy the man who waits and lives to see the completion of one thousand three hundred and thirty-five days! But go your way to the end and rest, and you shall arise to your destiny at the end of the age.[11]

The "abomination of desolation" is generally regarded by the Christian world as the Mosque of Omar or Dome of the Rock, which was "set up" on the temple mount in the year 691. The interval of 1,290 "days," interpreted by many scholars to be years, would bring the end time to 1981. But Daniel's enigmatic visitor also said that the man would be happy who waited to see the completion of 1,335 "days." The additional forty-five days, or years, extends the interval to the year 2026—very close indeed to the end time specified in Ruir's interpretation of the Nostradamus *Centuries*.

So, where are we?

Edgar Cayce predicted that the beginning of the end time could be identified by certain geological interruptions, which were verified during or around 1960. His prophecy is even more astonishing when we realize that he knew—in fact, the world knew—almost nothing about the science of plate tectonics at the time.

Both Malachi O'Morgain and Nostradamus have predicted the destruction of Rome either during or at the end of the last papacy, and both prophets agree that the last pope will be named Peter. According to these prophecies, that final pope is on the horizon—as is the final Dalai Lama.

The last of the Dalai Lamas, himself a living prophecy, is now in his sixties. He is still working for world peace and still planning for his return to the seat of government in Tibet, as was prophesied by those who preceded him.

The Brahan seer left us with the enigmatic suggestion of a nuclear accident, oddly enough, in Holy Loch. Mother Shipton predicted the end would come "400 years and some" after her death. The incredibly accurate forecasts she made during her lifetime compel us to look for the end time just about now.

The technology of humankind is, according to the Hopi, destroying the spiritual center of the land with huge power grids and a complete disregard for the Hopi warnings. What might their ancient prophets have seen that they would describe as a "gourd of ashes"?

Technology has further pushed us toward the very real possibility of the "mark of the beast." The capability to control access to various marketplaces is today a distinct reality. Whether or not that capability is transformed into reality remains to be seen.

Then, of course, there are the biblical prophecies, of which we have barely scratched the surface. Probably sixteen of the twenty-two chapters of Revelation alone deal with the disasters that will befall the earth and humankind in the last days. In an earlier chapter, we mentioned the flaming star called Wormwood that will poison a third of the rivers and streams, and we spoke of the mountain cast into the sea that will destroy a third of all life in and upon the waters. But we haven't explored the famous "four horsemen of the apocalypse": famine, pestilence, war, and death. To do so at this point would almost seem redundant. All of this, according to the prophecies, is just a warm-up for the last great battle of good and evil, the battle of Armageddon.

Ezekiel, Daniel, and John the Revelator are all remarkably similar in their visions of the last days and this great battle, but to get the full meaning and scope of the prophecies, one must read not only those prophets but Zechariah, Joel, Isaiah, Jeremiah, Haggai, and Zephaniah as well. It is perhaps a bit presumptuous to try to summarize all the events that they discuss. But it is necessary if we are to come to any understanding of the fate that, according to these prophets, awaits us all. (Scriptural references are provided so that you may fill in any gaps.)

First of all, the house of Israel is to be gathered and Israel itself rebuilt into a fruitful and productive land.[12] This condition, according to most observers, has already been met. Jerusalem is to be established as the capital city,[13] and Judah will become powerful in politics and war.[14] Most objective observers would probably agree that those prophecies have likewise been fulfilled. Then a combination of powerful forces (Gog and Magog) will come together with the avowed purpose of destroying Judah.[15] The Arab states have already stated that the destruction of the Jews is a prerequisite to world peace, but by themselves they do not comprise a force sufficient to meet the prophetic requirements. It is not only Gog but Magog as well who are to combine, and some biblical scholars interpret the prophetic clues to include Russia, Africa, and Europe. The climax of all this activity, of course, will be the great battle of Armageddon that is to occur before the second coming of Christ.

The enormous army that will be assembled will consist of 200 million men.[16] To give you some idea of the enormity of that number, the United States had approximately 14 million men under arms at the height of World War II. The army described by John will easily be the greatest army ever assembled.[17] It will be led by a powerful leader who will preach a false religion, work miracles, and deceive even the very elect.[18]

This is to be an assemblage of all the wicked nations of the world that have been given over to the power of Satan in one last, mighty attempt to destroy the remnant of God's chosen people. It is to be the ultimate conflict between good and evil, freedom and bondage. But for a time, this mighty army will be forestalled by two "witnesses" who have the power to shut up the heavens and breathe fire on their enemies[19] For three-and-a-half years, Jerusalem will be under siege. Then the two witnesses will be slain and the city will be overrun.[20] Two-thirds of the population will be killed while the evil nations rejoice and their leaders exchange gifts.[21]

But when all appears lost, the Lord himself will intervene. The two witnesses, whose bodies have remained lying in the street, are to be resurrected in full view of everyone[22] and called up to heaven. The Jews who remain will flee as the Mount of Olives is split in two by a giant earthquake[23] and the followers of Gog and Magog are deluged with 75-pound hailstones, pestilence, fire, and brimstone.[24] The "northern" army, decimated and defeated, will quit the field[25] and Israel will be left to clean up the mess. It will require seven months just to bury the dead, and the survivors will be able to live off the spoils for seven years.[26]

That sounds like a very definite end indeed. But wait, there's more. Before Christ comes to reclaim his world, it is to be transformed. There will be a worldwide earthquake, and all the landmasses are to be reunited, the valleys exalted, and the mountains made low.[27] The "great deep" will return to the north,[28] and a spring in Jerusalem will heal the Dead Sea.[29]

The monumental scope of these events, even in this brief summary, is truly mind-boggling. How could such things happen in so short a time? We are nearing the end of the twentieth century and the sixth millennium from the beginning of Adam and Eve's sojourn on this planet. Surely all of these cataclysmic events could not take place in so short a time. Besides, we can take comfort in the dictum of science: *Prophecy cannot be, therefore it isn't.*

Perhaps. But before we slip back into complacency, it might be well to remember that no one believed that the *Titanic* could sink, and no one thought that the Berlin Wall would come down in our lifetime. The French laughed when Nostradamus talked of an elected king, and generations of the Earl of Seaforth snubbed their noses at the prophecy of their own demise. No one expected islands to appear and disappear in the South Pacific while Mediterranean ports dried up, and no one believed that a civil war would be fought over slavery. John Kennedy didn't believe that his life was in danger when he boarded a plane for Dallas, and the Legionnaires didn't want to upset anyone by warning Robert Kennedy to stay away from the Ambassador Hotel. Yet, all of these events were prophesied and they all occurred with an uncanny devotion to the details of the prophecy.

In these few chapters, we have only touched on the many prophets, psychics, and seers who have seen visions of the future and had the courage to share those visions with the world. Over the years, these visionaries have managed to weave a tantalizing tale of unexplainably accurate forecasts. And lest we forget, they all agree in a most remarkable way about the timing of "the end."

Further Reading

Chapter One

Gibson, Walter B., and Litzka R. Gibson. *The Complete Illustrated Book of the Psychic Sciences.* New York: Pocket Books, 1969.

Puharich, Andrija. *URI, A Journal of the Mystery of Uri Geller.* Garden City, NY: Anchor Press, 1974.

Chapter Two

George, Llewellyn. *A to Z Horoscope Maker and Delineator, A Text Book of Astrology.* St. Paul, MN: Llewellyn Publications, 1970.

Hall, Angus. *Signs of Things to Come.* London: Danbury Press, Aldus Books Ltd., 1975.

Lynch, John, ed. *The Coffee Table Book of Astrology.* New York: Viking Press, 1967.

Zolar. *The Encyclopedia of Ancient and Forbidden Knowledge.* Los Angeles: Nash Publishing, 1970.

Chapter Three

Gibson, Walter B., and Litzka R. Gibson. *The Complete Illustrated Book of the Psychic Sciences.* New York: Pocket Books, 1969.

Hall, Angus. *Signs of Things to Come.* London: Danbury Press, Aldus Books Ltd., 1975.

Seligmann, Kurt. *Magic, Supernaturalism and Religion.* New York: Pantheon Books, 1971.

Wilson, Colin. *Mysterious Powers.* London: Danbury Press, Aldus Books Ltd., 1975.

Chapter Four

Cheetham, Erika. *The Further Prophecies of Nostradamus.*

Prieditis, Arthur. *The Fate of Nations.* St. Paul, MN: Llewellyn Publications, 1974.

ROBB, STEWART. *Prophecies on World Events.*

ROBERTS, HENRY C. *The Complete Prophecies of Nostradamus.*

ZOLAR. *The Encyclopedia of Ancient and Forbidden Knowledge.* Los Angeles: Nash Publishing, 1970.

CHAPTER FIVE

EDGAR CAYCE FOUNDATION. *Individual Reference File (The Black Book).* Virginia Beach, VA: Edgar Cayce Foundation, 1976.

KARP, REBA ANN. *Edgar Cayce Encyclopedia of Healing.* New York: Warner Books, 1986. (This is one of seventeen books by and about Edgar Cayce published by Warner Books.)

CHAPTER SIX

BRYANT, ALICE, AND PHYLLIS GALDE. *The Message of the Crystal Skull.* St. Paul, MN: Llewellyn Publications, 1989.

HALL, ANGUS. *Signs of Things to Come.* London: Danbury Press, Aldus Books Ltd., 1975.

HURLBURT, CORNELIUS S., JR. *Mineral Digest, The Journal of Mineralogy Vol. 1.* "Quartz." New York: Mineral Digest Ltd.

VAUGHAN, ALAN. *Patterns of Prophecy.* New York: Hawthorn Books, 1973.

CHAPTER SEVEN

DIAMOND, JOHN, M.D. *Your Body Doesn't Lie—Behavioral Kinesiology.* New York: Harper & Row, 1979.

GALDE, PHYLLIS. *Crystal Healing, The Next Step.* St. Paul, MN: Llewellyn Publications, 1989.

JOHNSON, RICHARD L., PH.D. *The Biogram Theory and the Healing Mind.* Oxnard, CA: Graham Page, 1995.

MYSS, CAROLINE, PH.D. *Anatomy of the Spirit.* New York: Harmony Books, 1996.

RAY, BARBARA, PH.D. *The Reiki Factor.* St. Petersburg, FL: Radiance Associates, 1985.

CHAPTER EIGHT

DIAMOND, JOHN. *Your Body Doesn't Lie—Behavioral Kinesiology.* New York: Harper & Row, 1979.

JOHNSON, RICHARD L. *The Biogram Theory and the Healing Mind.* Oxnard, CA: The Graham Page, 1995.

KINGSTON, JEREMY. *Healing Without Medicine.* London: Danbury Press, Aldus Books Ltd., 1975.

MYSS, CAROLINE. *Anatomy of the Spirit.* New York: Harmony Books, 1966.

VALENTINE, TOM. *Psychic Surgery.* Chicago: Henry Regnery, 1973.

CHAPTER NINE

STEARN, JESS. *The Power of Alpha Thinking—Miracle of the Mind.* New York: Morrow, 1976.

VAUGHAN, ALAN. *Patterns of Prophecy.* New York: Hawthorn Books, 1973.

WILSON, COLON. *Mysterious Powers.* London: Danbury Press, Aldus Books Ltd., 1975.

CHAPTER TEN

BERLITZ, CHARLES, AND WILLIAM MOORE. *The Philadelphia Experiment.* Panther, 1979.

JESSUP, MORRIS K. *The Case for the UFO.* VA: Saucerian Press, 1973.

KAKU, MICHIO. *Introductions to Superstrings.* New York:Springer-Verlag, 1988.

———. *Strings, Conformal Fields and Topology.* New York: Springer-Verlag, 1981.

———. *Quantum Field Theory: A Modern Introduction.* New York: Oxford University Press, 1993.

KAKU, MICHIO, WITH JEVICKI AND K. KIKKAWA. *Quarks, Symmetries and Strings.* World Scientific Publishers.

KAKU, MICHIO, WITH JENNIFER TRAINER. *Beyond Einstein.* Anchor Press, 1995.

———. *Nuclear Power: Both Sides.* New York: Norton.

MCMONEAGLE, JOSEPH. *MIND TREK, Exploring Consciousness, Time and Space Through Remote Viewing.* Charlottesville, VA: Roads Publishing, 1997.

SIMPSON GEORGE E. AND NEAL R. BURGER. *Ghost Boat.* Dell, 1985.

Chapter Eleven

Sellier, Charles E. *Miracles and Other Wonders*. New York: Dell, 1994.

Steiger, Sherry Hansen, and Brad Steiger. *Hollywood and the Supernatural*. New York: Berkley Books, 1992.

MacLaine, Shirley. *Going Within*. New York: Bantam Books, 1989.

Other books by Shirley MacLaine

Don't Fall Off the Mountain

You Can't Get There from Here

Out on a Limb

Dancing in the Light

It's All in the Playing

Chapter Twelve

Eddy, Betty. *Embraced by the Light*. Placerville, CA: Goldleaf Press, 1992.

Steiger, Sherry Hansen, and Brad Steiger. *Hollywood and the Supernatural*. New York: Berkley Books, 1992.

Moody, Raymond, with Paul Perry. *Reunions, Visionary Encounters with Departed Loved Ones*. New York: Villard Books, 1993.

Seligmann, Kurt. *Magic, Supernaturalism and Religion*. New York: Pantheon Books, 1948.

Steiger, Brad. *The World Beyond Death*. Norfolk/Virginia Beach, VA: The Donning Company, 1982.

Timms, Moira. *Beyond Prophecy and Predictions*. New York: Ballantine Books, 1994.

Zolar. *Zolar's Encyclopedia of Ancient and Forbidden Knowledge*. New York: Arco Publishing, 1984.

Chapter Thirteen

The Bible

Your favorite version. See the Books of Isaiah, Ezekiel, Daniel, Zechariah, the Four Gospels, and Revelations.

Dixon, Jeane, as told to Rene Noorbergen. *Jeane Dixon, My Life and Prophecies*. New York: Morrow, 1969.

GLASS, JUSTINE. *They Foresaw the Future.* New York: Putnam, 1969.

HALL, ANGUS. *Signs of Things to Come.* London: Danbury Press, Aldus Books Ltd., 1975.

SELIGMANN, KURT. *Magic, Supernaturalism and Religion.* New York: Pantheon Books, 1948.

CHAPTER FOURTEEN

HALL, ANGUS. *Signs of Things to Come.* London: Danbury Press, Aldus Books Ltd., 1975.

PRIEDITIS, ARTHUR. *The Fate of Nations.* St. Paul, MN: Llewellyn Publications, 1974.

SELLIER, CHARLES E. *Mysteries of the Ancient World.* New York: Dell, 1995.

ZOLAR. *The Encyclopedia of Ancient and Forbidden Knowledge.* Los Angeles: Nash, 1970.

CHAPTER FIFTEEN

DIXON, JEANE. *Yesterday, Today, and Forever.* New York: Morrow, 1975.

GLASS, JUSTINE. *They Foresaw the Future.* New York: Putnam, 1969.

HOLROYD, STUART. *Psychic Voyages.* London: Danbury Press, Aldus Books Ltd., 1976.

STEIGER, BRAD. *Brad Steiger Predicts the Future.* Gloucester, MA: Para Research Inc., 1984.

CHAPTER SIXTEEN

THE BIBLE, KING JAMES VERSION. *Revelations, Ezekiel, Daniel, and Isaiah.*

The New English Bible. New York: Oxford University Press, 1971.

GLASS, JUSTINE. *They Foresaw the Future.* New York: Putnam, 1969.

HALL, ANGUS. *Signs of Things to Come.* London: Danbury Press, Aldus Books Ltd., 1975.

PRIEDITIS, ARTHUR. *The Fate of Nations.* St. Paul, MN: Llewellyn Publications, 1974.

SELIGMANN, KURT. *Magic, Supernaturalism and Religion.* New York: Pantheon Books, 1948.

VAUGHAN, ALAN. *Patterns of Prophecy.* New York: Hawthorn Books, 1973.

Organizations and Web Sites

Chapter One

Astraea Psychic Center
33 Lower Pembroke Street
Dublin 2, Ireland
www.iol.ie/astraea
Learn skills on self-healing, tarot, and horoscope.

Miroslaw Magola
http://users.aol.com/mmagola/rightframe.html
A man with psychokinetic abilities who demonstrates them on his
Web page.

Mind Network
www.mindnetwork.com
On-line ESP experiment game.

The Most Unusual Store
www.mostunusual.com
Products relating to White Magic, New Age, ancient mysteries, etc.

Berkeley Psychic Institute
(510) 548-8020
www.berkeleypsychic.com
Preeminent institute for psychic training in the world. BPI teaches you how
to recognize and develop your psychic abilities.

Chapter Two

Astro Baby Choice
http://members.aol.com/clairbazin/homepage.htm
Use astrology and numerology to choose the gender of your baby before
conception.

Mystic Forest
http://members.aol.com/mysticforest/mystl.htm
Astrology, tarot cards, classes, workshops, gems, and crystals.

The Psychic Internet
www.wholarts.com/psychic
Tarot, *I Ching,* and astrological readings, provided on-line by qualified
psychic-intuitives.

Wildflowers Unique Books and Gifts
1512 Oakhurst Drive
Charleston, WV 25314
(304) 746-0100
www.wildflowerswv.com
Complete line of astrological, numerology, and tarot products and books;
crystal wands and balls, gems, and tapes.

Kepler College of Astrological Arts and Sciences
814 Greenwood Avenue North
Seattle, WA 98103
(206) 706-0658
www.aquarianage.org/edu/kepler/index.html
A nonprofit institution founded for the purpose of providing scholarly education and academic degrees in the field of astrology.

American Federation of Astrologers
www.astrologers.com
This Web site offers a complete picture of astrology. Learn about the
astrologers' national convention, see your monthly horoscope, visit the
astrology shop for the latest books and tools, plus a complete history of the
subject.

The Organization for Professional Astrology
401 East 34th Street
New York, NY 10016
www.prosig.com
This organization helps professional astrologers realize their potential.
Newsletter and telephone hotline for members.

Mission Astrology Group
StarCleaners
18 Sycamore Street
San Francisco, CA 94110
www.hooked.net/~sideal/mag.html
Studies the Western sidereal techniques introduced by Cyril Fagan, the Irish
astrologer and Egyptologist who rediscovered the sidereal zodiac.

National Council for Geocosmic Research
9307 Thornewood Drive
Baltimore, MD 21234
www.geocosmic.org
They offer a membership newsletter, books and guides, an educational program, and conferences.

CHAPTER THREE

The Palmistry Center
351 Victoria Avenue
Westmount, Quebec Canada H3Z 2N1
(541) 488-2292
www.palmistry.com
It is the oldest center in North America for palmistry. The center has over
60,000 handprints and charts of people and are tracking their lives. They
attract students from all over the world to their professional training and
research program.

Incredible Mystic Services
1-800-404-4384
www.alliance.net/~rtsdl/mystical.htm
This Web site operates a practice for telling fortunes and interpreting character by the lines and configuration of the palm of the person's hand.

JDR Ventures
918 Douglas Drive
Wooster, OH 44691
(330) 263-1308
www.jdrventures.com
Astrological, numerology, and tarot products and books; crystal balls, wands, gems, and tapes.

Astraea Psychic Center
33 Lower Pembroke Street
Dublin 2, Ireland
www.iol.ie/astraea
Teaches the skills of reading tarot cards.

Wildflowers Unique Books and Gifts
1512 Oakhurst Drive
Charleston, WV 25314
(304) 746-0100
www.wildflowerswv.com
Complete line of tarot card products.

The I-Tarot
http://manor.york.ac.uk/cgi-bin/cards.sh
This Web page lets you see your past, present, and future through the use of tarot cards.

Mystic Forest
http://members.aol.com/mysticforest/myst.html
Offers classes and workshops in the use of tarot cards.

Chapter Four

The Nostradamus Society of America
P.O. Box 101862
Fort Worth, TX 76185
www.nostradamususa.com
The society presents Nostradamus predictions and prophecy, together with current events and other topics of interest to its members.

In Defense of Nostradamus
www.sas.upenn.edu/~smfriedm/nostradamus.html
Presents proofs of the accuracy of Nostradamus's predictions.

The Nostradamus Link
www.infobahnos.com/~ledash/nostradamus.html
Gives you all the Web links to all Web sites that have Nostradamus information on the Internet.

Prophetic Insights
http://prophetic.simplenet.com
Presents all the latest analysis of current events and relates them to Nostradamus prophecy.

Chapter Five

The American Society of Dowsers
P.O. Box 24
Danville, VT 05828
(802) 684-3417
www.newhampshire.com/dowsers.org
Learn the ancient art of dowsing.

Association for Research and Enlightenment
P.O. Box 595
Virginia Beach, VA 23451
www.are.cayce.com
International headquarters for the work of Edgar Cayce; a nonprofit organization sponsoring activities, services, and outreach worldwide.

Edgar Cayce Books International Database
http://edgarcayce.com
The official Web site for ARE Press and the Edgar Cayce Foundation, custodian of the Edgar Cayce readings.

Sparky's Index of Edgar Cayce Readings
http://koke.net/~sparky/cayce.htm
The most complete source of Edgar Cayce readings on the internet; a complete index of all his writings.

CHAPTER SIX

Mystic Forest
http://members.aol.com/mysticforest/mystl.htm
Astrology, tarot cards, gems, and crystals; classes and workshops.

Chrysalis
www.lexingtonweb.com/chrysalis
A metaphysical store and gift shop offering healing and reading sessions, workshops, and classes.

Strange Worlds Bookstore
www.strangeworlds.com
Information and products for exploring the paranormal.

New Spirit Crystal Gallery
1918 E. Capitol Drive
Shorewood, WI 53211
1-888 255-1175
www.execpc.com/nuspirit
All sorts of crystals and crystal wands for sale.

CHAPTER SEVEN

Princeton Engineering Anomalies Research
C-131 Engineering Quadrangle
Princeton University
Princeton, NJ 08544
www.princeton.edu/~rdnelson/pear.html
Pursues rigorous scientific study of the interaction of human consciousness with sensitive physical devices, systems, and processes common to contemporary engineering practice.

Association for Research and Enlightenment
P.O. Box 595
Virginia Beach, VA 23451
www.are.cayce.com
The international headquarters of the work of Edgar Cayce; a nonprofit organization that sponsors activities, services, and outreach throughout the world.

Healing Properties of Gemstones and Crystals
www.gems4friends.com/~lorraine/therapy.html
This Web site explains the different gems and crystals and how they can aid in healing.

Paper Ships Books & Crystals
630 San Anselmo Avenue
San Anselmo, CA 94960
(415) 457-3799
www.papership.com
Specializing in books and crystals for psychic healing.

Divine Arts
P.O. Box 446
Ashland, OR 97520
(541) 482-8431
www.ashlandweb.com/divine
Psychic healing through vibrational attunement.

The Sanctuary
600 Sandtree Drive, Suite 104A
Palm Beach Gardens, FL 33403
(561) 775-0115
www.the-sanctuary.org
Its sole purpose is to promote and enhance physical, mental, and spiritual growth and healing through counseling, study, and meditation.

Complementary/Alternative Medical Association
3405 Gray Point Cove
Decatur, GA 30034
(404) 284-4843
www.insidetheweb.com/~abeis/page10.html
CAMA is a nonprofit association that brings complementary/alternative supporters and practitioners together.

CHAPTER EIGHT

Bare Hand Surgery
16 Dukes Wood Drive
Gerrards Cross Bucks SL9 7LR England
www.therapies.com/surgery
Arrange to have "bare hands surgeon" Laurence Cacteng of the Philippines do surgery on you.

Circle of Friends
www.circleoffriends.org
This Web site has a paraplegic forum that discusses biogram therapy.

Psychic Universes
Leon Grant
23 Center Street
San Rafael, CA 94901
(415) 459-4585
www.planetlink.com/universes
Clairvoyant readings and spiritual healings.

CHAPTER NINE

Office of Paranormal Investigations
www.mindreader.com
This site is operated by Lloyd Auerbach, a prolific author. He will be pleased to investigate honest reports of paranormal or supernatural activity.

Riley G. Psychic Detective
www.psicop.com
Riley G's highly developed psychic abilities have resulted in numerous important arrests and convictions. Along with his private and police cases, he gives lectures, demonstrations, and seminars.

Mind Network
www.mindnetwork.com
On-line ESP experiment game.

Uri Geller's Psychic City
www.urigeller.com
Find out about Uri Geller, his life story, and his consulting business services.
Test your psychic powers.

The Most Unusual Store
www.mostunusual.com
Products relating to white magic, new age, ancient mysteries, and more.

CHAPTER TEN

"The Constantine Report"
www.redshift.com/~wmason/lhreport/articles/const1.htm
Concrete evidence that electronic mind control was the true object of the
government study and that they did, in fact, succeed.

PSI Tech
P.O. Box 3762
Beverly Hills, CA 90212
(310) 657-9829
www.trv-psitech.com/to/news/pr1.htm
Major Ed Dames, who headed the government's remote viewing project,
now continues his research through PSI Tech. They work on such current
subjects as the TWA 800 crash and the Jon Benet Ramsey murder case. You
can see the results of their present investigations on their Web site.

Deja News
http://xl.dejanews.com/getdoc.xp
Government tests, aka remote viewing, aka stargate.

All Mine
338 S.E. 34th Circle
Troutdale, OR 97060
www.remoteview.com
Updates on the latest in remote viewing. Share experiences with others, sign
up for a course, find out current remote viewing sites, get an advanced copy
of "Farsight's Manual on Remote Viewing."

Probable Future Mall
http://probablefuture.com
Offers a course in remote viewing.

Remote Viewing Research Centre
Steve Crietzman, Research Director
www. Parabbs.demon.co.uk/index2.html
Provides information about remote viewing and anomolous cognition to
the public. The center publishes articles and answers questions about government intelligence operations and about the nature of disinformation.

The Farsight Institute
www.farsight.org
Offers history, sessions, and courses in scientific remote viewing.

The Montauk Project & Philadelphia Experiment
www.execpc.com/vjentpr/montauk.html

Controlled Remote Viewing
26944 Bosse Drive
Mechanicsville, MD *20659*
(301) 884-5856
www.ameritel.net/users/rviewer
Update of all those involved in some manner with ongoing history of the
controlled remote viewing project and research and new applications
development.

Altered States of Consciousness Center
www.ascc.org
Learn about astral projection, out-of-body travel, and mental travel. You can download files, read the on-line texts, and check out classes and workshops.

Mind Travel Plus
www.execpc.com/~mholmes/index.html
A nonprofit, worldwide Web site devoted to out-of-body experiences; astral projection, remote viewing, and other types of mind travel; table of contents and lots of excellent information.

Remote Viewing Web Index
www.io.com/~hambone/web/index.html
A complete index and directory of remote viewing; history, names, subjects, and issues.

Michio Kaku
www.dorsai.org/~maku/mk-biog.html
www.dorsai.org/~mkaku/mk-einst.html
www.dorsai.org/~mkaku/mk-artcl.html
The physicist responsible for the super string theory.

Beyond the Big Bang
www2.ari.net/home/odenwald/anthol/beyondbb.html

CHAPTER ELEVEN
National Council for Geocosmic Research
9307 Thornewood Drive
Baltimore, MD 21234
(410) 882-2856
www.geocosmic.org
They offer a membership newsletter, books, and guides. There is also an educational program and conferences.

MuseNet
http://users.aol.com/musefor/musl.html
Psychic readings, astral projection, clairvoyance, tarot; classes and workshops.

Quantum Quests International
www.quantumquests.com
Source for paranormal information and technology; books, gifts, readings, horoscopes, and workshops.

CHAPTER TWELVE

Paranormal Investigations
P.O. Box 1323
Bellevue, NE 68005-1323
(402) 553-1703
www.swiftsite.com/paranormal_investigation
Investigators of the paranormal.

Cosmic Society of Paranormal Investigation
P.O Box 336
Stratford, CT 06497-0336
(203) 378-2334
www.cosmicsociety.com
Ghost-hunt gatherings, workshops, newsletter, and presentations.

International Ghost Hunters Society
Dave Oester and Rev. Sharon Gill, Ghost Hunters
www.ghostweb.com
On-site ghost investigations and ghost conferences.

CHAPTER FOURTEEN

Association for Research and Enlightenment

P.O. Box 595

Virginia Beach, VA 23451

(757) 428-3588

www.are.cayce.com

The international headquarters of the work of Edgar Cayce; a nonprofit organization that sponsors activities, services, and outreach throughout the world.

Notes

Chapter Two

1. LYNCH, JOHN, ED. *The Coffee Table Book of Astrology.* New York: Viking Press, 1967.
2. Ibid.
3. HALL, ANGUS. *Signs of Things to Come.* London: Danbury Press, 1975.
4. Ibid.
5. LYNCH, JOHN, ED. *The Coffee Table Book of Astrology.* New York: Viking Press, 1967.
6. ZOLAR. *The Encyclopedia of Ancient and Forbidden Knowledge.* Los Angeles: Nash Publishing, 1970.
7. Ibid.
8. Ibid.
9. HALL, ANGUS. *Signs of Things to Come.* London: Danbury Press, 1975.
10. Ibid.
11. PRIEDITIS, ARTHUR. *The Fate of Nations.* St. Paul, MN: Llewellyn Publications, 1974.
12. Ibid.

Chapter Three

1. HALL, ANGUS. *Signs of Things to Come* London: Danbury Press, 1975.
2. Ibid.
3. Ibid.
4. Ibid.
5. GIBSON WALTER B., AND LITZKA R. GIBSON. *The Complete Illustrated Book of Psychic Sciences.* New York: Doubleday, 1966.
6. Ibid.
7. HALL, ANGUS. *Signs of Things to Come.* London: Danbury Press, 1975.
8. Ibid.
9. Ibid.

CHAPTER FOUR

1. PRIEDITIS, ARTHUR. *The Fate of the Nations.* St. Paul, MN: Llewellyn Publications, 1974.

CHAPTER FIVE

1. KARP, REBA ANN. *Edgar Cayce Encyclopedia of Healing.* New York: Warner Books, 1986.
2. Circulating file. *Nature of the Mind:* Virginia Beach, VA: Edgar Cayce Foundation, 1977.

CHAPTER SIX

1. HURLBURT, CORNELIUS S., JR. *"Quartz." Mineral Digest, Vol. 1.* New York: Mineral Digest Ltd.
2. BRYANT, ALICE, AND PHYLLIS GALDE. *The Message of the Crystal Skull.* St. Paul, Minn.: Llewellyn Publications, 1989.
3. HALL, ANGUS. *Signs of Things to Come.* London: Danbury Press, Aldus Books Ltd., 1975.
4. Ibid.

CHAPTER SEVEN

1. MYSS, CAROLINE. *Anatomy of the Spirit.* New York: Harmony Books, 1996.
2. GALDE, PHYLLIS. *Crystal Healing, The Next Step.* St. Paul, MN: Llewellyn Publications, 1989.
3. Ibid.
4. DIAMOND, DR. JOHN. *Your Body Doesn't Lie.* New York: Harper & Row, 1979, 23–24.
5. Ibid.
6. RAY, BARBARA, PH.D., *The Reiki Factor.* St. Petersburg, FL: 1986.
7. Ibid.
8. Ibid.
9. Ibid.

Chapter Eight

1. Valentine, Tom. *Psychic Surgery.* Chicago, IL: Henry Regnery, 1973.
2. Johnson, Richard L., Ph.D. *Biogram Therapy: A Quantum Leap in Mind/Body Healing.* Ventura, CA: MPower Press, 1997.
3. Johnson, Richard L., Ph.D. *Biogram Theory and the Healing Mind.* Oxnard, CA: The Graham Page, 1995.
4. Ibid. 19.
5. Ibid.
6. Ibid. 7.
8. Myss, Caroline. *Anatomy of the Spirit.* New York: Harmony Books, 1966.
9. Ibid.
10. Ibid.

Chapter Ten

1. "The Constantine Report No. 1," //www.redshift.com/~wmason/lhreport/articles/const1.htm.
2. Ibid.
3. Ibid.
4. *Mysteries of Mind, Space, and Time,* vol 18, "The Unexplained—The Philadelphia Experiment." Westport, CN: H.S. Stuttman, Inc., 1992.
5. Ibid.
6. Marciniak, Barbara. *Bringers of the Dawn.* Santa Fe, NM: Bear & Company Publishing, 1992.

Chapter Eleven

1. Steiger, Sherry Hansen, and Brad Steiger. *Hollywood and the Supernatural.* New York: Berkley Books, 1992.
2. MacLaine, Shirley, *Going Within.* New York: Bantam Books, 1989.
3. Ibid.
4. Ibid.

5. STEIGER, SHERRY HANSEN, AND BRAD STEIGER. *Hollywood and the Supernatural.* New York: Berkley Books, 1992.

6. Ibid.

7. Ibid.

CHAPTER TWELVE

1. MOODY, RAYMOND WITH PAUL PERRY. *Reunions, Visionary Encounters with Departed Loved Ones.* New York: Villard Books, 1993.

2. STEIGER, SHERRY HANSEN, AND BRAD STEIGER. *Hollywood and the Supernatural.* New York: Berkley Books, 1992.

3. Ibid.

4. SELIGMANN, KURT. *Magic, Supernaturalism, and Religion.* New York: Pantheon Books, 1948.

5. "New Visions of the Future, Prophecies III." The Learning Channel, 1997.

CHAPTER THIRTEEN

1. "I was dead and now I am alive forevermore," REV. 1:18.

2. Rev. 9:16.

3. Ezek. 38:16.

4. Zech. 14:13.

5. Ezek. 38:21.

6. Rev. 18:10.

7. Rev. 16:19.

8. Rev. 14:20.

9. Rev. 8.

10. Ezek. 37:12, 21–22.

11. HALL, ANGUS *Signs of Things to Come.* London: Danbury Press, Aldus Books Ltd., 1975.

CHAPTER FOURTEEN

1. HALL, ANGUS. *Signs of Things to Come.* London: Aldus Books Ltd., 1975, 125.

Chapter Sixteen

1. Roberts, B. H. *A Comprehensive History of the Church, vol 1.* Provo, Utah: Brigham University Press, 1965.
2. Rev. 13:7.
3. Hall, Angus. *Signs of Things to Come.* London: Danbury Press, Aldus Books Ltd., 1975, 140.
4. Ibid.
5. Rev. 13:3 New English Bible.
6. Hall, Angus. *Signs of Things to Come.* London: Danbury Press, Aldus Books Ltd., 1975, 140.
7. Dyer, Charles H. *The Rise of Babylon: Sign of the End Times.*
8. Ibid.
9. Dan. 12:7 Neb.
10. Dan. 12:8, 9 Neb.
11. Dan. 12:11–13 Neb.
12. Ezek. 36:37, 38.
13. Zech. 1:2, 12.
14. Isa. 19; Zech. 10.
15. Ezek. 38; Jer. 25.
16. Rev. 9:16.
17. Joel 2:3.
18. Rev. 13:19.
19. Rev. 11:3–6; Isa. 51: 19–20; Zech. 4:11–14.
20. Rev. 11:7–10.
21. Zech. 13:8–9, 14:1–2.
22. Rev. 11:11–12.
23. Zech. 14:4–5.
24. Rev. 11:13, 16:18–21; Ezek. 38:22; Hag. 2:6–7.
25. Ezek. 39:2; Joel 2:18–21.
26. Ezek. 39:8–16.
27. Zech. 14:8–10.
28. Rev. 16:17–21.
29. Ezek. 47:1–12; Rev. 22:1.

INDEX

Accidental seers, 49. *See also* Incidental seers; Intentional seers

Achilles Tatius (Greek writer), 23

Acupuncture, 16

Adair, David, 79

Adams, Evangeline (astrologer), 20, 26–28, 29, 30, 50

    court case against, 27–28

    predicts World War II, 29

Adams, John Quincy, 26

Afterlife, *See* Near-death experiences

Agpaoa, Antino "Tony" (psychic surgeon), 109–110

Aids (case study), use of intuition to heal, 118–119

Airplanes, taking trip through time, 202–203

Ali Agca, Mehmet, 243

Aliette (author), 46

All Mine (Web site), 271

Allen, Carl M., 144–145

Allende, Carlos Miguel, 144–148

Allison, Dorothy (psychic detective), 132–134

Altered States of Consciousness Center (Web site), 272

"Amazing World of Psychic Phenomena" (TV show), 9, 11, 159

American Federation of Astrologers, 26, 29

    Web site, 262

American Holistic Medical Association, 118

American Society of Dowsers, 265

An American Werewolf in Paris (movie), 160

Anatomy of an Illness (Cousins), 115

Anatomy of the Spirit (Myss), 99

Anti-Christ, 246–247

    year 2000 and, 17

Antoinette, Marie, 57–58

Apollonius (Roman sorcerer), 87

Apparitions, 174–175, 179

    defined, 174.

    See also Ghosts; Poltergeists

Aristotle (Greek philosopher), 24

Armendariz, Pedro, 165

Art of Chiromancy (Hartlieb), 33

Association for Research and Enlightenment (ARE), 66

    Web sites, 266, 267, 274. *See also* Cayce, Edgar

Astraea Psychic Center (Web site), 261

Astro Baby Choice (Web site), 261

Astrology, 18, 22

    books/magazines about, 26

    defined, 14

    ephemeris, 22

    founder of modern day, 26

    history of, 23–26

    scientific attitude toward, 28

    signing time of Constitution, 19

    stock market and, 27

Atlantis

    crystal skull and, 84

    Edgar Cayce's prophecies regarding, 69, 70, 77

Auerbach, Lloyd (parapsychologist), XIII–XIV, 178, 180

    Web site, 269

Babylon, Biblical prophecies and, 195, 248–249

Babylonians, use of astrology, 14, 22–23

Banyaca, Thomas, 197–198

Bare Hand Surgery (organization), 269

Batzel, Beth and Bob, encounters with poltergeists, 175–178

Baxter, George (poltergeist), 176–178

Bean, Jack, 169

Berkeley Psychic Institute (organization), 261

Berlitz, Charles (author), 157

Bermuda Triangle, 157

Bernhard, Father (Bishop of Clairvaux), 210–212

Beyond the Big Bang (Web site), 272

Bible

    end of the world prophecies, 194–198, 249

    Urim and Thummim, 87

Biblical prophecies, 194–198, 201, 207–208, 239, 250, 251–253

Bibliography (list of books), 255–259

    A to Z Horoscope Maker and Delineator, 255

    Anatomy of the Spirit, 256, 257

    Beyond Einstein, 257

    Beyond Prophecy and Predictions, 258

Bibliography, *cont.*

    Bible, The, 258

    Bible, King James Version, 259

    Biogram Theory and the Healing Mind, 256, 257

    Brad Steiger Predicts the Future, 259

    Case for the UFO, 257

    Coffee Table Book of Astrology, 255

    Complete Illustrated Book of the Psychic Sciences, 255

    Complete Prophecies of Nostradamus, 256

    Crystal Healing, the Next Step, 256

    Dancing in the Light, 258

    Don't Fall Off the Mountain, 258

    Edgar Cayce Encyclopedia of Healing, 256

    Embraced by the Light, 258

    Encyclopedia of Ancient and Forbidden Knowledge, 255, 256

    Fate of the Nations, 255, 259

    Further Prophecies of Nostradamus, 255

    Ghost Boat, 257

    Going Within, 258

    Healing Without Medicine, 257

    Hollywood and the Supernatural, 258

    Individual Reference File (Edgar Cayce), 256

    Introduction to Superstrings, 257

    It's All in the Playing, 258

    Jeane Dixon, My Life and Prophecies, 258

    Magic, Superstition and Religion, 255, 258, 259

    Message of the Crystal Skull, 256

    MIND TREK, 257

    Mineral Journal (Vol. 1 "Quartz"), 256

    Miracles and Other Wonders, 258

    Mysteries of the Ancient World, 259

    Mysterious Powers, 255, 257

    New English Bible, The, 259

    Out on a Limb, 258

    Patterns of Prophecy, 256, 257, 259

    Philadelphia Experiment, 257

    Power of Alpha Thinking, 257

    Prophecies on World Events, 256

    Psychic Surgery, 257

    Psychic Voyages, 259

Bibliography, *cont.*

    Quantum Field Theory, 257

    Quarks, Symmetries and Strings, 257

    Reunions, Visionary Encounters with Loved Ones, 258

    Rieki Factor, The 256

    Signs of Things to Come, 255, 256, 259

    Strings, Conformal Fields and Topology, 257

    They Foresaw the Future, 259

    URI, Journal of the Mystery of Uri Geller, 255

    World Beyond Death, The, 258

    Yesterday, Today and Forever, 259

    You Can't Get There From Here, 258

    Your Body Doesn't Lie-Behavioral Kinesiolgy, 256, 257

    Zolar's Encyclopedia of Ancient and Forbidden Knowledge, 258

Bielek, Al, 148–150, 152

Bielek, Duncan, 148–150

Biofeedback, 100, 111

Biogram Theory and the Healing Mind (Johnson), 114–115

Biogram therapy, 111, 112–115

    Web site, 269

Biogram Therapy: A Quantum Leap in Mind/Body Healing (Johnson), 100

Bioplasmic energy (life force), 107

Boban, M.E., 80

Bogart, Humphrey, ghostly image and, 17, 169

Bohr, Neils, 151

Book of Daniel, 250

Book of Genesis, 239

Book of Revelation, 194, 195, 196, 251

Book of Thoth, 42, 45

Borgnine, Ernest (actor), 161

Bosnia-Herzegovina, Medjugorje apparition and, 244–245

Boyer, Paul (professor), 196

Brahan seer. *See* Odhar, Kenneth

Brahe, Tycho (astrologer/astronomer), 24

Brain, achieving alpha state, 114

Bratter, Rosa (psychic), 166

Bringers of the Dawn (Marciniak), 152–153
Brutus, 221
Buddhism, 233
Buddhist prophecy, end of the world, 199
Bumps on head, reading. *See* Phrenology

Cabinet of Dr. Caligeri (movie), 160
Cactang, Lawrence (psychic surgeon), 269
Cade, Jessica (psychic), 185–186
Caesar Dominicus, 87
Campanus, Johannes (mathematician),
    inventor of the zodiac, 24
Campbell, Donald (speedboat racer),
    41–42, 46
Canterbury Tales (Chaucer), 16
Card games, origin of, 44
Caron, Jean, 107
Carradine, David (actor), 161
Caruso, Enrico (opera singer), 27
Case for the UFO (Jessup), 145
Catherine de Medicis (Queen), 55–56
Cayce, Carrie (mother of Edgar), 63
Cayce, Edgar, 16, 63–71, 99, 116, 205–208, 245
    ailments, readings that give causes and
        cures for, 66–68
    Atlantis, prophecies regarding, 69, 70,
        77, 86
    biographical sketch, 63–64
    criticism of, 70
    crystals, 86–97
    earth changes, predicts, 206–207, 251
    end of the world, prophecies, 205–208,
        219
    healing powers, discovers, 64–65
    paranormal experience, first, 63–64
    plate tectonics, foretells, 206–207
    predictions of, 67, 68
    psychic phenomena, defines, 69–70
    readings, number of given, 66, 205
    self-heals voice problems, 65–66
    trancelike states and, 66
    Wall Street crash, predicts, 68
    Web sites, 266
Cayce, Gertrude (wife of Edgar), 66
Cayce, Hugh Lynn (son of Edgar), 63

Cayce, Leslie (father), 63
Centuries (Nostradamus), 52, 53, 54, 58,
    214, 250
Chaldeans, use of astrology, 14, 22–23
Challenger (Space Shuttle), disaster and, 218
Channeling, by aliens from Pleiadian world,
    152–153
Charles II of France, 230, 231
Cheiro (palmist), 31–33, 34–38, 46, 50
    challenged by newspaper, 34–37
    predictions of, 37
Chi (energy flow), 107
Chinese
    Lo King (zodiac), 24
    use of acupuncture, 16
    use of astrology, 24
Chiromancy. *See* Palmistry
Chrysalis (Web site), 266
Churchill, Winston (Prime Minister), 26, 89
CIA, mind control experiments and, 143–144
Circle of Friends (Web site), 269
Clairvoyance, 12
    defined, 52
    developing, 71
Claudius Claudianus (poet), 87–88
Cleromancy (drawing of lots), 24
Cleveland, Grover (President), 37
Combe, George, 40
Complementary/Alternative Medical
    Association (Web site), 268
Complete Dictionary of Astrology (Wilson), 26
Confucius, 189
Conqueror (movie) filmed near nuclear test
    site, 164–165
Constantine, Alex, 143, 144
"Constantine Report", 270
Constitution, time of signing, astrological
    significance of, 19, 25
Controlled Remote Viewing (Web site), 271
Copernicus, 24
Cosmic Society of Paranormal Investigation
    (Web site), 273
Cousins, Norman (author), 115
Creation, theory of, 154
Croiset, Gerard (psychic detective), 134

Cromwell, Oliver, 225
Crowley, Aleister, 161
Crystal ball, 88, 90
Crystal skulls, 80–86
    Atlantis and, 82, 84
    characteristics of, 85–86
    channeling using, 84–85
    history behind, 80–83
    Mitchell-Hedges skull, 83–85
Crystals, healing power of, 100–103. *See also*
    Quartz crystals
Curie, Jacques, 79
Curie, Pierre, 79
Dalai Lama, 233–237, 251
    process to prove incarnations of,
        234–235

Dames, Major Edward, 140
    Web site, 270
Daniel (biblical figure), 12, 23
    prophecies and, 197, 249, 250
Dante, 3
D'Arpentigny, Casmir (palmist), 33, 34
Darwin, Charles, 39
Dauphin. *See* Charles II of France
d'Avignon, Marie (prophetess), 229
Debbie My Life (Reynolds), 165
Deja News (Web site), 270
Devil worshipers, 161
Diamond, John, 103, 106
Divine Arts (Web site), 268
Dixon, Jeane (psychic), 61, 88–90, 204
    anti-Christ, predicts birth of, 246–247
    first psychic experience, 88
    John F. Kennedy, predicts assassination
        of, 192
    predictions of, 89–90
DNA, 115
Dorland, Frank, 85
Dorland, Mabel, 85
Dowsing, 63, 72–74
    making a dowsing rod, 73
    testing for ability, 72–74
    Web site, 265
dreams, using for psychic healing, 116

Druids, 221
Dunne, John William, 202
Durham, Elaine, 185
    visions for the future, 185
Dyer, Charles H., 248, 249

Earl of Seaforth, prophecies regarding,
    227–229, 253
Earthquakes, as cataclysmic earth changes,
    207, 208
Eddy, Betty, 183
Edgar Cayce Books International Database
    (Web site), 266
Egyptians, use of astrology, 23
Einstein, Albert, 28, 148, 151, 152
Embraced by the Light (Eddy), 183
End of the world prophecies, 193–201,
    205–208, 239–254. *See also* Millenium;
    Year 2000
Ephemeris, defined, 22
ESP. *See* Extrasensory Perception
Eukrate, 181
Evans, Linda (actress), 161
Exorcist (movie), 170
Experiment in Time (Dunne), 202
*Expression of the Emotions in Men and
    Animals* (Darwin), 39
Extrasensory perception (ESP), 12
Ezekiel (prophet), 194, 196

Face reading. *See* Physiognomy
Faith healing, 14–15
Farsight Institute (Web site), 271
Fatima Prophecy, 241–243, 244, 245. *See also*
    Virgin Mary
Fingerprints, 33, 38
Ford, Glenn (actor), 161
Four Books on the Influence of the Stars
    (Claudius Ptolemy), 23
Franco (Spanish dictator), 59
Fresci, John H., 27
Freud, Sigmund, 33

Galde, Phyllis, 101

Gayle (psychic), 47–50, 71–72, 93–97, 121–125,
        135–140
Galileo, 8, 52
Gall, Franz Joseph, discovers practice of
        phrenology, 39–40
Gandhi, Mahatma, 89
Gates, Bill, 247
Gaynor, Mitzi (actress), 169, 175
Gebelin, Antoine Court de (author), 45
Geller, Larry, 170
Geller, Uri, 9–11, 157
        key bending abilities, 10–11
        Web site, 270
Ghosts, 174–175, 179, 180, 181–183
        causes for appearances of, 179–180
        defined, 174. See also Apparitions;
                Poltergeists
Gibbens,Bill, 182–183
Gill, Sharon, 273
Goddard, Victor, 202
Government use of psychics, 140–144
Graham, Billy (evangelist) has vision of
        Marilyn Monroe's death, 165–166
Greeks,
        astrology, use of , 24
        cleromancy, use of, 24
        cult of the dead, 181
Guardian angels, 168–169
Guilaroff, Sidney, 165–166

Hamilton, George (actor)
        paranormal encounter and, 16–17
Hammarskjold, Dag, 89
Hamon, Count Louis Le Warner de. See Cheiro
Harris, Henrietta (astrologer), 20–22
Hartlieb, John, 33
Hauk, Dennis, 183
Haunted Places (Hauk), 183
Hauntings, 181–183
Hauy, Rene Just, 78
Hayward, Susan (actress), 165
Healing, using holistic approach, 101
Healing Properties of Gemstones and Crystals
        (Web site), 267
Heisenberg, Werner, 151

Henry VIII. See King Henry VIII
Hermitic Order of the Golden Dawn,
        45–46
Hitler, Adolf
        astrologers and, 13, 26
        Nostradamus and, 60–61
Hollywood, psychic phenomena and, 160–171
Hoover, George W., 146
Hopi (Native American tribe)
        Black Mesa, 200–201
        prophecies for the end of the world,
                197–201, 251
Hoyt, John, 165
Hudson, Rock, 160
Hurkos, Peter (psychic detective), xiv,
        127–129, 157
Hussein, Saddam, 195, 247–249
        as possible anti-Christ, 248–249
Huygens, Christian, 78
Hyperspace, 151, 154

I Ching, 189, 190
Implants, microchip, 247
In Defense of Nostradamus (Web site), 265
Incidental seers, 49. See also Accidental seers;
        Intentional seers
Incredible Mystic Services (Web site), 264
Information, value of, 17–18
Ingram, Rex, 161
Intentional seers, 50. See also Accidental
        seers; Incidental seers
International Ghost Hunters Society (Web
        site), 273
Intuition, to help the healing process, 116–120
Isaiah (Biblical prophet), 196
Israel, prophecy foretelling formation of,
        196–197
I-Tarot (Web site), 264

James I, 34
JDR Ventures (Web site), 264
Jessup, Morris Ketchum, 144–147
Jesus Christ
        faith and, 14–15
        life energy, 107

Joan of Arc, 229–232
    burned at the stake, 232
    charged with heresy, 232
    hears voices, 230, 231, 232
    prophetic visions of, 230
John Paul II, Fatima Prophecy and, 243
John the Revelator, end of the world
    prophecy and, 194, 195, 239, 240, 246
Johnson, Richard L, 100, 101, 111–116
Julius Caesar, 221
Jung, Carl, 33

Kabbalah, 45–46, 118
Kaku, Michio, 151, 152, 153
Kennedy, John F., predictions of
    assassination of, 61, 192, 253–254
Kennedy, Robert, predictions of
    assassination of, 90, 254
Kepler College of Astrological Arts and
    Sciences, (Web site), 262
Kepler, Johannes, 24–25
Keys, bending of through psychokinesis, 10–11
Khayyam, Omar, 201
Kinesiology, importance of for healing
    process, 103–105, 106
King Charles VI, 44
King Edward VII, 28
King Frederick II, 24
King Henry II, 55–56
King Henry VIII, 33–34, 42
    prophecies regarding, 224–225
King, Larry (talk show host), 233
King Louis II, 214
King, Martin Luther, 90
Kitchener, Horatio, 31–33, 46
Koslov, Dr. Sam, 143

Lansa, John, 199–201
Late Great Planet Earth (Lindsey), 208
Lavater, Johann Kaspar, 38–39
Lee, Steve, 181–183
Lennon, John, 160
Lenormand, Marie, 45
L'evi, Eliphas, 45
Life After Life (Moody), 173

Lilly, William, 191
Lindsey, Hal (author), 208
Lisle, Rome de, 78
Lo King (Chinese zodiac), 24
Louis XVI, 57–58
Luke (apostle), 197
Lupino, Ida (actress), 162–163
Lupino, Stanley (father of Ida), 162–163
Lynn, Loretta, 161

MacLaine, Shirley, 17, 161, 163–164
    role of Madame Sousatzka, 163–164
Macrocosmic, theory of, 153
Magician, The (Maugham), 161
Maimonides (Jewish philosopher), 239
Mana (life force), 107
Manson, Charles, 161
Mantegazza, Paolo (anthropologist), 39
Marciniak, Barbara (author), 152–153
"Marion apparitions". *See* Virgin Mary
"Mark of the beast", 246, 251
Marvin, Lee (actor), 160
Mata Hari, 37
Maugham, W. Somerset (author), 161
Maximilian I (German emperor), 224–225
McCambridge, Mercedes (actress), 170–171
McMoneagle, Joseph, 141
Merlin (Druid seer), 87, 221–222, 226, 229
    Joan of Arc, prophecy regarding, 231
    Richard the Lionheart, prophecy
        regarding, 222
Meyer, Dr. (convicted murderer), 34–36
Microcosm, theory of, 153
Mictlantecutli (Aztec god of death), 81
Millenium, prophecies regarding, 17, 193–201
    Nostradamus predictions regarding,
        218–219
    See also End of the world; Year 2000
Miller, Ann, 168
Mind-body connection. *See* Intuition
Mind control experiments, CIA and, 143–144
Mind Network (Web site), 261
Mind Travel Plus (Web site), 272
Mineo, Sal (actor), 160
Miroslaw, Magola, 261

Mirravalle, Mark (theologian), 245
Mirror gazing, 173
Mission Astrology Group, 263
Mitchell-Hedges, Ann (daughter of F.A.), 83–85
Mitchell-Hedges, F.A., 83–85
Moles on body, reading, 41
Monroe, Marilyn, 89, 160, 165–166
Montauk Project, 149, 150
    Web site, 271
Montgomery, Count de, 55–56
Moody, Raymond (author), 157, 173–174
Moorehead, Agnes (actress), 165
Moreau, Madame Adele, 34
Morgan, J.P., 20, 27
Most Unusual Store (Web site), 261, 270
Mother Shipton (English seer), 222–225, 251
    prophecies of, 223–225
Muller, Johann, 24
MuseNet (Web site), 273
Musgrave, Cassandra, 184
    visions for the future, 184
Mussolini, Benito, Nostradamus foretells rise
    of, 61
Myss, Caroline (author), 99–100, 116–120
Mystic Forest (Web site), 262, 265, 266

Napoleon Bonaparte, 45, 58
National Council for Geocosmic Research
    (Web site), 263, 272
Near-death experiences, 183–187
Nebuchadrezzar (Chaldean king), 23, 248,
    249
Nefertiti (queen), 246, 247
Nelson, Willie, 161
Nepal, importance of astrology, 19
New Spirit Crystal Gallery, 267
"New Visions of the Future Prophecies III",
    (TV show), 184
New York City, predictions regarding
    destruction of, 218–219
Newton, Sir Isaac, 25, 28, 152
Nicerino, Nick, 179–180
Nichols, T.L., 103
Niven, David, 170

Nostradamus, 51–62, 191, 212–219
    Adolf Hitler, predicts rise of, 60–61
    biographical sketch, 51–52, 214–215
    Centuries, 52, 53, 54, 58, 214, 250
    criticism of, 57, 58
    French Revolution, predicts, 57–58
    future technology, predicts, 61
    John F. Kennedy, predicts death of, 61
    King Henry II's death, predicts, 55–56
    medical background, 214–215
    Mussolini, predicts rise of, 61
    Napoleon's reign, predicts, 57–58
    papal prophecy of, 212–213
    pasteurization process, predicts, 59–60
    Quatrains, 52, 53, 61, 217–218, 250
    source of clairvoyance, 52–53
    Spanish Civil War, predicts, 59
    Web sites, 265
    year 2000 predictions, 218–219, 249–250
Nostradamus Link (Web site), 265
Nostradamus Society of America (Web site),
    265
Nostredame, Michel de. See Nostradamus

Odhar, Kenneth (Brahan Seer), 226–229, 251
Oester, Dave, 273
Office of Paranormal Investigations (Web
    site), 269
O'Morgain, Malachi, 209–212, 251
    papal prophecy and, 209–212, 213
Oracle of Delphi, 24
Organization for Professional Astrology, 263

Palmistry. See also Cheiro
    criticism of, 33–34
    gypsies and, 33–34
    history of, 33–34
    oldest manuscript on, 33
Palmistry Center (Web site), 263
Paper Ships Books & Crystals (Web site), 268
Paranormal
    defined, xi
    organizations, list of, 261–274
    Web sites, list of, 261–274
Paranormal Investigations (Web site), 273

Past lives, celebrities that believe in, 161
Pasteur, Louis, 8, 60
Pasteurization, Nostradamus predicts, 59–60
Patmos (island), 194, 195
Pauli, Wolfgang, 151
Peretti, Felice (Pope Sixtus V), 212
Pert, Candace (neurobiologist), 115
Philadelphia Experiment, 145–150
Philadelphia Experiment and other UFO Conspiracies (Bielek), 148
Philippines, use of psychic surgeons, 14, 109–111
Phrenology (reading bumps on head), 38, 39–41
    discoverer of, 39–40
Physiognomical Fragments (Lavater), 38
Physiognomy (face reading), 38–39, 40
Pickford, Mary (actress), 27
Plate tectonics, Edgar Cayce and, 206–207
Plato (Greek philosopher), 24
    Atlantis and, 69, 77
Pleiadian definition of time, 152–153
Poltergeists, 174, 175–178, 179. *See also* Apparitions; Ghosts
Pommer, Erich, 160
Pope Paul VI, Fatima Prophecy and, 243
Pope Pius XII, 242
Pope Urban IV, 24
Popes
    papal prophecy of Malachi O'Morgain, 209–212, 213
    papal prophecy of Nostradamus, 212–213
Powell, Dick 165
Prana (life force), 107
Presley, Elvis, paranormal experience and, 170
Pribram, Dr. Karl, 143
Prieditis, Arthur, 28
Primo de Rivera, 59
Princeton Engineering Anomalies Research (Web site), 267
Princess Grace of Monaco, 160, 170
Probable Future Mall (Web site), 271
Prophecies, 191–193
    end of the world, 193–201, 205–208, 239–254
Prophetic Insights (Web site), 265

Prophetic Messenger (magazine), 26
Prophets, Psychics, and Seers, 200
Przbycien, Irene, 109, 110
PSI Tech (Web site), 270
Psychic abilities, testing using a crystal, 90–91
Psychic awareness, exercise to test for, 15
Psychic, defined, xiii
Psychic detectives, xiv, 5–7, 127–134
Psychic Dictatorship in the U.S.A. (Constantine), 143
Psychic healing, 14, 99–120
    exercise to diagnose ailments and cures, 104–105
Psychic Internet (Web site), 262
Psychic phenomena, defined, 69–70
Psychic surgery, 14, 100, 109–111
Psychic Universes (Web site), 269
Psychokinesis, 12
    keys, bending of, 10–11
Psychometry, 1–2, 5–6
Ptolemy, 23, 24
Pythagoras (Greek philosopher), 24

Quantum Quests International (Web site), 273
Quantum theory of physics, 153
Quartz crystals, 77–80. *See also* Crystals
    characteristics of, 78–79, 87–88
    historical use of, 87
    healing powers of, 100–103
    outer space and, 79
    piezoelectricity and, 79
    testing psychic abilities using, 90–91
"Queen of sciences". *See* Astrology

Rambova, Natasha, 160
Ramirez, Richard (Night Stalker), 161
Rapael's Almanac of Prophetic Messenger and Weather Guide, 26
Rathbone, Basil, prophetic dreams and, 161–162
Ratzinger, Joseph Cardinal, 243–244
Rausher, Elizabeth, 200
Ray, Barbara, 106, 107–108

Reagan, Ronald (President), 25
Reeve,Christopher (actor), 116
Reiki, 99–100, 106–108
    defined, 106
Reiki Factor (Ray), 106
Remote viewing, 140–142
Remote Viewing Research Centre (Web site),
    271
Remote Viewing Web Index (Web site), 272
*Reunions, Visionary Encounters with
    Departed Loved Ones* (Moody), 173, 174
Reynolds, Debbie (actress), 165
Richard the Lionheart, 222
Riley G. Psychic Detective (Web site), 269
Rise of Babylon: Sign of the End Times (Dyer), 248
Rivers, Joan, 17
Robertson, Morgan (author), 191–192
Robin Hood, 222
Rooney, Mickey, encounter with a guardian
    angel, 167–168
Roosevelt, Franklin Delano, 26, 89
Rubaiyat (Omar Khayyam), 201
Ruir, E., 250

Sagan, Carl, 173
Sanctuary, The (Web site), 268
Saunders, Richard (British author), 34
Schlesinger, John (film director), 164
Schweitzer, Albert, 112
Scientific attitude towards paranormal, 8, 14
Scrying (form of divination), 33
Seances, 176
Seers, different types, 49–50. *See also*
    Accidental seers; Incidental Seers;
    Intentional seers
Sellers, Peter (actor), 17, 160
Sellier, Charles (author/producer)
    death of son, 158
    "visitation" by son, 159
Shealy, C. Norman, 118, 119
Sherby, Sidney, 146
Shipton, Tobias (husband of Mother
    Shipton), 223
Skepticism, 12–13
"Sleeping Prophet". *See* Cayce, Edgar

Smith, J. Herbert, 27
Smith, Joseph (Mormon leader)
    Civil War, predicts, 240–241
    prophecies of, 240–241
Smith, Robert Cross, 26
Socrates (Greek philosopher), 77
Sommer, Elke (actress), 166–167
Southhill Agatha, 222
Sparky's Index of Edgar Cayce Readings
    (Web site), 266
Spielberg, Steven (film director), 179
Spurrina, Vestricius (Druid seer), 221
Spurzheim, Johann Kaspar, 40
Sputnik, launching of, 89
St. Augustine, 25–26
St. Bernadin of Sienna, 45
Stalin, Joseph, 60
Stallone, Sylvester (actor), 161
Stanford Research Institute, mind control
    experiments and, 143
Stargate Project, government use of
    psychics, 140–142, 144
Stead, W.T. (British writer)
    prophetic dream regarding Titanic, 193
    victim of Titanic, 193
Strabo (Greek philosopher), 22
Strange Worlds Bookstore (Web site), 266
Strasberg, Susan, 160
Strom, Andrew, 148
Sumerians, use of astrology and, 23
Super Collider, 154
Superstring theory, 151–154. *See also* Unified
    field theory

Tarot cards, 42–46
    Church criticism of, 44, 45
    greater arcana, 43
    gypsies and, 42
    history of, 42
    Kabbalah, relationship to, 45–46
    lesser arcana, 44
    Web site, 264
Technology, prophecies regarding future, 68,
    69, 225, 227
Teleportation, xiii

Television shows, interest in paranormal, 16–17
Ten dimensions in universe, 154
Tesla, Nikola, 148, 149
Tests for psychic awareness, 15, 104–106
Theory of relativity, 153. *See also* Einstein, Albert
Thomas, Northcote, 174
Thymus gland, using to test for overall vitality, 105–106
Tibet, Chinese takeover of, 233, 236–237
Time
    Pleiadian definition of, 152–153
    theory regarding, 202–203
Time travel paradox, 152
Titan (fictional ocean liner), similarities to *Titanic*, 191–192
Titanic (ocean liner), 193, 253
    comparisons with earlier disaster novel, 191–192
Travolta, John (actor), 160–161
Turner, Gladys Davis, 66
Twain, Mark, 37
Two Thousand. *See* Year 2000

Unified field theory, 148, 151–152. *See also* Superstring theory
Universe
    concept of time and, 152–153
    ten dimensions and, 154
Upwall, Sue Apitz (astrologer), 29
Uri Geller's Psychic City (Web site), 270
U.S. Government
    mind control experiments, 143–144
U.S. Government, *Cont.*,
    remote viewing experiments, 140–142
    use of psychics, 140–155
U.S.S. Eldridge (naval ship), 147, 148, 149. *See also* Philadelphia Experiment
Valentine, Tom (author), 110

Valentino, Rudolph (silent film star), channeled messages to wife, 160
Virgin Mary, visions of, 174, 241–242, 244–245. *See also* Fatima Prophecy
Vivekananda (Indian teacher), 27
Von Daniken, Erich (author), 157
Von Neumann, John, 149, 150

Wagner, Lindsay (actress), 161
Walker, Clint (actor), 161
Waters, Frank (author), 198–199
    Hopi prophecies and, 198–199
Wayne, John, 160, 165
Web sites, list of, 261–274
West, Mae (actress), 160
Wildflowers Unique Books and Gifts (website), 262
Williams, Robin (actor), 161
Wilson, Carol (psychic), 84
Windsor Hotel, destroyed by fire, 27
Wolper, David (TV producer), 9
Wolsey, Cardinal Bishop, 223–224
Wormholes, 151, 152
Wreck of the Titan, The (Robertson), 191

Year 2000
    Edgar Cayce's predictions regarding, 219
    Nostradamus's predictions regarding, 218–219
    prophecies and, 17, 195, 225, 229, 239–254
Your Body Doesn't Lie (Diamond), 103

Zechariah (Biblical prophet), end of the world prophecy, 194–195, 249
Zodiac
    invention of, 24
    Lo King, 24